WAR AND HUNGER

WAR AND HUNGER

RETHINKING INTERNATIONAL RESPONSES TO COMPLEX EMERGENCIES

Edited by

JOANNA MACRAE *and* ANTHONY ZWI

with Mark Duffield and Hugo Slim

Foreword by M.M. Sahnoun

ZED BOOKS
London & New Jersey

in association with
SAVE THE CHILDREN FUND (UK)

War and Hunger was first published in 1994 by:

Zed Books Ltd, 7 Cynthia Street, London N1 9JF, UK, and
165 First Avenue, Atlantic Highlands, New Jersey 07716, USA,
in association with
Save the Children Fund (UK), 17 Grove Lane, London SE5 8RD.

Cover designed by Andrew Corbett.
Typeset in Monotype Garamond by Lucy Morton, London SE12.
Printed and bound in the United Kingdom
by Biddles Ltd, Guildford and King's Lynn.

A catalogue record for this book is available from the British Library
US CIP data is available from the Library of Congress

ISBN 1 85649 291 5 Hb
ISBN 1 85649 292 3 Pb

Contents

Acknowledgements   viii

Preface   ix

Foreword *M.M. Sahnoun*   xi

Introduction *Joanna Macrae and Anthony Zwi*   1

PART I WAR AND HUNGER: AN INTRODUCTORY FRAMEWORK

1 Famine, Complex Emergencies and International Policy
   in Africa: An Overview *Joanna Macrae and Anthony Zwi*   6

   Basic Concepts of Famine and War 6
   The Use of Food as a Weapon 11
   Towards a New Approach to Conflict and Famine 20
   Complex Emergencies: A Framework for Policy Action 21
   Conclusion 31

2 The Course of the Four Horsemen: Costs of War and
   Its Aftermath in Sub-Saharan Africa *Reginald Herbold Green*   37

   Introduction: Anguish to Apocalypse 37
   War Types and War Costs 39
   Survival During War: Preserving and Ameliorating 42
   Drought 1991–93: Calamity, Catastrophic Response 44
   The Cost Continues: The Case for Focusing on Rehabilitation 45
   A Note on Governance 47
   Conclusion 48

3 The Political Economy of Internal War: Asset Transfer,
   Complex Emergencies and International Aid *Mark Duffield*   50

   Introduction 50
   Political Survival in a Permanent Emergency 50
   The Internationalisation of Public Welfare 57
   Conclusion: The Challenge of Internal War 64

4 Human Rights and Wars of Starvation *Katerina Tomasevski* 70

    Human-Rights Protection against Purposeful Starvation 70
    International Policy: Relief, Development and Human Rights 76
    Preventing Purposeful Starvation 78
    Stretching the Limits of Human Rights: Which Way? 82
    Conclusion and Summary 86

PART II FIVE AFRICAN CASE STUDIES

5 Angola: Surviving against Rollback and Petrodollars
   David Sogge 92

    Introduction 92
    Origins of Vulnerability 93
    Breakdown and Descent into Widespread War 96
    Conclusion 106

6 The Functions of Famine in Southwestern Sudan:
   Implications for Relief *David Keen* 111

    Introduction 111
    A Combination of Exploitative Processes 112
    Donors' Limited Agendas and their "Room for Manoeuvre" 116
    Concluding Remarks 121

7 Relief behind the Lines: The Cross-Border
   Operation in Tigray *Barbara Hendrie* 125

    Introduction 125
    Context of the Cross-Border Operation 126
    The Cross-Border Operation: 1984–85 130
    Conclusion 136

8 Dangerous Precedents? Famine Relief in Somalia 1991–93
   Alex de Waal 139

    Introduction 139
    Social Geography of the Famine 140
    Chronology of the Famine 141
    Local Relief Initiatives 143
    The United Nations Programme 147
    The NGO Record 150
    Countdown to Intervention 152
    Record of the Intervention 154
    Conclusion 158

9 The Impact of War on Food Security in Eritrea:
Prospects for Recovery *Lionel Cliffe*   160

   Assessing the Impact of War 160
   Strategies for Recovery 167
   Towards Sustainable Recovery 176

PART III TOWARDS NEW APPROACHES:
IMPLICATIONS FOR POLICY AND PRACTICE

10 Gender, War and Food
Judy el Bushra and Eugenia Piza-Lopez   180

   Introduction 180
   Women as Household Providers during Wartime 181
   Long-Term Changes to Gender Relations 187
   Development in Conflict: The Challenge to the Aid Community 190

11 UN Reform in a Changing World: Responding to Complex
Emergencies *Hugo Slim and Angela Penrose*   194

   Introduction 194
   New Scope for Humanitarian Response 195
   Obstacles to UN Engagement in Complex Emergencies 196
   Reform: Responding to the New Political Landscape 198
   Conclusion 206

12 Engaging with Violence: A Reassessment of
Relief in Wartime *David Keen and Ken Wilson*   209

   Introduction 209
   Depopulation: Functions and Response 210
   Relief and the Dynamics of Violence 214
   Conclusion 219

Conclusion *Mark Duffield, Joanna Macrae and Anthony Zwi*   222

   Introduction 222
   Complex Emergencies: Changing Contexts and Changing Concepts 222
   The International Response to Complex Emergencies 226
   The Challenge of Complex Emergencies: Priorities for Action 230
   Conclusion 232

About the Contributors   233

Index   236

Acknowledgements

In the summer of 1991, the editors of this book, Joanna Macrae and Anthony Zwi, conducted a review of the literature concerning famine and conflict in Africa with the financial support of Save the Children Fund (UK). This project resulted in a workshop, co-convened by SCF and the London School of Hygiene and Tropical Medicine in March 1992, which brought together a diverse group of donor agencies, NGOs, academics and human-rights workers, a number of whom have contributed to this volume. The editors gratefully acknowledge Save the Children Fund's financial and moral support for this work, and in particular the contribution of Celia Petty, John Seaman and Mark Bowden to its success.

The Health Policy Unit of the London School of Hygiene, and specifically the ODA-funded Health Economics and Financing Programme in which the two editors are based, provided an opportunity for this volume to be edited alongside their other commitments and research activities. For this, and the support of others, notably within the International Health Policy Programme, we are most grateful. This book forms part of an ongoing agenda to examine the health impact and policy implications arising in situations of extreme political instability.

Our thanks are also due to Robert Molteno at Zed Books for his patience during the preparation of the book and his editorial support.

Preface

Save the Children Fund welcomes the opportunity to support the publication of this book. The issues it raises about today's humanitarian crises and the current conduct of international relief efforts are important ones. The analysis in the various contributions is informed and broad-ranging. It is also extremely challenging and raises many dilemmas for those, including NGOs, who play an increasing role in humanitarian efforts.

The book's main message is that today's humanitarian emergencies are protracted and politically complex, and that the present efforts of the international community to meet these challenges are inadequate. UN agencies and NGOs alike must re-examine the models of humanitarian assistance they have long taken for granted. Above all, they must recognise that providing relief is not just a logistical exercise. In today's emergencies, the provision of relief requires a high level of social and political analysis, combined with a long-term commitment to communities affected by conflict.

War and Hunger poses many questions. Can humanitarian aid ever be neutral? Can ill-conceived relief aid institutionalise conflict and increase inequality and hardship? Can the UN's structures be reformed? Is there a framework for guaranteeing people's rights in humanitarian emergencies? Do NGOs need to develop new paradigms of humanitarian assistance? Does Africa's colonial legacy, its economic decline and its increasing international isolation mean that conflict and hunger are inevitable? These are all hard questions, not least for NGOs like Save the Children, but we believe that it is vital that they are kept at the forefront of humanitarian policy and practice in the years ahead. There are no simple answers to such questions, and no doubt many of the arguments contained in this book will be challenged. Save the Children Fund itself would challenge some of the assumptions made about NGOs in conflict-related emergencies, and the relationships between NGOs, donor agencies and African governments. Nevertheless, informed debate and hard analysis are prerequisites for progress in the field of humanitarian assistance. It is our hope that this book will contribute to debate and action in this crucial area.

M.J. Aaronson, Head of Overseas Department,
Save the Children Fund (UK)

Foreword
M.M. Sahnoun

As we examine the saga of humanitarian efforts in conflict situations, we are struck by two important facts. First, these efforts achieve today a remarkable result under increasingly difficult conditions. Second, while some attention is being given to the activities of international agencies such as UNHCR, UNICEF and WFP, little is known of what non-governmental organisations can accomplish with relatively limited resources and also the considerable knowledge of local situations they acquire in the process.

This book is one of the few attempts to shed light on a number of crucial issues related to humanitarian tragedies in war situations and analyses the experiences of a number of NGOs and UN agencies working in these contexts. Although focusing on Africa, the lessons drawn are of vital interest for the rest of the world. The international community needs to assess the characteristics and causes of humanitarian crises everywhere, and to develop new concepts and approaches to cope with these trag-edies. This book also reminds us that prevention is, unfortunately, far from being a priority today. Current strategies of conflict management focus primarily on intervention once a conflict and emergency have started, largely ignoring the vital aspects of prevention and resolution.

Historically, the function of UN peacekeeping was to observe truce agreements and police the disengagement of warring parties. A basic prerequisite of these operations was that it required the consent of the parties concerned. Most of the conflicts on the UN agenda were those fought between states. Today the international community is also expected to intervene in internal conflicts, either to make peace between contending parties and preserve national and regional peace and security, or to put an end to human-rights abuses and mitigate a humanitarian tragedy.

With the end of the Cold War, policy aspects of the big powers, and the proliferation of new challenges such as the deterioration of the envi-ronment and government deficits, these internal conflicts are bound to continue to erupt worldwide for the foreseeable future. Questions of why, how and when to intervene are presenting major dilemmas for the inter-national community.

The Security Council of the United Nations has demonstrated a pattern of behaviour over the last three to four years which deserves closer scrutiny. Its massive interventions in Iraq, Somalia, Cambodia and Bosnia have produced new and problematic grey areas between peacekeeping and peace enforcement which can lead to tragic consequences and cause immense difficulties to officers in the field. The UN management has been inadequately prepared for such vast operations, yet it was partly responsible for pushing through new peacekeeping agendas. The operation in Somalia alone has cost around US$2 billion to protect less than US$50 million of effective relief. According to the *New York Times* (8 December 1993), about six thousand Somalis and eighty-three UN peacekeepers have died in the clashes between UN forces and Somali armed groups since the UN took over from Operation Restore Hope in April 1993. This is a tragedy, and one which deserves full investigation in order that we learn important lessons for the future.

So what should be our attitude to humanitarian intervention? Armed intervention in a humanitarian tragedy in my view should not be ruled out. We should, however, exercise maximum caution and restraint and exhaust all other possibilities before using this option. On the other hand, it is important that all aggravating factors must be dealt with firmly. Interferences from outside, such as the role of Serbia in the Croatian and Bosnian conflicts, or arms supplies to all parties such as in Somalia, must be stopped first, as is the case in international conflicts. The United Nations and regional organisations must develop guidelines specifying when and how they would become engaged and what kind of instruments they may use – diplomatic, economic, humanitarian and military.

At present, UN capabilities fall tragically short of needs. In 1981, Secretary-General de Cuellar set up an office for research and information with primary responsibility for early warning. In early 1992, his successor decided to abolish it. A proposal to set up observation posts in explosive areas of the world has never been implemented. Yet the international community needs these and other innovative structures. Most importantly, a comprehensive preventive approach that involves all international development and humanitarian organisations, regional associations as well as national development agencies and NGOs, offers the only real hope for many communities threatened by civil war, humanitarian tragedy or structural collapse. We cannot continue to approach these and other global problems with old-fashioned solutions and obsolete structures which seek only short-term, unsustainable fixes.

The former Polish leader General Jaruzelski described concisely the dilemma facing a large part of humanity today: "Bread without democracy is bitter, but democracy without bread is fragile." The Western world welcomed with some jubilation the collapse of the Soviet Empire. Mixed with a feeling of vindication, there was strong hope that the world would become more amenable to Western values and democracy and hence more peaceful. President Bush announced a "new world order", and Prime Minister Thatcher pronounced that there was a "unique opportunity to extend the bounds of true democracy on a rule of law and free markets". Soon, however, it became clear that if bread without democracy is bitter, democracy – and I might add peace – without bread is indeed very fragile.

It is true that the challenges to peace and democracy do not necessarily take the shape of large manifestations of the hungry, homeless and job- less. These challenges work their own way to the surface through inflation, riots, nationalism and ethnic cleansing in Eastern Europe, or through famine, factionalism and large-scale civil wars in the Third World.

While in Somalia I was struck by the fact that there was nothing inherent within Somali society that contained the germs of serious divi- sion. Its population comprises a single ethnic group, which shares largely the same language and religious beliefs. Yet there was total dislocation of the society along clan, sub-clan and even family lines. I have absolutely no doubt in my mind that the instinct of survival in a threatening political and economic environment was the basic motivation in the behaviour pattern of the Somali people. The instinct becomes acute when repeated drought further worsens such a hostile environment. The rationale behind the Somali experience is very much present in other conflict situations in a more or less elaborate way.

These conflicts are not necessarily endemic. However, under certain circumstances the ingredients of the crisis gather like clouds before the storm. It is clear that these circumstances have much to do with economic and resource issues. The continuing deterioration of the resource base in many Third World countries is undermining the possibility of checking and resolving most of these conflicts. Environmental degradation and deterioration of the economic and social situation force people to move and thereby to impinge on the limited resources of the host populations in their own countries or countries of asylum. The violent conflicts that ensue result in serious strains on natural ecosystems and further threaten their capacity to support life and livelihood. It is no surprise that these conflicts occur most frequently in Africa, Latin America and Asia. UN statistics indicate that as a percentage of developed countries, Africa's GDP declined by about 50 per cent between 1960 and 1990; Latin America shared similar trends.

The circumstances that catalyse the ingredients for conflict and crisis also include what I have called the governance deficit. Not only are govern- ments in most of these areas unable to monitor and plan for food security, and to instigate appropriate emergency measures to cope with natural catastrophes; they themselves are often a factor promoting conflict. Power elites seek to protect particular economic and political interests, even if this should result in the increasing of existing ethnic, religious or social tensions. It is a vicious cycle that we need to break. Ideally, with the end of the Cold War, the international community should take stock of the consequences of this worldwide confrontation and look at the present historical phase of humanity and the challenges it poses. We should draw a map of all existing and potential crises, examine their immediate and remote causes, and draw lessons from past experience to understand the factors which ignite and compound conflict. This kind of vision and leadership is not yet present. So far, the UN and its member states have responded in routine fashion, and sometimes with dangerous improvisations which fail to acknowledge the depth and complexity of the problems posed by war-related humanitarian crises around the globe.

Introduction
Joanna Macrae and Anthony Zwi

Images of war and hunger are flashed daily on our television screens, and encapsulated in banner headlines quantifying the latest horrors from the civilian battlefields of Bosnia, Rwanda and Somalia, and, less often, Angola, East Timor and Sudan, to name but a few. The optimism for peace inspired by the collapse of the Berlin Wall and former Soviet Union lies in tatters. The old battlefields of the Third World, where the proxy wars of the United States and USSR were played out, are still bloodied by conflict in countries such as Afghanistan and Angola. In other countries, new waves of violence are accompanying the birth of a post-Cold War (dis)order.

Civilians, not military personnel, are the prime victims of these conflicts. They are threatened not only by bullets and bombs, but by the massive social and economic dislocation engendered by war. War undermines those very social, economic and political systems upon which we rely to secure our basic human needs, including the most basic – food. The conventional view of famine as an essentially environmental and economic disaster has been shattered by events such as the siege of Sarajevo and the appalling refugee city of Goma. These events have brought the issue of conflict and its accompanying humanitarian crises to the forefront of public attention. They have also placed new strains on the international community, embodied in organisations such as the United Nations and NATO. In the early 1990s, the humanitarian system has become increasingly linked to wider agendas of foreign policy and military strategy. In Somalia, for example, images of hunger were used by the United States to justify military intervention on an unprecedented scale.

Yet, despite the extensive coverage and debate of these complex, conflict-driven emergencies, we are often left with more questions than answers about the nature of contemporary conflicts and famines and about the international response to them. Why is the momentum for conflict intensifying in so many corners of the world? Why does war generate humanitarian crises of such terrible intensity? What can be done to prevent them? How should they be addressed by the international community? These questions lie at the heart of debates surrounding the organisation of international political and economic life at the end of the millennium.

I

This book is a modest contribution to these debates on war, hunger and international policy. While focusing on Africa, many of the ideas, concepts and issues it raises are relevant across continental boundaries. As this book goes to press, events in the former Yugoslavia and the ex-Soviet Union and Afghanistan spring to mind. Africa has suffered an undue share of war and hunger in recent decades. The diversity of experience of conflict and famine which has emerged through the suffering of millions on the continent offers salutary lessons at a time when the international community is struggling to define global policies for conflict prevention, mitigation and resolution. In particular, it highlights the need for a more critical understanding of the nature and dynamics of conflicts and their implications for food security, and a reappraisal of current paradigms which govern international action in complex emergencies.

This volume draws on analyses of conflict and famine across the continent and highlights their implications for the development of international humanitarian policy. Given the multifaceted nature of the problem, it is not surprising that this collection of essays draws on a diverse range of disciplines – anthropology, political science, international human-rights law, public health and policy sciences. Across these disciplinary divides comes a constant theme: the urgent need to reframe the concepts we use to describe and analyse conflict-related disasters.

Structure of the Book

The book is divided into three substantive parts: Part I provides a framework for analysis of war and hunger in Africa. Joanna Macrae and Anthony Zwi provide an introductory overview of the relationship between conflict and famine. This chapter highlights many of the key themes addressed by this volume. It begins with some comments on models and concepts of famine, and then relates these to the nature and form of conflict in Africa. It considers the specific uses of food as a weapon, and analyses local and international responses to conflict-related famines. The implications of these analyses for local and international attempts at conflict prevention, mitigation and resolution are then explored. Reginald Green details the origins of vulnerability to food crises in sub-Saharan Africa and analyses the role of conflict in slowing the pace of economic development on the continent. He considers how the costs of conflict can be estimated, emphasising the need to support rehabilitation efforts in countries recovering from conflict. Mark Duffield explores the development of political and economic systems which systematically target and exploit discrete population groups and result in cultural genocide, stressing that conflicts have both winners and losers and that understanding this will be central to development of appropriate policy in these contexts. He uses this analysis to question prevailing international paradigms of development and relief. Katerina Tomasevski comprehensively outlines the changing frameworks of international law and development policy and their implications for international responses to conflict in the developing world. Current frameworks provide the legitimacy for a variety of forms of action, but, as indicated in the chapter, the application of human rights and humanitarian law is often selectively applied.

Part II draws on case-study material from five African countries to examine key issues in complex emergencies. David Sogge's historical analysis of the roots of hunger and violence in Angola points to the role of colonialism, inappropriate development strategies, the Cold War, and inequitable North–South relations in creating the country's vulnerability to complex and permanent emergencies. He highlights the neglect of the needs of peasant farmers and the deep structural factors that will have to be overcome if conflict resolution and development are to take place. David Keen's powerful analysis of the conflict-famine in south-west Sudan vividly describes how the creation of famine can benefit powerful economic and political interest groups, to the great cost of the politically marginalised whom they exploit. This is one of relatively few studies that provides us with considerable insight into how vested interest groups may use scarcity to their own ends. Barbara Hendrie examines the role of indigenous relief agencies in mitigating the successive famines that accompanied the war in Tigray. She analyses the complex factors underlying the international community's slow response to conflict-producing famines in the region, and counts the human costs of prevailing policy paradigms and approaches to planning famine relief. The theme of the role of indigenous organisations in famine relief and conflict resolution continues in Alex de Waal's chapter on the Somali famine in 1991–93: he contrasts the relative effectiveness of these organisations in the delivery of relief aid with the failure of the UN and its military-supported humanitarian efforts. His contribution also highlights the dangers of the increased militarisation of humanitarian relief efforts, and in particular how it may fail to support the redevelopment of civil society in conflict-affected countries. The long-term impact of conflict on food security is starkly portrayed by Lionel Cliffe in his case study of Eritrea. He highlights the political determinants of sustainable rehabilitation and development of food systems, and examines the linkages between environmental protection, equitable land tenure and sustainable peace.

The final section of the book builds upon these earlier analyses to highlight the key policy issues currently facing the international community as it seeks to redefine its response to complex emergencies in the post-Cold War era. Judy el Bushra and Eugenia Piza-Lopez highlight the gender dimensions of conflict and famine within African households, and their implications for humanitarian policy and operations. Gender awareness is frequently lacking, but is shown to be a pivotal component of appropriate policy-making. David Keen and Ken Wilson call for a reappraisal of the objectives of relief interventions, pointing to the need for more accurate analysis of the nature of conflict and the role that international aid plays in its maintenance and resolution. They warn that existing policy frameworks risk reinforcing the very factors that sustain conflict and the creation of humanitarian disasters. The authors go on to identify strategies which might better serve the weak than the strong. The reform of the United Nations is described by Angela Penrose and Hugo Slim, who map out the potential and limitations of existing efforts to improve the effectiveness and accountability of this rapidly changing set of institutions.

The conclusion draws these multiple strands together, identifying trends and issues likely to dominate future debate surrounding complex emergencies and outlining strategies to influence national and international policy.

No volume, however weighty, could produce "ten easy answers" to the horrors and complexity of conflict-related emergencies. A constant theme of this book is the need for a basic first step: to question current paradigms for analysing the nature of, and responses to, complex emergencies. This needs to be done not simply by testing their validity empirically, but by understanding why such paradigms prevail, whose interests they serve, and how they can be challenged and modified. Ensuring the development of an appropriate discourse on the nature of contemporary conflicts is not therefore simply an exercise in academic correctness; it will be a precondition for improving the effectiveness of international assistance and developing new strategies of conflict prevention and resolution. Finally, such a discourse is part of a process of creating improved mechanisms of accountability and effectiveness in a world order which has so far promised, but failed, to deliver equity and peace.

PART I

War and Hunger:
An Introductory Framework

Famine, Complex Emergencies and International Policy in Africa: An Overview
Joanna Macrae and Anthony Zwi

The right to food represents the very symbol of the right to life and to livelihood.[1] Adequate nutrition is a condition of physical survival. Our capacity to access sufficient nourishment is determined by a complex set of economic, cultural, social and political factors, which in turn reflect our relationship with a wider world, locally, nationally and internationally. War threatens the right to food, but it is equally about the relationships which enable us to meet the basic needs that determine survival and development.

This chapter provides an overview of the relationship between war and hunger in Africa. It is divided into two substantive parts: the first explores concepts of famine and conflict and analyses their linkages; the second offers a framework for considering the key issues facing households, governments and the international community in conflict-related emergencies.

Basic Concepts of Famine and War

Models of famine

Famine is commonly attributed to dramatic reductions in food availability and has become associated with natural disasters such as drought, floods and crop pests. Amartya Sen (1986) demonstrated, however, that scarcity of food alone is insufficient to explain the occurrence of famine. His entitlement theory reflected on the economic relationships which determine access to food: he argued that "endowment bundles" provide access either through one's own production or through the market. These bundles, divided between assets (investments and stores) and claims (patronage and kinship ties which provide a means of support), enable the individual to procure or produce adequate food. In periods of scarcity, entitlement is threatened since prices for staple grains are characteristically high, while the value of assets diminishes as the market becomes swamped with crisis sales. Similarly, wages in the commercial sector may not rise sufficiently to meet the higher prices of staple crops. Famine occurs when there is a collapse of entitlement, restricting access to food, leading to a decline of nutritional status, and culminating in starvation.

This model has been questioned by writers such as Rangasami (1985) and De Waal (1990a), who suggest that it retains the features of more conventional Western models in viewing famine-stricken populations as passive victims of external shocks. They have also argued that definitions which identify famine with widespread starvation deaths conceptualise famine as an enviro-economic event culminating in an *individual* biological crisis, and that this ignores the essentially *social* nature of the disaster. This fails to acknowledge the perceptions of famine-stricken communities themselves for whom famine is a collective experience which poses a threat not only to their lives, but also to their livelihood.

All famines are not the same, and people's responses to food production and distribution failures vary according to the intensity and depth of the crisis, as well as to the initial vulnerability of households and communities. Famine can be defined along a continuum which ranges from vulnerability to external shocks such as drought and economic instability, to starvation and death. The early stages of famine are not easily distinguishable from endemic poverty. Green (1986; see Chapter 2 in this volume) for example, argues that mass starvation in sub-Saharan Africa has been triggered by the interaction of drought, poor transport systems and war, and that the narrow margin between "normal" food supply and famine has left communities especially vulnerable to even minor shocks.

As the subsistence economy comes under environmental and economic stress, the production base is rendered more fragile, and African communities become increasingly dependent upon securing alternative sources of income. Entire families, or significant parts of them, may migrate from their home areas in search of employment opportunities, patronage or charity. In situations of acute stress, reliance on these strategies intensifies. De Waal (1989) has suggested that the key objective of these coping mechanisms is to avoid destitution and to enable communities to resume production once the crisis has passed, rather than primarily to avoid starvation. Thus, famine-stricken communities in the 1984–85 famine in Darfur, Sudan, spent substantially more of their income, gained through wage labour and asset sales, on productive investments, such as seeds and tools, than on food itself. Despite their own hunger, they also sought to maintain key assets such as plough oxen, to ensure that they would be able to plant and produce in the following season. The coping strategies implemented by famine-affected communities therefore strive not merely to ensure biological survival, but to maintain livelihood and production capability, and, wherever possible, attempt to address those factors which led to their vulnerability to famine.

Survival strategies entail considerable risks, which are evaluated with respect to the survival of the household, group or community, rather than with exclusive reference to the individual. Increased risks of disease, for example, are associated with the large-scale population movements prompted in times of stress (Prothero, 1977), as migrants and refugees seek work or patronage. It has been suggested that it is this changed disease environment, not starvation itself, which is largely responsible for the excess deaths associated with the majority of recent famines (De Waal, 1989).

The nature of famine changes dramatically if coping strategies fail and entitlement to food collapses entirely. Communities which lose or dispose of all their assets, and which are unable to generate alternative sources of income, lose not only access to food, but also their ability to return to pre-crisis levels of production. If communities have insufficient purchasing power, market flows of food into the deficit region will cease, thus causing an absolute scarcity of food. Such a collapse of entitlement is associated with the risk of widespread starvation, as well as increasing vulnerability to communicable diseases, and represents the final stage of the famine process. De Waal (1990a) suggests further that coping strategies fail most often when associated with violence. In such circumstances, strategies which normally enable communities to survive environmental and economic shocks are systematically undermined, hastening the pace of decline from scarcity to destitution. Famines associated with conflict are therefore more likely to conform rapidly to the final stages of the famine process (starvation) than those caused exclusively by enviro-economic factors.

Conflict in Africa

The instability of subsistence life throughout Africa has increased its vulnerability to political instability. A multitude of factors underlie this economic and political vulnerability, some predating colonialism, others following in its wake. Still others can be attributed to climatic change and environmental degradation. As households, communities and states have come under greater economic and social pressure, so has there been an increase in violent conflict.

Access to, and control over, resources are the key to the maintenance of a particular way of life, including cultural and political identity. It follows, therefore, that threats to the physical means of production, which occur in violent, localized conflicts, have severe repercussions for the overall survival of communities and their way of life (Duffield, 1990a; Turton, 1989). Such threats have always been present within and between African communities, yet the nature of these conflicts and local capacity for conflict resolution were changed during the colonial period and have come under still further pressure since independence.

Changes in the mode of governance and the emergence of nation-states have resulted in the nationalisation of localised conflict, as governments seek to protect particular economic and political interests, often by manipulating existing ethnic and religious tensions (Duffield, 1990a). This trend was maintained during the Cold War era by international forces, which in turn incorporated nationalised conflicts into global struggles to gain political hegemony. Military and economic support by the United States, the former USSR and, in southern Africa, South Africa, sustained the internal and interstate conflicts which have haunted the continent.

A diverse range of conflicts was spawned under the conditions of the Cold War, leading governments in some cases to mount violent counter-insurgency campaigns among their own populations. Counterinsurgency wars throughout the world seek to inflict not simply a military defeat, but to disempower the opposition, to deny it an identity and to undermine its ability to maintain political and economic integrity (Summerfield, 1991). This remains true of civil wars and those where external forces seek to undermine the legitimacy of governments such as those in Angola and Mozambique. Attacks on food systems represent one facet of this process of personal, political, cultural and social disempowerment. Others include attacks on health services, as experienced in Mozambique (Cliff and Noormahomed, 1988) and in Sudan and Uganda (Dodge, 1990). The conditions of war also threaten the future ability of communities to partici-pate in the economic and political life of the country, as whole generations of children are deprived of access to education. The violation of women by rape, the re-emergence of slavery, and widespread war-related disability have further contributed to the process of social dislocation and dis-empowerment of the war-affected.

The demise of the Soviet Union and the apartheid state in South Africa may have irrevocably changed the nature of such superpower-related conflicts, but there is little to suggest that other forms of conflict, equally devastating, will not emerge. The slaughter in Angola, following the UN-supervised elections in 1992 and their rejection by the losing UNITA party, is testimony to the destructiveness present even after the with-drawal of active support by the superpowers. Ethnic cleansing in Zaire, the intense levels of political violence in South Africa, and the conflicts between Hutus and Tutsis in Rwanda and Burundi, to name but a few, illustrate the harsh variety of forms that conflict may take.

The disengagement of the global and regional superpowers has not resulted in the reduction of conflict in countries such as Somalia or Angola: the factors promoting national and local-level conflicts have not been resolved, and groups created during conflict driven by superpower inter-ests often continue to reap gains. In some regions, such as the Horn of Africa, the withdrawal of the superpowers may be seen as temporary: the renationalisation of conflict has been followed by a new international framework for military involvement, albeit justified under a new humani-tarian rubric. In Angola and Somalia, the inadequacy of the UN's peace-

keeping and peacemaking activities has increased awareness of the limitations and complexities of this new phase of international engagement on
the battlefields of the Third World. Of course, this is no longer limited
to Africa: the UN's failures in the former Yugoslavia are eloquent testimony
to that.

Conventional approaches to conflict analysis have tended to focus on
the international, macro-level dimensions, ignoring the local-level rationale, and the impact of low-intensity strategies on individuals and households (Deng and Zartman, 1991; Stockton, 1989). However, without an
understanding of the local political and cultural complexities, and of the
motivations of individuals and groups for sustaining struggles, the means
of preventing and resolving them, as well as of relieving their effects, will
remain elusive. This lack of political analysis has limited the understanding
of food-security issues in Africa. The human-rights dimension of famine
has been underplayed in favour of environmental and economic factors,
seen as politically neutral. The public face of famine, at least until the
early 1990s, has thus been maintained primarily as an enviro-economic
crisis, rather than that of a legal, social and political disaster, with integral
environmental and economic components. Although each conflict and its
effects are unique, some common trends in the aetiology of conflict-
famines in Africa are discernible.

The aetiology of conflict-famines

Food serves three primary functions in insurgency and counterinsurgency,
or "low-intensity" wars: political, economic and military. Undermining the
ability of communities to produce and procure food renders them destitute, dependent on the state or welfare agencies, and thus politically compliant. Conversely, providing food, and being seen to do so in times of
scarcity, places one in a powerful position to win "hearts and minds".

Attacks on the food supply may also serve economic interests.
Rangasami (1985) has pointed out that in all famines there are both victims
and beneficiaries. Merchants and other powerful groups, often allied to
political and military interests in conflict situations, may make substantial
profits out of scarcity. There is good evidence of this in a number of
settings, most notably Sudan (Keen, 1991; see also Chapter 6).

The military function of attacks on food is the most obvious use of
food as a weapon in many contemporary conflicts. Rebel forces are
dependent upon civilian populations for food and shelter: in the eyes of
a threatened state, the distinction between opposition military personnel
and the civilians who provide them with support becomes blurred. As a
result, civilians come to be seen as a legitimate target for attack: this is
part of the explanation for the rising proportion of civilians killed in
conflict in the latter part of this century (Sivard, 1991).

Comparing different famines in different wars in different countries, each with their own histories, must be undertaken cautiously. Nevertheless, as this review shows, it is the similarities of a number of recent African conflict-famines, rather than their differences, that stand out. In Angola, Mozambique, Ethiopia, Sudan and Somalia, famine was not simply a consequence of conflict, but represented its goal (Duffield, 1990a).

The Use of Food as a Weapon

Attacks on food security – in effect, the use of food as a weapon – may be categorised under three headings: omission, commission and provision.

Acts of omission: failures to act

By "omission" we mean instances of food misuse where governments fail to monitor adequately and plan for food security in all sections of a country; it identifies the failure of governments to manage food reserves and to instigate and facilitate appropriate emergency measures.

Facilitation of relief operations

In 1988, the United Nations passed a resolution urging governments to enable the delivery of humanitarian assistance to the victims of disasters (UN resolution 43/131). It invited all states to profit from the international community's ability to provide aid and assistance, and identified the need for cooperation from national governments in coordinating and expediting aid to their citizens. In both this and a subsequent resolution (UN resolution 45/100), the UN's right to intervene remained compromised, however, by the continued primacy of government sovereignty and the usual requirement for government permission to mobilise humanitarian assistance. Where governments fail to protect the interests of the mass of the people, or, worse still, are repressive or discriminatory, this creates substantial problems in making relief available.

Among the best-known examples of government noncooperation in delivering relief assistance was the refusal of Ethiopia's President Mengistu to allow emergency aid into rebel-held areas of Eritrea and Tigray during the 1984 famine (Jansson et al., 1987). Donor unwillingness to violate national sovereignty and channel assistance across the border was partially responsible for the displacement of over 400,000 Tigrayans across the border to Sudan (ibid.).

Similarly, in 1988 the government of Sudan refused to grant international agencies access to war-displaced communities in southern Kordofan; tens of thousands of people weakened by the war-famine were denied aid, leading to some of the highest starvation death rates ever reliably recorded. Slightly over 7 per cent of the displaced population died every

week at the peak of the crisis in Meiram (Keen, 1991). In 1990, the World
Food Programme estimated a shortfall of 1.2 million metric tonnes of
grain in Sudan, while the government acknowledged a national shortfall
of only 75,000 metric tonnes (*Proceedings of "Famine Now" Conference*, 1991).
The war-displaced around Khartoum and conflict-affected communities,
particularly in the Nuba mountains, were severely affected by this failure
to declare a food emergency and facilitate the delivery of aid.

In Angola, the government on a number of occasions blocked attempts
to establish a safe corridor for relief supplies which traversed rebel-held
areas. The delay in implementing the Special Relief Program for Angola
(SPRA) slowed the establishment of village-level relief operations, forcing
communities to move to the towns. The rapid increase in the urban
population in Luanda placed considerable strain on health and environmental services, and health status is extremely poor for the vast majority
of the population (Kanji and Harpham, 1992). These stresses have been
exacerbated by the resumption of the war following the elections, which
continued to take a heavy toll as this book went to press.

The importance attached to sovereignty enables governments to withhold the right to assistance which their citizens could otherwise claim
from the UN and other humanitarian agencies. Without government
consent, bilateral and multilateral agencies are technically unable to operate
within a nation's borders. Similarly, NGOs which seek to support famine-
affected areas despite government policy may face expulsion or other
penalties, jeopardizing their operations in other areas of the country. If
they remain committed to providing assistance, they may seek to channel
aid through a third party. The Emergency Relief Desk (ERD), based in
Khartoum, Sudan, provides one such example: the ERD channelled assistance across the border into rebel-held territory in neighbouring Eritrea
and Tigray from 1985 to 1991, without the permission of the Ethiopian
authorities. The identity of the NGOs which managed the consortium
remained confidential throughout its operation, thus protecting their
interests within government-held areas of Ethiopia (Hendrie, 1989; see
also Chapter 7 in this volume).

While in some areas opposition forces have established relief organisations that have successfully channelled food aid, in many of the conflicts in sub-Saharan Africa rebels share responsibility for omissions which
have led to famine. Their failure to participate in ceasefire agreements has
limited the implementation of effective relief programmes. Such failures
are particularly significant in those famines which coincide with a total
collapse of government: in Liberia, and more recently in Somalia and
substantial parts of Angola, the peak food crises have coincided with the
failure of governmental structures. It is unclear in such situations who is
responsible for ensuring the legal right to adequate food; rebel forces that
control large areas of the country do, however, have a particular respon-

sibility for ensuring that the citizens under their control have access to humanitarian supplies.

Management of existing food resources

Governments also have a responsibility to prevent famine by utilising national resources effectively and encouraging accurate national food security planning. In Sudan the government failed on both fronts. In 1990, the export of the strategic grain reserve prior to the 1991 harvest created dependence on imports to meet the nation's food requirements. The income generated by export sales was channelled to the military, leaving the government with insufficient funds to import food to meet the deficit (Africa Watch, 1990a). By blocking aid, the only alternative means of breaching the food gap and of rebuilding strategic grain reserves was withheld. There have also been suggestions that government staff responsible for preparing agricultural reports and monitoring food security worked in a climate of fear: their findings were politically sensitive, and they perceived themselves to be at risk of imprisonment or of losing their jobs if they delivered reports contradicting government policy (Buchanan-Smith et al., 1991). Governments have exploited the structural vulnerability of regions such as Eritrea (Bondestam et al., 1987), Tigray (De Waal, 1991) and southern Sudan (Keen, 1991), which have traditionally depended on imports of grain from other areas of the country. By hampering commercial and relief grain flows into deficit areas, governments have created actual scarcities of food, resulting in the collapse of marketing systems, and forcing communities to move out of the regions.

De Waal (1987) has estimated that in the 1984–85 famine in Darfur, food aid met only 10 per cent of food consumption needs, the remainder coming from the depleted harvest, wild fruits and grasses, and purchases bought with income from wage-labour and the sale of assets. Insufficient research has been carried out to assess the role that food aid plays in preventing starvation in conflict-famines. However, it is clear that the creation of absolute scarcity, which results from attacks on production and marketing systems, as well as on the means of coping with such crises, may render civilian populations in conflict-famines more dependent on food aid than those affected by environmental disasters. The failure of governments to declare an emergency and facilitate the delivery of food aid is thus particularly serious in such situations.

Acts of commission: attacks on the means of producing and procuring food

We define acts of commission as attacks on the means of producing and procuring food. They include actions which undermine agricultural production and hinder coping strategies, including attacks on relief convoys, safe corridors and markets. Campaigns of terror, designed to depopulate specific areas, are not explicitly included, although their negative effects on the food security of those forced to abandon their assets and means of livelihood cannot be overemphasised. Attacks on food production and consumption are central to the process of famine creation. The tactics employed in a variety of conflicts show alarming similarities. The most important feature of these is that they quicken the pace of destitution by blocking coping strategies, thus pushing communities further from the threshold of survival.

Attacks on production

Scorched-earth tactics have been widely employed both by ground troops and by aerial bombing with napalm and other incendiary devices. Accurate data concerning such attacks are difficult to collect and assess; De Waal (1991) has, however, reported that 142,000 hectares of land in Tigray were destroyed by Ethiopian government forces in only two months in 1980, while Bondestam et al. (1987) record a further 90,000 tsimdi (approximately 23,000 hectares) of land destroyed in Eritrea in 1987.

The threat of aerial attack forced farmers in Tigray and Eritrea to cultivate at night, thus limiting their productivity (Hendrie, 1991). In Angola the threat to peasants working in their fields was so acute as to prompt the army to insist that they accompanied workers to the fields; when military escorts were not available, farmers were not able to tend their crops. Grain stores have also been subject to attack by both government and rebel forces in many countries: these attacks have acted as a disincentive to community efforts to establish grain stores, a traditional feature of food security structures (Spooner and Walsh, 1991).

In southern Sudan the most important attack on production was the confiscation and killing of large numbers of livestock, the central feature of the rural economy. The long-term effects of these raids may be more severe than those of one-off attacks on sedentary farmers. Pastoralists exchange livestock for grain, and in drought years are severely affected when the terms of trade decline as the market becomes swamped with crisis sales of livestock. These sales are, however, managed by herders who usually selectively sell livestock according to the age and sex of the animal in order to protect the core of the herd, which acts as a base for future production. In contrast, livestock killed or seized by raiders may severely deplete herds without allowing for further reproduction, plunging communities into destitution. Thus pastoralist communities may be forced out of subsistence production permanently if they lack sufficient resources to rebuild their herds. The struggle to regain a productive base may itself lead to violent raids, as has occurred in south-western Sudan and the northern regions of Uganda (see, for example, Keen, Chapter 6 in this volume).

During the rule of the Barre regime in Somalia, government troops attacked herders at wells and watering points. Wells were frequently poisoned and water tankers destroyed. These attacks forced pastoralists to move their herds nearer to towns in search of water and protection; this has occurred also in Sudan. This resulted in abnormal concentrations of livestock in certain areas, intensifying environmental degradation and increasing the threat of disease (UN and GoS, 1990). Changes in grazing patterns have also been recorded in Eritrea: Bondestam et al. (1987) record how the war cut off some of the best grazing, forcing communities to move to new pastures which were often unsuitable for the particular kind of livestock. The imposition of curfews in government-held areas further limited the range of grazing as people were unable to look for stray animals after dark (ibid.).

The use of land mines has had a devastating effect on the agricultural and pastoral economy of large areas of Africa. It has been estimated that there are between 18 and 30 million mines scattered in various parts of Africa: most seriously affected are the countries of the Horn, Angola and Mozambique (MacLeod, 1993). In Eritrea, 10 per cent of agricultural land had been taken out of production by 1987 because of mines (Bondestam et al., 1987). Over one million mines have been planted in Somalia (SCF, 1991), and especially in Somaliland (northern Somalia), many of them since the adoption of the Land Mines Protocol by the United Nations in 1981 (African Rights and Mines Advisory Group, 1993). Angola has one of the highest rates of mine-disabled populations anywhere: it has been estimated that there are at least 15,000 mine-related amputees in the country (Africa Watch, 1993). Others (MacLeod, 1993) put the figure far higher, at a minimum of 38,500. Like UNITA, Renamo has also used anti-personnel mines with devastating effect: mine-related injuries, like direct atrocities, reinforce community awareness of Renamo presence, and place a substantial burden on already overstretched medical resources (Vines, 1991).

Mines represent a threat to sedentary farmer and pastoralist alike, and large numbers of livestock have joined the dead and disabled human victims. Mines also limit the ability of communities to migrate; yet movement is often the key to survival in production crises, as it enables people to seek wild foods, grain, markets, employment and security. In southern Sudan access to wild foods was curtailed, particularly around garrison towns (Africa Watch, 1990a); people were unable to leave the towns because of roadblocks and mines, and trees and bushes, the source of berries and bark, were felled to deny opposition forces access to cover. Garrison towns were encircled by double rings of mines, the first laid by the army, the second by rebels: those attempting to flee risked explosion or being shot by both sides (ibid.).

Disruption of other coping mechanisms represents an additional burden. Wild foods, for example, serve as a means of exchange for other commodities, including grain. In Eritrea, collection of wild foods was reserved for army forces who lacked other sources of provisions (Africa Watch, 1990b). In Angola, community attempts to gather wild foods were blocked by UNITA (Africa Watch, 1989). In southern Sudan, those most affected by the famine frequently had their wares confiscated, thus denying them a potential source of income (Hutchinson, 1991).

Restrictions on movement affect groups differentially according to age, gender and wealth. Men may avoid movement to particular areas to evade enforced conscription, detention or harassment by opposition forces. Women may face assault and rape, and their perception of this threat has limited their freedom to move. Fear of harassment by government troops was cited as the primary cause of restriction on movement by Eritrean women and men interviewed by Bondestam et al. (1987). Tigrayan fears of resettlement and forcible conscription similarly led to their opting to walk for four to six weeks across the Sudanese border, rather than seek relief in government held towns, two or three hours away (Hendrie, 1991).

Those fleeing attacks on their homes and property have also been subject to further military action by aerial bombardment and ground troops. Refugees returning to Sudan from Ethiopia were greeted by aerial attacks. The strafing of refugees has also been reported in Tigray (Hendrie, 1991), Eritrea (Africa Watch, 1990b) and Somalia (Africa Watch, 1990c). Roadblocks are often established, with soldiers attempting to extract bribes, which the poorest may be unable to afford. In Ethiopia, taxes and "voluntary contributions" were forcibly sought from populations seeking food and refuge in government-held areas; these acted as a further disincentive for people to travel (Hendrie, 1991). In Liberia, displaced rural communities have been stripped of their food and remaining assets by rebel troops before being allowed to enter Monrovia (Africa Watch, 1990d).

In periods of production failure, communities which usually practice subsistence agriculture become increasingly dependent on markets, as households seek to realise assets such as livestock and jewellery in exchange for grain. Markets also provide employment and trading opportunities, and act as important centres for the exchange of information, vital to the decision-making processes that determine survival. The collapse of markets, therefore, serves as a key indicator in assessing the impact of conflict on food security (De Waal, 1990b).

Restrictions on movement contribute to the breakdown of the marketing systems, as merchants fear transporting produce into insecure regions. Markets have also been the direct targets of attack as military forces seek to disrupt the social and economic cornerstone of rural communities. Operation Red Star in Ethiopia in 1982 is, perhaps, the best example of such tactics, as the army sought to isolate Eritrea from surplus-producing areas within Tigray, and to block flows of food from Sudan (Hendrie, 1991). The threat of such attacks prompted the rebel forces to hold markets throughout the region on the same night each week, on the assumption that the air force would be unable to bomb all markets simultaneously. This meant, however, that merchants were unable to circulate effectively between markets, and spent several idle days each week. Holding markets under cover of darkness brought other problems, as people could not clearly see what they were buying, nor how it was measured. Aerial and ground attacks also destroyed scales and grain mills vital to the maintenance of the grain trade (De Waal, 1990b).

Sieges of key towns and cities represent one of the most dramatic restrictions on movement and the ability of populations to secure adequate food. They have been used in countless conflicts, most recently highlighted in Sarajevo in Bosnia. Towns typically provide the bases for government actions within the conflict zone; their incursions into the surrounding rural areas may force civilians to seek refuge and employment in towns, bringing them under government control. Government-held towns are subject to siege by opposition forces who may seek to starve the military into submission by restricting flows of food into the town. A siege lasting about a year took place around the Eritrean capital of Asmara, as the Eritrean Peoples Liberation Front sought to recapture the city, causing unknown numbers of civilian deaths (Africa Watch, 1990b).

Within towns, military and commercial interests may become allied; profiteering has been widely reported in garrison towns in Sudan, Eritrea and Somalia. Such practices further inflate grain prices, restricting the entitlement of the poorest to staple foods. Attacks on relief supplies by military personnel to maintain high grain prices is reported to have occurred in Torit, southern Sudan, in September 1988 (Africa Watch, 1990a). Keen (1991) describes the complex set of commercial and private interests served by maintaining the blockade on food into the region. Civilians living within garrison towns are also liable to have their property and food looted, as was experienced in Monrovia (Liberia), Asmara (Eritrea) and Hargeisa (Somalia).

Garrison towns are also often centres for relief, as governments may restrict the delivery of food into rural areas held by rebel forces. Food aid is frequently targeted: both government and rebel forces argue that their attacks on relief convoys are justified because such convoys serve as a cover to supply the opposition forces with weapons and other provisions. Such events may be, in some cases, unintentional, but they nevertheless lead to a loss of good faith. A plane that UNICEF had chartered to fly supplies from Nairobi to Mogadishu was impounded by Kenyan police after it was found to be flying money and military uniforms to Ali Mahdi while still bearing UN markings and using the UN flight code. The failure to ensure the removal of UN markings from a hired plane prejudiced further UN flight activities (Human Rights Watch, 1993). This problem of military attacks on relief becomes particularly acute if food aid does indeed move as part of military convoys. In southern Sudan the military insisted that relief trucks required protection from rebel attack; and humanitarian supplies often became incorporated into military convoys, which were moving army personnel and military equipment.

The threat of aerial attack on relief convoys in Eritrea and Tigray led to lorries travelling at night, slowing their movement considerably, and halving their coverage and efficiency (Hendrie, 1991). Often, feeding centres are also targeted. Camps in Somalia, which housed Ogadeni refugees, were frequently attacked by Somali National Movement rebels, on the grounds that opposing Western Somalian Liberation Front troops were provisioned within the camps. Although young men were particularly targeted, such attacks undermined the sense of security of the entire community. The militarisation of the camps led to the withdrawal of the United Nations High Commission for Refugees in 1989 (Africa Watch, 1990c). Similarly, Ethiopian air-force MIG bombers strafed ICRC feeding camps in Tigray, dropping incendiary devices and napalm. In just one incident fifty-two people were killed and an orphan centre destroyed (Hendrie, 1991).

Forced population relocation

Both government and rebel forces have forcibly displaced large civilian populations. All displaced communities, particularly those within camps and towns, are at risk both from the lack of access to their lands and means of subsistence, and from the changed disease environment. However, where people maintain their freedom to move in and around the area they can trade grain for other commodities, and may be able to supplement rations with wild foods. They can also take advantage of employment and trade opportunities, or claim patronage from kin, and may thus be able to access food supplies and health services.

Forced resettlement of populations has been characterised by high levels of violence, inadequate logistical and health planning, and restrictions on people's ability to diversify their sources of food and income. Ethiopia's resettlement programme is the most publicised example of such a policy (see, for example, Clay and Holcomb, 1985). One of the aims of the programme was to depopulate large areas of northern Wollo and Southern Tigray, areas of rebel activity. Transport arrangements were appalling, with large numbers of people dying from crush injuries and thirst. The lack of adequate food and health services in host areas placed enormous stresses on the indigenous communities.

In October 1990, the Sudanese government forcibly removed the population of Hilat Shook, a settlement for displaced southerners, near Khartoum. They were relocated twenty-five miles away from the city centre and left without adequate access to water, food and employment. In Angola, Africa Watch (1989) estimated that the majority of the 600,000 people living in UNITA-held areas had been abducted and forcibly resettled. Government forces also moved hundreds of thousands of people

out of rural areas into militarised towns, ostensibly for "their protection",
but also to deny UNITA a base and prevent communities from providing
details of government troop movements (Africa Watch, 1991). UNITA
has been accused of failing to allow displaced populations to return home
in order to ensure that relief aid is channelled through the organisation,
and thus maintain the population's dependence upon it (Brittain, 1992).

In Mozambique, Renamo brutally enslaved large sectors of the population, forcing them to work as agricultural labourers or porters. The
Mozambican government relocated substantial numbers of people, initially
in an attempt to collectivise agriculture but, as the war progressed, also in
an attempt to provide security and services to these populations. In certain areas the resettlement programme may have been motivated by the
desire to remove potential sources of support from the insurgents (see
Chapter 12 in this volume).

Such population movements undoubtedly represent one of the most
severe health and nutritional risks to war-affected communities. They also
constitute a threat to future food security, as it takes considerable time for
farmers to rehabilitate their farms after prolonged absence. If others settle
their land, this may provide a recipe for future conflict. Displaced communities are among the most vulnerable groups in conflict-related famines.
Populations forced to move away from their homes by the dual pressures
of hunger and violence have often been stripped of their assets and suffer
harassment as they attempt to move in search of food and security. They
become dependent on the goodwill of their host communities to provide
employment and to facilitate their access to food supplies, including food
aid. This dependency renders displaced communities vulnerable to exploitation – the re-emergence of slavery in Southern Sudan is the most extreme
example of this. Slaves are often inadequately fed, and risk severe punishment or even death if they try to escape (Keen, 1991; Hutchinson, 1991).

Acts of provision: differential supply of food

Food may be selectively provided to government supporters, to those
from whom support is sought, or to lure sections of the population to
areas controlled by the military. Selective provision of food is poorly
documented, perhaps reflecting donors' reluctance to publicise the abuse
of food aid, as well as the difficulties of distinguishing between abuses as
part of a "hearts and minds" campaign and the humanitarian activities of
either side.

Differential provisioning of military and civilian populations has been
reported in Somalia where food aid, donated by USAID, was regularly
diverted to the armed forces and government bodies. Only 12 per cent of
the food aid reached the civilian population for whom it was destined
(Askin, 1987). In garrison towns held under siege, differential provisioning

is commonplace. In Wau, southern Sudan, Fertit people were encouraged to steal grain at the expense of Dinka communities (Africa Watch, 1990a). Similarly, merchants in Meiram refused to sell grain to displaced Dinka, despite their severe undernutrition; food aid in the area was diverted to Baggara herdsmen to use as fodder (Keen, 1991). In Asmara, the capital of Eritrea, the government militia were paid in grain, and all military personnel received larger rations than civilians (Africa Watch, 1990b).

Food has been used to lure civilian populations into areas controlled by government or rebel forces: in Tigray, for example, feeding centres acted as collection sites for the government's resettlement programme. Similarly, by blocking relief aid into rural, rebel-held areas and centring relief efforts in garrison towns, famine-affected populations may be forced to move into government-held areas.

Food is regularly used as part of propaganda campaigns. In Liberia, Charles Taylor sought to regain the support of Mandingo muslims by distributing sheep and extra rations of grain (*West Africa*, 1990). The differential provisioning of refugees from the Ogaden proved a major source of conflict among the indigenous communities, reflecting the importance of providing compensatory aid for host communities (Duffield, 1990a).

Towards a New Approach to Conflict and Famine

This review indicates that deliberate interventions in food marketing, distribution and aid flows, and attacks on production have contributed to, and in some cases caused, successive famines in Ethiopia, Angola, Southern Sudan, Somalia and Mozambique. In many of these famines, terror and attacks on food systems were superimposed on natural disasters such as drought. In Liberia, the initial phase of a counterinsurgency war gave way to widespread banditry; here food was not systematically used as a proxy weapon, but the small size of the country and comparative accessibility of rural areas enabled rebel and government troops to depopulate rapidly large swathes of the countryside, precipitating a food security crisis among the displaced communities as well as in urban centres.

It is not always possible to ascertain whether it is fear or hunger which ultimately drives war-affected people to flee their homes and farms: in most cases one can safely assume a combination of the two. Much of the work reviewed is descriptive and lacks quantitative estimates of the impact of conflict on food supply. It also tends to be selective in that it is dependent upon relatively few sources of information. The history of few communities affected by wars of hunger has been documented. Such limitations are inherent within such violent and unstable environments, and much more work needs to be done to establish more effective systems for monitoring food insecurity in conflict areas. The work of De Waal (1990a) and Duffield (1990a) does, however, offer the beginnings of a model that traces the complex impact of low-intensity war on the socio-economic structures that support food production and distribution. Attacks on health care, the denial of education and technical services, and the traumatisation of large sectors of the civilian population all compound this negative impact.

The crises promoted by such military strategies are therefore much more than crises of food supply. Rather, they represent the systematic and deliberate violation of individual rights to biological survival, and social and economic rights to produce and to secure an adequate livelihood. Humanitarian crises are intentionally created, and powerful political and economic pressures strive to ensure that they are sustained in order to achieve their objectives of cultural genocide and political and economic power. It is this potent combination of political and economic factors driving and maintaining disaster-producing conflicts which creates what are increasingly referred to as "complex emergencies". Such emergencies differ from those spawned by natural disasters in a context where the state has the capacity and willingness to provide emergency assistance. In conflict-related humanitarian crises not only are the means of independent survival blocked, but the means to mitigate the threat are often deliberately denied or manipulated.

Complex emergencies are further distinguished from environmental disasters by their persistence over long periods of time, thus threatening the capacity of those affected to return to production. Migration patterns associated with flight from terror differ from the coping strategies normally employed under enviro-economic crises. Their magnitude brings particular health risks, and these movements away from conflict areas are often more long-lasting than those associated with enviro-economic disasters, where families seek to return quickly to their homes and farms to plant. The tactics of low-intensity warfare aim to control civilian populations by restricting movement and rendering communities destitute through asset-stripping: the choices open to famine victims are steadily narrowed, and they become more dependent upon a potentially hostile commercial sector and market economy to sustain themselves and their families. The very complexity of these emergencies suggests that it is time to reframe models of disaster-mitigation developed largely to contain the effects of enviro-economic crisis, and that urgent attention must be paid to understanding the conditions required for conflict prevention and resolution.

Complex Emergencies: A Framework for Policy Action

As discussed above, conflict-generated emergencies by their very nature are complex. Their causes can be traced back to what Duffield calls the "active underdevelopment" and breakdown of the state, and its replacement by a political culture which reinforces and condones the use of violence to secure assets and maintain power (Duffield, Chapter 3 in this volume). Preventing, mitigating and resolving such conflicts, and the humanitarian crises which they provoke, therefore require far more than a technical, logistical fix. Rather, such crises raise questions that lie at the very heart of contemporary international relations and reverberate to the core of conflict-affected communities.

This section highlights the limitations of the policy paradigms currently in place with regard to the prevention, mitigation and resolution of conflict and famine. These three processes should not be seen as mutually exclusive: they are significantly affected by, and significantly affect, one another. We attempt here to explore their relationships, rather than to present firm boundaries between them.

Prevention of complex emergencies

Addressing structural vulnerability

Underlying the visible crises generated by war are the less visible but deeper structural crises of underdevelopment and maldevelopment. As David Sogge (Chapter 5 in this volume) powerfully argues with regard to Angola, the roots of vulnerability to conflict and its humanitarian consequences can be traced far back to the colonial era and to the strategies for development employed by newly independent states and their international backers. The rural and urban poor have become steadily marginalised, forced back onto their own limited resources to eke out a precarious living, disconnected from the formal political and economic life of the state.

Multilateral and bilateral donors have responded to the economic crisis bedevilling the continent through the introduction of structural adjustment programmes; these sought to reform the role of the state in production and economic management. The relative failure of these programmes to achieve their objectives led development economists to explore further the political conditions influencing the design and implementation of reform measures (Meier, 1993). The introduction of market reforms has come to be seen as contingent upon the adoption of Western-style democracy, which would boost private investment and increase the accountability of the state.

The human-rights records of Third World governments have therefore come under closer scrutiny and to serve as a proxy indicator for levels of democracy. Conditionality policies increasingly seek to reward "good governments" with additional development funds and to support legislative, constitutional and penal reform (Chalker, 1991). Those governments which fail to conform to donor criteria may be subject to cuts or suspension of aid until suitable reforms are implemented. However, the imposition of a multitude of conditionalities on aid – from those concerning economic policy to environmental impact, to human rights and military expenditure – may simply overburden states whose capacity and willingness to engage in formal, long-term planning for development is limited by their need simply to survive. Mark Duffield notes the irrelevance of international posturing to governments such as those in Sudan, which have developed powerful economic and political tools, often including violence, to maintain their grip on power (Chapter 3 in this volume).

Furthermore, it is important to note that the imposition of these conditions has taken the form of a one-way dialogue, which omits international responsibility for improving the global environment within which national policy must operate. Conspicuously absent from the agenda are economic obligations on the industrialised countries to ensure fair trade and reduce the Third World's debt burden, as well as environmental measures to control pollutants and ensure the more equitable and appropriate use of natural resources. Both these factors may have a substantial impact on a nation's ability to create the political, economic and environmental conditions within which its populations can thrive.

To date, the international community has placed greater emphasis on conditions regarding macro-economic reform than on those concerned to protect human rights. Where human-rights and governance issues have been addressed, concern has focused on the monitoring of individual civil and political rights. The remits of human-rights agencies such as Amnesty International and the UN Centre for Human Rights in Geneva reflect this concentration on the protection of largely "negative" rights, that is, those which seek to limit the state's control over the life of the individual. Far less donor attention has been paid to the importance of protecting "positive" social, economic and cultural rights, such as the right to adequate food, health and education. The failure of the donor community to address this broader human-rights dimension has been attributed to their reluctance to accept the costly obligations associated with the right to development (see Tomasevksi, Chapter 4 in this volume).

It is also important to recognise that democracy per se does not guarantee accountability or prosperity (ODI, 1992). The maintenance of elected parliaments rests upon economic stability, and their ability to resolve conflicts which may emerge as different groups claim their right to increased autonomy or secession (Rupesinge, 1990). The viability of reinventing and imposing the Western democratic tradition is sorely questioned in the current African context. Models of development which fail to acknowledge the presence of powerful actors who have a vested interest in undermining the productive capacity and development of large regions, or who seek to disempower distinct population groups, ignore the potential for conflict that exists and the subsequent threat to sustainable and equitable development.

Addressing the structural factors that increase societies' vulnerability to conflict and associated humanitarian disasters will require a reappraisal of models of development which largely ignore the changing nature of the state in many countries experiencing acute economic and political stress. The informalisation of the economy, and the subsequent fragmentation of political power as ethnicity and religious ties are manipulated to secure access to assets and land, present a major threat to development prospects in Africa and elsewhere. Responding to these threats will require alleviating the stress placed on these fragile economies by international debt and the imposition of unproven economic prescriptions. It will also demand improved mechanisms for monitoring potential points of conflict at the national and community levels and the development of innovative, transparent and appropriate civil institutions to resolve tensions.

Planning against conflict

Prevention of conflict must be included within the design of development projects at the community level. Implicitly this may already be included in considerations of equity; yet explicit acknowledgement of actual tensions between ethnic, religious and political groups may be vital in ensuring that violent conflict is avoided. Nnoli (1990) and Horowitz (1989) have urged development planners to recognise the effects of differential development patterns in creating sources of tension among communities who are under environmental and economic stress. The example of northern Somalia or that of southern Sudan should act as a powerful reminder to development planners of the perils of differential development and relief inputs. Such lessons are relevant to many parts of the world: the rebellion of the indigenous communities of Chiapas, Mexico in 1994 brought this lesson home to neighbouring states.

Mitigation

Getting the questions right

Complex emergencies related to conflict may be considered slow-onset disasters (Shears, 1991). As a given crisis is linked to the cumulative impact of structural factors and violence on a population, defining its beginning (and its end) is likely to be difficult. This is compounded where emergencies and famine are defined primarily in terms of their impact on population mortality rates, rather than in terms of the broader social, political and economic conditions that are integral features of such disasters.

De Waal (1987) has argued with respect to food crises more generally that equating famine with starvation reduces it to an individual biological crisis, ignoring its socio-economic precursors and consequences. Famine, and by implication complex emergencies more specifically, can be defined as a process rooted in vulnerability to environmental, economic and politi-

cal shocks, which extends to acute stress, prompting new strategies of
survival and culminating in death.

Considerable attention has been paid to understanding the process of
famine development in non-conflict situations and to devising methods of
supporting the initial attempts by communities to cope with enviro-
economic shocks. Much less attention, however, has been paid to the
processes that create complex emergencies and to designing appropriate
methods of mitigation (Duffield, Chapter 3 in this volume). This failure
relates to the fundamental misconception within the international community of the nature of complex emergencies, which systematically ignores
the inherently political dimensions of these disasters, and subsequently
fails to acknowledge that these situations are characterised not only by
groups of losers, but also by groups of winners. Not recognising the
winners in particular means that the factors perpetuating violence are not
identified. Furthermore, there is a lack of recognition of the fact that
international aid interventions may serve to reinforce inequalities in power,
further contributing to the political and economic marginalisation of the
losers in conflict-famines. The limitations of the humanitarian framework
internationally have major implications for the design of political, legal
and operational responses to conflict-generated disasters.

Political framework for mitigation

Ignoring the political factors underlying the creation and maintenance of
famine does not imply that international attempts to mitigate its effects
are not themselves highly political. The British government excludes humanitarian assistance from ODA political conditionality, believing that
"ordinary people should [not] suffer twice" (Chalker, 1991). This argument
suggests that the withdrawal of development aid does not contribute to
increasing vulnerability to disasters such as famine, and that therefore
people have not already "suffered twice", a problematic assumption.
Second, by excluding relief aid from the political agenda it suggests that
the provisioning of food aid is an apolitical act, motivated exclusively by
humanitarian concerns.

Clearly, however, donors are aware of the vital political role of food
aid. In 1984, despite the failure of the Nimeiri regime to declare a famine,
USAID mobilised food aid to avert a crisis for the Sudanese government.
In 1985, USAID was willing to support the cross-border operation into
the northern region of Ethiopia, despite its questionable legality (in international law), in order to remove the potential destabilising effect of the
substantial population movements into Sudan (Hendrie, 1989). By 1990
the complexion of the Sudanese government had changed, and donors
were no longer willing to bypass conventional protocols about waiting for
formal declaration of the famine within Sudan; it has been suggested that
donors were using food aid as a political weapon to cause a major food

crisis, and so undermine the government (*Proceedings of "Famine Now" Conference*, 1991).

In 1983, many if not most of the 100,000 famine deaths occurring in Mozambique could have been averted had food aid been provided to the Mozambican government to distribute or by risking personnel and vehicles in areas under attack from Renamo (Green, 1986). However, the aid agencies had made a political decision not to grant such aid: when they did a year later, in a more adverse security situation, deaths in the affected population were sharply reduced. If such informal conditionality does operate on relief aid, donors have a responsibility to acknowledge the policy and to state the reasons publicly.

The public face of emergency aid is presented as apolitical, designed to relieve human suffering whatever the political conditions that have caused it. However, the lack of a coherent and transparent international policy framework to guide intervention and distribution of resources has resulted in ad hoc decisions motivated by strategic political and institutional concerns, and even by the personal attitudes of policy-makers rather than the needs of conflict-affected populations (Hendrie, Chapter 7 in this volume).

The trend towards the politicisation of humanitarian assistance is most marked where the provision of emergency aid is combined with military intervention, as in the cases of Kurdistan, Bosnia and Somalia. As the boundaries between humanitarian assistance and peace-making are blurred, so the capacity of aid agencies to reach their constituencies may be reduced. The risks are increased where international strategic objectives are overly simplistic and fail to take account of the nature of the conflict itself. The tendency of the international community to identify conflicts with individual leaders, such as General Aideed in Somalia, and to seek their removal from power, underestimates the complex dynamics of war and the need to support the development of alternative civil institutions which can provide a more sustainable basis for peace (see Keen and Wilson, Chapter 12 in this volume).

Legal framework for mitigation

These changes in the international political environment are reflected in changes to the international legal context within which relief operations are being framed. Tomasevski (Chapter 4 in this volume), argues that the legislative framework within which interventions are implemented is itself contributing to the problem of complex emergencies. In particular, the emphasis in international law is being placed less on the rights of conflict-affected communities to *receive* assistance, and more on ensuring the rights of the international community to *deliver* emergency aid. This emerging bias in legal provision potentially further undermines attempts to develop an international framework of entitlement to assistance and protection, and provides the international community with yet more political space to justify ad hoc military interventions in order to enforce their right to access victims.

International aid: part of the conflict dynamic?

Aid, far from being politically neutral, is a political and economic resource. David Keen's exposition of the process of famine creation and maintenance in south-western Sudan explains how conflict was sustained by efforts to control and co-opt efforts to relieve the famine (see Chapter 6 in this volume; Keen, 1991). This is not surprising given that the groups and institutions responsible for violence and oppression are often the same as those involved in the distribution of relief aid (Duffield, Chapter 3 in this volume). Existing mechanisms for the delivery of aid therefore reinforce inequalities of power, benefiting the winners and denying the losers.

Wilson and Keen (Chapter 12 in this volume), for example, describe the appalling similarities in the design of international relief operations and those used by military forces to control populations. The creation of emergency relief camps persists, despite the well-documented public health risks of such structures: control of populations, whether by international aid agencies concerned with maximising the effectiveness of food distribution and the visibility of their inputs, or by soldiers concerned to depopulate specific areas, exposes the powerless to major health risks, while allowing the powerful (internationally and nationally) to meet their objectives.

Institutions for aid delivery

The choice of institutions to deliver emergency aid can have a profound effect both on the effectiveness of the intervention and on the course of the conflict. Internationally, donors are choosing increasingly to support development initiatives implemented by the non-governmental organisations (NGOs) (Meyer, 1992). This trend, reinforced by the ideology of privatisation during the 1980s, is based on the assumption that the alternative structures offered by NGOs are more responsive to the needs of Third World communities. An important part of this process of transfer of institutional responsibility and donor support has been the emergence of what Korten (1990) describes as "public-service contracting", arrangements which typically involve a major bilateral or multilateral donor paying Northern NGOs to implement a predetermined package of assistance (Duffield, 1990a; and Chapter 3 in this volume).

This concept is particularly well developed in complex emergencies where national government structures either lack the capacity to implement relief programmes or are perceived to be actively hostile to relief interventions. In countries where bilateral development aid has been suspended, donor relief aid is commonly provided through multilateral agencies such as the World Food Programme and the United Nations High Commissioner for Refugees, which in turn may subcontract work to

Northern NGOs such as CARE, Oxfam, and Save the Children Fund. Northern NGOs are seen as neutral channels for humanitarian assistance without political allegiance, and may implement operations which, under international law, multilateral and bilateral agencies might not wish to support directly. However, many Northern NGOs also fear alienating national governments in order to protect their long-term development and relief interests in government-held areas of the country. Human Rights Watch has criticised the failure of international agencies, specifically the United Nations, to condemn human-rights abuses in order to maintain other ongoing projects (Human Rights Watch, 1993). It argues that being consistent about human-rights principles and opposing all forms of black-mail will lead to improvements in the longer term.

The reliance of the international community on private agencies to implement disaster-relief programmes may exert pressure on Northern NGOs to refrain from publicising the conditions that have created famine and that block relief operations. It has been suggested that the role of NGOs as contractors to bilateral and multilateral agencies may serve to maintain their silence if they fear that their comments are likely to elicit sanctions (Duffield, personal communication). Within their home countries, Northern NGOs may face constraints to publicising the political causes of contemporary famines. In Britain the charity laws limit the advocacy work of agencies to "apolitical" campaigning activities, and charities may fear alienating their constituents if they reveal the full extent of man's involvement in the process of famine creation.

Northern NGOs and organisations such as the ICRC are increasingly forced to bear the public face of donor policy as they become the proxy means of maintaining aid flows. They face a multitude of ethical and political influences, yet their programmes are not subject to public scrutiny and accountability; nor are they openly evaluated. Most important of all, there is no international ombudsman to whom the intended beneficiaries of such programmes can appeal if they have reason to complain. The criteria according to which donors decide on the suitability of provisioning particular forces or the means of delivering aid are not always guided by international law, and are only scrutinised by their home parliaments, if by anyone at all.

Northern voluntary agencies may rely upon indigenous relief agencies, such as the Eritrean Relief Association (ERA), the Relief Society of Tigray (REST); and the Sudan Relief and Rehabilitation Association (SRRA) in southern Sudan, to deliver relief into rebel-held areas. Such groups may have clear political allegiances. The provision of food into rebel-held areas may serve numerous functions over and above the humanitarian: by maintaining food supplies, civilian communities are able to remain in their homes, or at least within the region. This is significant not only for their own health, but also serves to legitimise the rebel force. The ability of such forces to feed the people under their control is a primary concern in wars that depend on popular support. As Green (1986) puts it, "providing food aid saves lives and bolsters the authority of the political institutions through which it is provided. Not providing it kills human beings and erodes the political strength of those who are unable to feed their people." Second, food aid may be used to feed military personnel. While this may help reduce the likelihood that grain stores will be plundered or homes raided, food aid that sustains a particular fighting force can determine the outcome of the conflict. Interestingly, in the lead up to the Angolan elections the UN agencies agreed to provide food for both government and UNITA forces. Where rebels do not benefit from the legitimising role of food aid, they may be forced to accept a premature or unfavourable settlement, as occurred in Biafra (Gorndeker and Weiss, 1989) and in Zimbabwe (Sanders, 1982).

International agencies may also face dilemmas about which rebel-held areas they choose to supply. For example, would humanitarian aid in Renamo-held areas of Mozambique be as appropriate as that given to ERA in Eritrea? Which populations should suffer the "double punishment" of violence and hunger? Some agencies such as the ICRC are bound under their constitution to be impartial in their provisioning of aid and therefore attempt to provide relief to both sides. In an attempt to be "neutral", however, such action may inadvertently lend support to forces which do not operate in the interests of the community, but which nevertheless gain some credibility by being seen to be associated with the provision of food to the population. Such situations present a formidable challenge to the concept of "active neutrality" currently being promoted by many humanitarian agencies. Advocates of this approach argue that by providing both sides of the conflict with equal access to relief aid the security of humanitarian operations can be enhanced, potential conflicts between opposing parties over access to relief resources can be mitigated, and civilian populations can be equitably provided with assistance irrespective of their location (Jean, 1992). While the concept of active neutrality may facilitate the delivery of relief, it is unclear what its potential impact may be on the dynamics of conflict. If such neutrality is operationalised directly or indirectly through the same institutions that are promoting violence against civilian populations, as was the case with Renamo, it may be argued that relief may serve to fuel, rather than resolve, conflict. It is clear that such decisions will have to be made on a case-by-case basis, and each presents formidable moral and operational dilemmas.

In the case of Somalia, De Waal argues that Northern NGOs and UN agencies have undermined the development of indigenous civilian institutions that provide a basis for mitigating disaster. Given that many contemporary conflicts are synonymous with the breakdown of these civil institutions, and that the resolution of conflict will be contingent upon creating more effective and representative civilian bodies, such failures will have important implications both for the operational effectiveness of interventions in the intra-conflict period and for longer-term development.

Increasing the accountability of relief efforts will depend upon including the intended beneficiaries in the processes of planning and distribution. It will also be contingent upon securing more accurate analysis of the political landscape: evaluating the potentials and limitations of different organisational structures in different contexts, assessing their capacities and the risks they face. In the cases of Tigray and Somalia, the importance of supporting indigenous humanitarian agencies and institutions clearly lies in their capacity both to develop effective mechanisms for the delivery of relief and to contribute to rebuilding devastated civil societies.

Mitigation: towards alternative strategies

It has been suggested that the weakness of the international response to complex emergencies results from two distinct but related factors. First, the nature of the problem has been inadequately conceptualised: in particular the humanitarian disasters promoted by conflict are being seen as the consequence of, rather than the objective of, political and military strategies. Such an analysis fails to identify those who gain from promoting humanitarian disasters. This misconception has resulted in an international political system which simultaneously denies its own role in sustaining complex emergencies and threatens further the capacity of victims of conflict-related disasters to access humanitarian assistance. The refusal to acknowledge explicitly the political function of relief in conflict situations contributes to the maintenance of violence, playing into the hands of the powerful, while the politicisation of humanitarian assistance, through selective provision and the militarisation of delivery, increases the security threat to humanitarian agencies.

Reversing the failures of existing policies will be contingent upon clarifying both the nature of conflict and the function of assistance (nationally and internationally) in these conflicts. Keen and Wilson (Chapter 12 in this volume) develop such an analysis which might be used to inform operational design. They postulate that if certain patterns of relief can contribute to increasing violence, so alternative patterns could serve to reduce conflict. Their approach relies upon understanding the context within which relief takes place and the responses it provokes. They note, for example, that ensuring equitable allocation of resources between opposing parties may serve to reduce those instances of violence that take place when relief goods are delivered to only one side. They go on to question the type of resources typically provided to conflict-affected communities: the delivery of free relief food may simply undermine local markets, while failing to provide other inputs such as health care and commodities which communities could use to rebuild their asset base.

Resolution

Just as complex emergencies are slow to begin, so are they slow to end. The structural changes in the social, political and economic environments engendered by conflict are not reversed by the signing of formal peace treaties, nor by the election of new governments. Reginald Green (Chapter 2 in this volume) and Lionel Cliffe (Chapter 9) discuss the long-term costs of conflict and their implications for the restoration of food security and the reduction of vulnerability to conflict.

As structural threats and shocks to food security systems persist, such as drought and fluctuations in commodity prices, so too do threats to political security. As Cliffe points out with regard to Eritrea, the potential for violent disputes regarding land tenure arrangements in the "post"-conflict period is significant as large numbers of people displaced by the war return, threatening the delicate equilibrium of land-holding in the country. Anti-personnel mines litter vast swathes of Eritrea, Angola and Somalia. The laying of mines represents a serious threat to future production. Their deactivation is a skilled and hazardous job. Often those trained in the art are unwilling to utilise their skill, recognising the danger (McGrath, 1990); Ahlstrom (1990) estimated that one person would die and two be injured for every 5,000 mines deactivated, let alone those accidentally detonated by the unwary. Yet there are literally millions of mines clustered in specific areas across the African continent.

Similarly, in the absence of adequate planning for the demobilisation of military forces on both sides of a conflict, the presence of significant quantities of small arms in the hands of young men, often denied adequate employment opportunities, can quickly promote widespread and violent banditry. There are indications that increasingly violence may be used to settle all forms of conflict, whether in the home, where women are most often the victims, or elsewhere in the community.

"Post"-conflict rehabilitation therefore requires not just significant resources if the legacy of violence and food crises are to be reversed: institutions will need to be rebuilt if potential sources of conflict are to be recognised and resolved before violence re-emerges. As discussed earlier with regard to Somalia and Tigray, the capacity of such institutions to contribute to post-conflict recovery may be enhanced or undermined in the intra-conflict period depending on the way in which relief is organised nationally and internationally.

Conclusion

Conflict-related humanitarian emergencies are not new phenomena, but they have achieved renewed prominence in recent years. The relative silence among international policy-makers, practitioners and academics concerning political violence is being broken amidst headlines of horror from around the world and the flurry of meetings by the Security Council. Yet the voices of those affected by conflict and hunger are still not being heard. Once again, solutions to Third World problems are being devised in Geneva, Washington, New York and London; once again, the paradigms informing policy choices are being driven by international, not local, imperatives.

The early 1990s have witnessed a series of experiments, largely conducted under the umbrella of the United Nations, which have sought to develop new approaches to mitigating conflict-related disasters. In Iraqi Kurdistan the creation of "safe havens" in 1992, protected by military forces, constituted the first tentative step towards redefining the new global order. UN military involvement in Bosnia has sought to secure delivery of humanitarian assistance, but has strived to avoid direct military engagement to achieve its objectives. By contrast, US intervention in Somalia aimed to make peace, purportedly in order to facilitate the delivery of humanitarian assistance. Few would consider any of these operations a humanitarian success story.

These events are of profound importance and mark radical changes in relations between the North and South which will have major implications for communities throughout the Third World. They exemplify an approach to conflict-management which is concerned much less with prevention, than with military and enforced resolution. Yet such strategies clearly underplay the complexity of the factors promoting and underlying many contemporary conflicts, which include structural inequalities, poverty and environmental change. They aim to address the crisis of material provision – food, basic health care and shelter – but they ignore the societal, political and development crises which culminate in complex emergencies. This is in contrast to the UN Secretary-General's *Agenda for Peace*, which clearly identifies prevention and early resolution of conflict, peacemaking, peacebuilding and peacekeeping, as well as the need to address the fundamental causes of conflict, amongst which are "economic despair, social injustice and political oppression" (United Nations Development Programme, 1993).

Given the complexity of contemporary conflicts throughout the world, and the potentially negative impact of international intervention, whether military or ostensibly humanitarian, it is surely time for a fresh appraisal of current approaches to complex emergencies – which includes the voices of those for whom wars are purportedly fought. Only by building upon nascent civil institutions, and by placing greater emphasis on the rights of "victims" rather than those of international agencies, can the process of disempowerment engendered by conflict begin to be reversed.

Note

1. This chapter is a much revised version of an earlier paper: J. Macrae and A.B. Zwi, "Food as an Instrument of War: A Review of the Evidence in Contemporary African Famines", *Disasters* 16 (4) 1992: 299–321.

References

Africa Watch (1989) *Angola: Violations of the Laws of War by Both Sides*, April.
———— (1990a) *Denying the Honor of the Living*, London, New York, Washington.
———— (1990b) "Ethiopia: 200 Days in the Death of Asmara", 20 September.
———— (1990c) "Somalia, Evading Reality: Government Announces Cosmetic Changes as Abuses Continue and Challenge to Regime Intensifies", 12 September.
———— (1990d) "Flight from Terror: Testimony of Abuses in Nimba County", April.
———— (1991) "Angola: Civilians Devastated by 15 Year War", 5 February.
———— (1993) *Land Mines in Angola*, New York.
African Rights and Mines Advisory Group (1993) "Violent Deeds Live On. Land Mines in Somalia and Somaliland", December.
Ahlstrom, C. (1990) "Casualties of Conflict", Report for the World Campaign for the Protection of Victims of War, Department of Peace and Conflict Research, Uppsala University, Sweden.
Askin, S. (1987) "Food Aid Diversion", *Middle East Report*, March–April, pp. 38–9.
Awua-Asmoa, M. (1991) "Implications and Repercussions of the Arms Race in Africa", *Voices from Africa*, 3, NGLS, 1991.
Bondestam, L., Cliffe, L. and White, P. (1987) "Eritrea Food and Agricultural Production Study", Agriculture and Rural Development Unit, University of Leeds.
Brittain, V. (1992) "UN Aid Helps UNITA Defy Peace Terms", *Guardian*, 23 March, p.7.
Buchanan-Smith, M., Bailey, J. and Maxwell, S. (1991) "Famine in Sudan", a symposium held at the Institute for Development Studies, University of Sussex, 23 October 1990, *Disasters*, 15 (2): 196–202.
Chalker, L. (1991) "Good Government and the Aid Programme", speech by the Minister for Overseas Development, Royal Institute of International Affairs, 25 July.
Clay, J. and Holcomb, B. (1985) "Politics and the Ethiopian Famine 1984–1985", Cultural Survival Inc., December.
Cliff, J. and Noormahamed, A.R. (1988) "South Africa's Destabilisation of Mozambique", *Social Science and Medicine*, 27 (7):717–22.
Deng and Zartman (1991) *Conflict Resolution in Africa*, Washington, Brookings Institute.
De Waal, A. (1987) *Famine That Kills: Darfur, Sudan, 1984–1985*, Oxford, Oxford University Press.
———— (1989) "Famine Mortality: A Case Study of Darfur, Sudan 1984–85, *Population Studies*, 43: 5–24.
———— (1990a) "A Reassessment of Entitlement Theory in the Light of Recent Famines in Africa", *Development and Change*, 21: 469–90.
———— (1990b) "Tigray Grain Markets and Internal Purchase", Oxford, Oxfam.

———— (1991) "Counter-population Warfare and Famine in Tigray and Its Border-lands 1980–1984", mimeo.

———— (n.d.) "War and Famine in Africa", mimeo.

Dodge, C. (1990) "Public Health Implications of War in Uganda and Sudan", *Social Science and Medicine*, 31: 691–8.

Dreze, J. and Sen, A. (1989) *Hunger and Public Action*, Oxford, Oxford University Press.

D'Souza, F. (1989) "Famine and the Art of Early Warning: The African Experience", Economics and Social Research Division, Overseas Development Administration.

Duffield, M. (1990a) "War and Famine in Africa: An Exploratory Report for Oxfam", Oxford, November.

———— (1990b) "Sudan at the Crossroads: From Emergency Preparedness to Social Security", *Discussion Paper* 275, Institute of Development Studies, University of Sussex.

———— (1992) "Notes on the Parallel Economy, Conflict and Disaster Relief in the Post-Cold War Era", paper presented at a working meeting on "Conflict and International Relief in Contemporary African Famines", London School of Hygiene and Tropical Medicine and Save the Children Fund, London, 26 March.

Gersony, R. (1988) "Summary of Mozambican Refugee Accounts of Principally Conflict Related Experiences in Mozambique", mimeo.

Gorndeker, L. and Weiss, T. (1989) "Humanitarian Emergencies and Military Help: Some Conceptual Observations", *Disasters*, 13 (2): 118–33.

Green, R.H. (1986) "Hunger, Poverty and Food Aid in Sub-Saharan Africa: Retro-spect and Potential", *Disasters*, 10 (4): 288–310.

———— (1987) "Killing the Dream: The Political Economy of War", *Discussion Paper* 238, Institute of Development Studies, University of Sussex.

———— (1989) "Human Rights, Human Conditions and Law: Some Explorations towards Interaction", *Discussion Paper* 267, Institute of Development Studies, University of Sussex.

Hanlon, J. (1991) *Mozambique – Who Calls the Shots?*, London, James Currey.

Hendrie, B. (1989) "Cross-Border Operations in Eritrea and Tigray", *Disasters*, 13 (4): 351–60.

———— (1991) "Impact of War in Tigray, Ethiopia", Nairobi, draft report for the Inter-Africa Group.

Horowitz, M. (1989) "Victims of Development", *Development Anthropology Network*, 7 (2).

Human Rights Watch (1993) *The Lost Agenda: Human Rights and UN Field Operations*, New York.

Hutchinson, S. (1991) "War Through the Eyes of the Dispossessed: Three Stories of Survival", *Disasters*, 15 (2).

Jansson, K., Harris, M. and Penrose, A. (1987) *The Ethiopian Famine*, London, Zed Books.

Jean, F., ed. (1992) *Populations in Danger*, London, Médecins Sans Frontières and John Libby.

Kanji, N. and Harpham, T. (1992) "From Chronic Emergency to Development: An Analysis of the Health of the Urban Poor in Luanda, Angola", *International Journal of Health Services*, 22 (2): 349–63.

Keen, D. (1991) "A Disaster for Whom?: Local Interests and International Donors during Famine among the Dinka of Sudan", *Disasters*, 15 (2): 150–65.

Korten, D.C. (1990) *Getting to the 21st Century: Voluntary Action and the Global Agenda*, Connecticut, Kumarian Press.

McGrath, R. (1990) "Land Mines", *Refugee Participation Network*, 9.

MacLeod, S. (1993) "And Still They Kill", *Time Magazine*, 50: 14–19.

Meier, G. (1993) "The New Political Economy and Policy Reform", *Journal of International Development*, 5 (4): 381–9.

Meyer, C. (1992) "A Step Back as Donors Shift Institution Buildings from the 'Public' to the Private Sector", *World Development*, 20 (8): 1115–26.

Mourey, A. (1991) "Famine and War", *International Review of the Red Cross*, 284.

Nnoli, O. (1990) "Desertification, Refugees and Regional Conflict in West Africa", *Disasters*, 14 (2).

Overseas Development Institute (ODI)(1992) "AID and Political Reform", briefing paper, London, January.

Prothero, A. (1977) "Disease and Mobility: A Neglected Factor in Epidemiology", *International Journal of Epidemiology*, 6: 259–67.

Proceedings of "Famine Now" Conference (1991), Convened by *Sudan Update*, London, May.

Rangasami, A. (1985) "Failure of Exchange Entitlements Theory of Famine, A Response", *Political and Economic Weekly*, XX (41): 1747–53; XX (42): 1797–1800.

Rupesinge, K. (1990) "The Disappearing Boundaries between Internal and External Conflicts", plenary paper submitted to the International Peace Research Association, Prio.

Sanders, D. (1982) "Nutrition and the Use of Food as a Weapon in Zimbabwe and Southern Africa", *International Journal of Health Services*, 12 (2): 201–13.

Save the Children Fund (SCF) (1991) "Emergency Updates" – Sudan, Ethiopia, Somalia, Overseas Department, London.

Sen, A. (1986) *Famines and Poverty*, Oxford, Oxford University Press.

Schutz, B. and Slater, R. (1990) *Revolution and Political Change in the Third World*, Boulder, Col. and London, Lynne Rienner and Adamantine Press.

Shears, P. (1991) "Epidemiology and Infection in Famines and Disasters", *Epidemiology and Infection*, 107: 241–51.

Sivard, R. (1991) *World Military and Social Expenditures 1991*, 14th edn, Washington, World Priorities.

Spooner, B. and Walsh, N. (1991) "Fighting for Survival: Insecurity, People and the Environment in the Horn of Africa", Vols 1 and 2 (Draft) , International Union for the Conservation of Nature.

Stockton, N. (1989) "Understanding Conflict in Africa", mimeo, Oxford, Oxfam.

Summerfield, D. (1991) "The Psychosocial Effects of Conflict in the Third World", *Development in Practice*, 1 (3): 159–73.

Tomasevski, K. (1990) "Human Rights Violations and Development Aid: From Politics towards Policy", occasional paper, London, Commonwealth Secretariat, Human Rights Unit.

Toole, M. and Waldman, R. (1990) "Prevention of Excess Mortality in Refugee and Displaced Populations in Developing Countries", *Journal of the American Medical Association*, 263 (24): 3296–302.

Turton, D. (1989) "Warfare, Vulnerability and Survival: A Case Study from Southern Ethiopia", *Cambridge Anthropology*, 13 (2): 67–85.

United Nations (UN) (1988) *United Nations Actions in the Field of Human Rights*, UN Centre for Human Rights, Geneva.

United Nations Development Programme (UNDP) (1991) *United Nations Development Report*, UNDP.

——— (1993) *Human Development Report*, New York and Oxford, Oxford University Press.

United Nations and Government of Sudan (UN and GoS) (1990) "Operation Lifeline Sudan Phase II – Background Appeal Document", Khartoum.

Vines, A. (1991) *Renamo: Terrorism in Mozambique*, London, James Currey.

West Africa, (1990) "Killing Fields", 20–26 August.

Wilson, K. (1991) "Food vs Cash Aid", paper submitted to the Nutrition Symposium, Refugee Studies Centre, Oxford, March.

Zwi, A. and Ugalde, A. (1989) "Towards an Epidemiology of Violence", *Social Science and Medicine*, 28 (7): 633–42.

——— (1991) "Political Violence in the Third World: A Public Health Issue", *Health Policy and Planning*, 6 (3): 203–17.

——— (1992) "Should Military Expenditure and Development Aid be Linked?", *British Medical Journal*, 304: 1421–22.

The Course of the Four Horsemen:
The Costs of War and Its Aftermath
in Sub-Saharan Africa
Reginald Herbold Green

We see our future in the smiling faces of our children,
the flowers that do not wither.

SAMORA MACHEL

This is terrorism, but it is not mindless.
They [the warmakers] seek to kill the dream.

JOSEPH HANLON

Introduction: Anguish to Apocalypse

Wars in sub-Saharan Africa are often perceived as small, low impact, and low technology. The last is often, but not by any means always, true; the first two are inversions of reality. In each of Ethiopia, Sudan, Angola and Mozambique, "excess" deaths since 1980 resulting from war are nearing or above one million lives. In two more countries, Eritrea and Somalia, they exceed 500,000 (UNICEF, 1987; 1989). For the last four countries named that loss is of the order of a tenth of the living population of 1993; the same ghastly proportion probably applies to Liberia. For the subcontinent as a whole, any estimate of deaths resulting from war since 1980 that is much below eight million would be unrealistic: these wars are therefore neither "small" nor "low impact".

Using data compiled from UNHCR and UNICEF sources, the number of persons (internally and externally) displaced by war at its 1992 peak exceeded thirty million, much of the burden concentrated among nationals of the same six countries. In the cases of Mozambique, Somalia, Eritrea and Angola, at least half the living population have had to flee at least once; the proportion in Sudan, Liberia, Togo and Uganda may not be much lower.

The deaths resulting from war bear little relation to loss of life of armed personnel or even civilians massacred or killed in crossfire. Dramatic as these manifestations are, estimates for Angola and Mozambique suggest that they account for as little as 5 per cent of the war-related deaths (UNICEF, 1989). There is little reason to suppose detailed study would show great differences in most other cases. Uganda in the 1970s is an exception, because Idi Amin's forces directly massacred up to 500,000 civilians, as are Rwanda and Burundi in the 1990s.

This sombre fact was well known to medieval symbolism: the Four Horsemen of the Apocalypse – Famine, Pestilence, Death and War – ride out together. Without war, drought in Africa (except in Ethiopia) over the past half century has rarely resulted in massive loss of life. Similarly, the collapse of immunisation and primary health care, together with extreme malnutrition, make measles, respiratory diseases and diarrhoea lethal. The health services, like food production and relief food supplies, are casualties of combat zones, mass dislocation, wrecked or blocked transport routes and bankrupted governments. Lack of food and of medical services, combined with the physical stress of flight, kill about twenty times as many human beings in Africa as do bombs, bullets and cold steel. In particular they kill the very young, the elderly and the infirm, and the disabled. In Somalia during 1992 over half, by some estimates almost three quarters, of the children under five alive on 1 January were dead by 31 December, the majority of whom (90 per cent) died from the interaction of extreme malnutrition and disease. Literally dividing deaths in a war and drought zone on a counterfactual estimation of drought deaths in the absence of war is not particularly useful. However, it is crucial to recognise that war impedes relief delivery and may well prevent post-drought output recovery. Furthermore, the end of war will not contribute much to restoring output without substantial livelihood rehabilitation relief unless the period of dislocation has been brief and physical damage limited. As long as war continues, survival assistance is central; only after the achievement of relative peace can (and should) it be converted to livelihood rehabilitation relief, except in secure areas.

Similarly drought, by itself, does not usually lead to significant challenges to governance whether in terms of legitimacy or of loss of capacity to function. Extended war on national territory, though not necessarily solidarity and forward defence campaigns in neighbouring states, does severely erode capacity. This may or may not reduce legitimacy during the war, but, in the absence of speedy reconstruction and livelihood rehabilitation, is likely to do so in its aftermath.

War-related deaths occur predominantly within war-ravaged countries and amongst refugees from them. There are, however, also indirect deaths inflicted on people of countries which are forced to incur heavy (relative to resources) defence expenditure on their own or their neighbours' behalf, with resultant damage to the absolute level, or the rate of expansion, of basic health services. Tanzania is the most evident case in point: loss of life has resulted primarily from the economic and fiscal burden of war choking off and setting back food security and, more especially, expansion of effective primary health services. These deaths are far more numerous than those of Tanzanian soldiers who died in action in Uganda and Mozambique, or even the ten thousand people massacred by Idi Amin's forces when they invaded Kagera in 1979.

Similarly, economic costs are not limited to direct war damage, massive as this has been in Angola, Mozambique, Eritrea, Somalia, southern Sudan and northern Ethiopia. The destruction of capital stock has led to lost output. The high costs of militarisation and the provision of assistance for displaced populations has also necessitated a reduction in imports for consumption, production and investment, and budget constrictions on health services and food security. However, even the import or relief bills do not capture the full scope of the economic loss. For example, reduction in rubber imports causes a loss of domestic value-added in tyres and subsequently of value-added in transport (as tyreless vehicles are grounded), and of agricultural production (as crops cannot be marketed).

For households, direct war damage is low relative to output loss. The destruction of livelihood results primarily from inability to farm normally or, in many cases, to remain in or near homes and farms. It also arises from the costs of assisting displaced persons. For the ten independent states of southern Africa, gross domestic product losses have been estimated at above $60,000 million over the period 1980–91 (in 1991 prices), running at nearly $12,000 million annually by 1991 or over 40 per cent of achieved output. In the cases of Mozambique and Angola, actual 1991 output was around half of what might reasonably have been expected in the absence of war.

War Types and War Costs

War costs vary with the type of war. However, the basic differences do not appear to depend as much on the level of technology (especially if the imported arms are "paid" for on credit), as on the location and duration of the war. The technology level of the war primarily affects the import bill and the fiscal balance. The high-technology war in Angola and the relatively low-technology conflict in Mozambique have been equally lethal; the same applies in comparing the conflicts in Ethiopia and Eritrea, or Ethiopia and Somalia. The immediate economic impact depends on whether medium-term external credit is available; in the longer term it hinges on whether the credit is paid. But, as war deaths in Africa are only peripherally the direct result of combat, high technology and highly trained personnel have only a limited impact on mortality levels.

Whether a war had primarily external or internal initial dynamics, or, as is more usual, a combination of both, is not self-evidently a major factor in cost levels or the composition of the costs. Exceptions to this rule include brief invasions followed by a quick settlement by those invaded, or a rapid repulse or overthrow of a regime by an externally backed domestic exile force. Of these the only significant case is the Tanzanian–Ugandan response to the Amin invasion of Tanzania, which had (excluding later war in Uganda) low human and economic costs for both parties, despite the scale of operations.

Clearly the size of the war relative to area and population is relevant, as is its duration. In Angola, Mozambique, Eritrea (prior to independence), Ethiopia and Sudan, the duration has lasted decades; in the last two cases high proportions of the population have resided in areas not directly afflicted. On the other hand, while the Somalian war can be dated at least to 1987, the real descent into horror was in the three years since 1991 and the collapse of the Barre regime. The tactics adopted also have an impact on the economic and human consequences. The use of strategies such as laying siege and starving out towns and cities, or disrupting rural life for all members of the community, increases the human costs in terms of displacement and food insecurity, compared with those which occur in a conventional war between army troops.

The degree of brutality adds to the horror, traumatic impact and barriers to reconciliation, but may not significantly affect the impact. UNITA, in Angola, sought to mobilise and relocate civilian supporters to create food production bases and sowed large areas with anti-personnel mines to prevent the populations of government-controlled towns from engaging in rural aspects of their lives. UNITA's rural attacks focused on hard as well as soft (health, water, education and extension work) targets. In Mozambique, Renamo used forced labour to produce food and focused rural attacks on soft targets to create terror and enforce flight to towns or dislocated person camps. Unlike UNITA, Renamo has regularly massacred rural civilian households as part of its strategy. Despite these variations in levels of brutality, the human dislocation, famine and physical destruction have been similar in both countries.

The most significant difference relates to whether the war takes place within a state's territory or abroad. The territory in which the conflict is being fought suffers far greater costs, especially in human relative to economic costs, than a conflict fought abroad. In military terms, both Zimbabwe and Tanzania engaged in very substantial combat operations as well as building up deterrent capacity in order to support the Mozambican government against Renamo insurgency. The fiscal and macro-economic costs have been enormous, probably of the order of $5,000 million in 1991 prices over the period 1961–1991 for Tanzania (Green, 1987). However, they do not compare even in macro-economic terms with the burden on Mozambique, and most certainly not in terms of hunger, collapse of basic services, excess civilian deaths resulting from displacement, and the collapse of public services and transport.

A note on numbers and magnitudes

War cost data are either imprecise, incomplete or both. This results from the need first to conceptualise what they are and then to devise proxy methods for measuring many of them. It is also affected by the near impossibility of estimating counterfactual levels of food security, economic performance or health status in the absence of war. The direct output loss and the multiplier effect through reduced demand for purchases and both fiscal and foreign-exchange diversions can pose major economic burdens. For example, in Zimbabwe in 1992, perhaps $150 million was lost due to direct output loss, and at least an equivalent amount lost through high foreign-exchange and expenditure diversions. In the absence of war, however, even struggling economies can hold human mortality to low levels.

Civilian deaths in conflict situations result primarily from the inter-action of forced migration, lack of basic health services and malnutrition. They are concentrated among the very young and the old. It is usually possible to secure some estimates of famine deaths and enough fragments of under-five mortality data to make some reasoned estimates of its level, despite the fact that the data available are biased towards lower levels as they are often drawn from more accessible and safer areas. It is therefore possible to make a rough estimate of indirect excess deaths if one can estimate what nonwar under-five mortality would have been. One method is to project the likely trend taking into account prewar health and food security priorities and dynamics.

On the economic side, estimates of costs associated with physical damage can usually be made. These, however, do not cover the loss of output resulting from the interruption of free movement, which makes it literally impossible, or intolerably risky, to live or work in many rural and small town areas. Similarly, the multiplier effect or income-flow impact of lost capital stock is undeterminable. On the other hand, military expenditure estimates can often be derived, albeit with great difficulty, as can those for domestic resources at budget level which have been reallocated to survival support. It is possible to infer the foreign-exchange cost of war-related imports and the higher cost of transport routes. However, these do not measure the multiplier losses of, for example, crops not grown because seed or distribution and extension services collapsed, or of agricultural inputs which were not available because foreign exchange has been used to import guns.

Two routes are possible. One is to estimate and add specific items and make rough "guesstimates" of the multiplier impact. The other is to make a reasoned estimate of probable overall output growth in the absence of war (UN Inter-Agency Task Force, 1990). While neither method is precise or uncontentious, they have both been applied to other economic modelling applications. The only systematic use of these approaches in sub-Saharan Africa to date are UNICEF's for Southern Africa in the *Children On The Front Line* series (and the related 1989 UN calculations), and even in this case the full methodology was used only for Angola, Mozambique and Namibia. The results do show that data of much higher quality than those obtained from random observation and speculation are attainable.

The lack of precision of such estimates, as of many other macro-economic estimates including food output and gross domestic product, is apparent. They are valid, however, in terms of order of magnitude, and no plausible modification of assumptions or improvement in data collection would lead to any other conclusion than that war was the dominant factor influencing mortality, food insecurity, absolute poverty and macro-economic decline in Mozambique and Angola in the 1980s. The budgetary impact, both fiscal and external, in Zimbabwe, Zambia and Tanzania, which had little or no domestic fighting, indicated that any plausible non-war scenario would have resulted in higher output growth trends in the 1980s, which would have had a significant impact on poverty alleviation and access to basic services.

In the case of Tanzania, analogous costs were incurred earlier, particularly in respect of contingency defence spending, the 1970s support operation in Mozambique, and the 1978/82 military and peace-building activities following the Amin invasion. While dwarfed by the costs of those states directly afflicted by war, these expenditures have clearly been of sufficient magnitude to impede macro-economic growth, as well as diverting policy and analytical attention away from macro-economic and development issues, especially over the period 1978–82.

Survival During War: Preserving and Ameliorating

Programmes directed at saving lives in war-ravaged sub-Saharan African countries require substantial levels of external resources. War ensures that domestic fiscal and foreign-exchange flows cannot be mobilised even on the government side, and insurgent movements often have no capacity (and low priority) for civilian survival operations. The record has been, at best, mediocre. Substantial sums have flowed since 1985: perhaps over $1,000 million to sub-Saharan African countries and $250 million to refugee support in most years. But even in the most adequately financed case, Mozambique, only about 50 per cent of basic requirements could be from such funds. Proposals tended to be trimmed to what donors "would wear", then pledges were below what was required, and, finally, delivery was both further reduced and often delayed. Even after receiving foreign assistance, there was a 20 to 30 per cent annual shortfall of gross food availability against need, even assuming literally equal distribution. A third to a half of this domestic shortfall could be attributed to war-imposed delivery barriers, but at least half was the result of inability to secure additional food aid.

The level of external logistical and personnel resources varies substantially: more important is the marginalisation of state structures, often compounded by aid processes which create multiple parallel structures or expatriate-run enclaves within nominally national ones. Such practices further erode national capacity to manage food crises both during conflict and in its immediate aftermath.

The nature of efforts by states, opposition forces and international agencies to support those affected by conflict vary radically from territory to territory. Their effectiveness is critically dependent on three key factors: the priority accorded to meeting survival needs by the respective sides in the conflict; the type of military strategy pursued; and technical capacity. For example, the Mozambican government has consistently given very high priority to feeding and providing health services to war-affected people, including civilians in areas controlled by Renamo. Despite its technical and logistical weaknesses and the lack of substantial fiscal resources, that prioritisation, combined with effective canvassing of external governments, institutions and audiences, has saved at least as many lives as have been lost. The government of Angola has not placed as high a priority on meeting food needs (particularly in UNITA-controlled areas before 1989), partly because of the very different economic structure and the physical nature of the war. It has also been far less successful in mobilising external support for its assistance programme than Mozambique (Green, 1994), despite its strong human and fiscal resource base. In southern Somalia, the total absence of a government in 1992, and the near total lack of civil governance capacity by the armed parties, created a vacuum in nationally organised efforts for disaster mitigation, resulting in the highest death rates among displaced persons ever recorded in sub-Saharan Africa.

In Sudan, both the Khartoum regime and the warring factions of the southern leadership accord higher priority literally to starving out enemy combatants than they do to feeding the civilians in areas they control, let alone those in enemy-controlled areas. International efforts are constantly at risk both of disruption and of physical destruction; the impact of programmes of assistance are much reduced. In contrast, the Eritrean People's Liberation Front (EPLF) always accorded priority to providing food and health care to its followers. In the last days of the Mengistu regime, it allowed food into Asmara because it would not accept the price of depriving Eritrean civilians of food in order to hasten the surrender of the Ethiopian forces controlling the town.

In food-scarce war zones, it is nonsensical to suppose food relief will not go first to meet the needs of combatants if they are not accommodated by their own supply lines. Thereafter, the needs of the transporters, distributors and guards will be met. If, as in one province of Mozambique, all of these groups, and probably two-thirds of the total population, were acutely short of food, any attempt to target food aid to a sixth of the population in dislocated-person camps and relocated-person areas resembles trying to carry water in a sieve. That about 50 per cent did reach the dislocated and affected should have been the surprise, not that hungry drivers, guards, clerks, militia members and their households took half of it. In private, some bilateral donors and international organisations recognised this and provided rations to the armed forces. However, openly acknowledging this and planning accordingly was considered impossible. The Mozambican government accepted food aid and vaccines for Renamo as long as the distributor had cause to believe that a substantial share went to civilians. After the peace accord in late 1992, it asked WFP and UNICEF to give priority to feeding Renamo ex-combatants, as well as the 10 per cent of the civilian population under their control.

Drought 1991–93: Calamity, Catastrophic Response

The 1991–92 drought in southern Africa leading to the 1992–93 food and water shortage crisis was evidently not caused by war. Nor, with the worst regional harvest in a century, would the challenges it posed have been readily surmounted even in the absence of war. An increase in food import requirements of almost five and a half million tonnes would have posed severe foreign-exchange, fiscal, logistical and institutional problems, even under optimal conditions. However, the differences in how countries responded to this challenge underscores the interaction of war, famine and death. The two war-ravaged countries in the region, Angola and Mozambique, already had substantial food imports, although these were inadequate and food deficits remained. Most of the other states had much lower levels of food deficit and could, in previous years, finance most of their purchases commercially.

The wars in Mozambique and Angola presented significant logistical problems: many routes were unusable or unsafe, and the mechanics of delivery interacted with the politics of conflict. Initially, the Angolan context was less complex as the peace programme was in process. However, in 1992, following UNITA's refusal to accept its electoral defeat, and the signing of the Rome Accords by the government of Mozambique and Renamo, which led to a massive decline in violence, their relative positions reversed. Logistical problems of landlocked Zimbabwe and Zambia were exacerbated by the destruction and damage to Angolan and Mozambican transit routes.

Institutional capacity for distribution was, in some senses, greater in Angola and Mozambique than in several other states, because war had made this a necessity. However, Botswana, Tanzania and Zimbabwe also functioned well: by late 1992 Zimbabwe was serving five million persons compared with around half that by the Mozambicans before the Rome peace accords, and perhaps three to three and a half million at its peak in early 1993. In the case of Swaziland and Zambia, the relatively rapid creation of an ad hoc distribution structure worked reasonably well; only in Malawi was there a major institutional capacity gap, apparently related to the low priority accorded to relief by their government.

Economically, Zimbabwe and Botswana succeeded in bridging the gap between food requirements and domestic availability plus emergency aid deliveries by markedly increasing commercial imports. Mozambique had no means to make such imports; Angola had limited means to do so. How much the lack of interim commercial imports limited Mozambican deliveries, given that the Rome Accords began to relax security constraints at the same time that food-aid flows rose markedly, is unclear. Their value in speeding the number of food distribution recipients in Zimbabwe from under 100,000 in February/March to five million by September/October is indisputable, as is the fact that the fiscal constraints imposed by the still high military budget did limit distribution significantly in some months.

Of the 1992–93 drought-related deaths, largely resulting from malnutrition, disease, water shortages, forced migration and their interactions, around 90 per cent occurred in Angola and Mozambique, despite the fact that, in the case of Angola, there was only a limited drought area. To a great extent, the inability of domestic output to feed rural populations in Angola was the result of the lingering consequences of the 1980–90 war, including land mines, lack of inputs and limited security.

The Cost Continues: The Case for Focusing on Rehabilitation

The end of any war is not the end of its cost. In one sense the costs do not end until levels of output per capita, infant mortality, access to basic services, food security and poverty alleviation are achieved which correspond to those that would have been predicted in the absence of war. In terms of output per capita, that is a very long-term objective, since after a long severe war growth starts from a much lower base. In recent years Mozambique has had a 4 per cent trend growth rate, but from a base halved by war so that the cumulative loss of GDP attributable to war is still growing rapidly. However, postwar reconstruction and rehabilitation planning is not primarily about regaining projected prewar or nonwar output levels. In sub-Saharan Africa this is neither plausible, given the impracticability of this objective, nor necessarily desirable, as prewar structures and balances in the economy and services were not necessarily optimal.

Postwar, like post-drought, rehabilitation and reconstruction, strategic initiatives and their articulation are at present subject to a plethora of weaknesses (Green 1993a; 1993b):

- too little attention has been paid to the package of measures needed to restore rural and small-scale urban activity – in particular, the need to restore the commercial and marketing systems;
- the adoption of a short-term superficial approach, which tends to treat symptoms and be concerned with immediate survival but fails to place adequate priority on restoring livelihoods in a sustainable way;
- inadequate participation by refugees, displaced and war-affected people and communities in priority determination, identifying opportunities and needs, programme formulation, detailed design, implementation and monitoring;
- overemphasis on large-scale physical infrastructure rehabilitation, which is inadequately linked to provision of basic health, education, and water services (basic human and social investment), household production support and facilitating market access;
- inadequate incorporation of livelihood rehabilitation and rural re-construction in overall growth and other macro-economic strategies;
- consequential marginalisation of rehabilitation as an add-on to the "serious" core macro-economic programme rather than as integral to and in some cases (for example, Somalia, Mozambique, Liberia, Ethiopia and Eritrea) its largest core component.

There is nothing inevitable about these weaknesses, any more than about the parallel problems afflicting absolute poverty reduction and food security planning. However, addressing these weaknesses in the initial years will cost money. For Mozambique a rough five-year projection for a full programme is $2,000 million, according to National Planning Commission estimates (unpublished source). Especially in the first three years, national output and fiscal gains will not cover the import and budget bills. The concept of a peace dividend is valid, but takes time to collect, especially as demobilising combatants without reintegrating them into livelihoods and communities is likely to prove a very costly "economy". However, in the case of Mozambique, by the sixth year after commencement, total additional output related to the rehabilitation could exceed $900 million, and the fiscal and foreign balance impact could have become neutral or slightly positive.

Much more dramatically, the combined food deficit "met" by imports and hunger could be reduced from over one and a half million to under half a million tonnes, consistent with a reduction of food aid from half to a fifth of a million tonnes; access to basic primary health care could be near-universal, and to water and primary education two-thirds complete; while absolute poverty could be reduced from 65 per cent to 25 per cent. More fragmentary data and projections in respect of Somalia are not dissimilar (Green, 1993c). Indeed, they suggest that Somalia's pre-1988 basic food self-sufficiency in non-drought years, with livestock exports well in excess of non-refugee-related food imports, could be restored within three years of attainment of peace.

Based on such assessments, de facto conversion of survival assistance to war-torn countries and the support given to refugee nationals abroad, plus some reallocation within capital assistance flows, would cover most of the initial higher costs beyond those for interim international peace-stabilising operations. On economic as well as human calculations that would appear a good bargain. Rehabilitation injections securing peace and livelihood recovery can phase down; survival assistance to war-affected populations and territories has no such in-built cutoff.

A Note on Governance

This chapter has not focused on issues of legitimacy, structure or competence of governance, nor their relation to the causes of, or means to, end wars. However, governance is integral to reconstruction and rehabilitation. This goes well beyond the issue of achieving a government generally regarded as legitimate, normally by some form of election process allowing competition, with some degree of international observation and supervision. That is a necessary condition, but in no sense sufficient: Angola is testimony to that. Reconciliation requires the involvement of all significant communities in governance. Namibia and Zimbabwe represent successes in this respect. The gains in terms of relative peace and stability carry a price of slower structural reform and less ability to finance, or to pursue, policies designed to increase access and equity of basic services and, especially, livelihoods.

Competence is necessary: reconstruction and rehabilitation alone place major demands on public-service-delivery institutions. These have, in many cases, such as in Liberia, Somalia, Eritrea and Ethiopia, always been weak and have been further decimated by war. Their rebuilding, along with that of the enterprise sector, is integral to postwar recovery and progress. Participation is necessary for three significant reasons: to underpin reconciliation, to create a permanent basis for legitimacy, and to increase efficiency in the articulation of priorities and operational response to them. Especially in respect of reconstruction and livelihood rehabilitation, identification of what to do and mobilisation of communities and households to do it can only be done rapidly and efficiently if they are involved in the data collection, programmatic articulation and prioritisation processes, as well as in physical implementation and resource contribution.

Decentralisation, of elections and of decision-taking, as well as of the executive side of administration and service provision, is likely to be a necessary component of effective reconstruction and of longer-term governance. This is partly a matter of efficiency and overcoming the colonial and early independence period of overcentralisation. But it is also a matter of making participation more practicable and more visibly meaningful and, where significant regional interests exist, of strengthening legitimacy. The nature and form of decentralisation, beyond urban and rural districts and provinces, is context-specific. Sudan may need some form of federal or confederal structure, while such an approach would be less plausible in either Liberia or Mozambique.

Finally, one – rather old-fashioned – aspect of governance for reconstruction is law and order. Rehabilitation requires that ordinary people are able to go about their daily lives within a set of rules which are transparent and predictably construed, free from the fear of frequent violence from anyone (rebels, government troops, bandits, hostile communities), and confident the state can and will act to prevent, halt and punish those who resort to violence. In virtually all war-ravaged countries that requires more, better-trained, and better-equipped police, as well as better-codified laws. A more accessible, more efficient, and more consistent judiciary of higher perceived probity is also necessary. Law and order is never enough, but if it is largely absent there is not likely to be much else either.

Conclusion

War in sub-Saharan Africa has had very high death, hunger, illness and macro-economic costs. In the 1980s and early 1990s, these were concentrated in, but not limited to, Angola, Mozambique, Ethiopia, Eritrea, Somalia, Sudan and Liberia (now joined by Rwanda and Burundi), where excess war-linked deaths since 1980 exceed five million and annual war-related loss of output exceeds $12,500 million annually. Deaths related to war are not primarily of combatants, nor even of bystanders killed in the course of conflict. Nor is lost output primarily related to physical war damage. The deaths come from extreme malnutrition and collapse of basic medical services resulting from the destruction of rural life and transport and the loss of state capacity. They are concentrated among the very young, the old and dislocated persons forced to flee long distances.

The output and government capacity losses arise largely from the destruction of the rural economy by war, especially when terror tactics are used to deny food to the other side, and 40 per cent to 75 per cent of available fiscal and foreign-exchange resources are diverted to fighting the war. After a decade of war the largest cause of lower output and capacity is investment not made, including basic human investment in education, health, water and nutrition, because war consumed the resources. Physical damage and population dislocation, pushing up to half of households out of their livelihoods, compound the loss from noninvestment as long as the war lasts.

That contextual setting has several practical implications for saving lives, rehabilitating livelihoods and restoring economies. During the war survival support and basic human investment must have priority, as rehabilitation and restoration are largely out of reach. However, the end of the war will not automatically end loss of life or loss of output. Rural infrastructure restoration, livelihood promotion and government are central to reversing the higher loss of life and to restoring household and, usually, national food security. Their short-term role in overall output recovery is also high unless, as in Angola, there is a dominant enclave sector. Survival support during wartime therefore needs to be transformed into postwar rehabilitation assistance, both at national and donor strategic planning and implementation levels. Finally, among the key issues is rebuilding the capacity of the civil operations of war-debilitated states, not least because the failure of new governments to produce visible postwar recovery at household level will rapidly erode legitimacy and prevent the rebuilding of civil society and accountable governance.

References

Green, R.H. (1987). "Killing the Dream: The Political and Human Economy of War in Sub-Saharan Africa", *Discussion Paper* 238, Institute of Development Studies, University of Sussex.

—— (1993a) "The Political Economy of Drought in Southern Africa 1991–1993", *Health Policy And Planning*, 8 (3).

—— (1993b)"Calamities and Catastrophes: Extending the UN Response", *Third World Quarterly*, 14 (1).

—— (1993c) "Somalia: Toward 1994–96 Reconstruction, Rehabilitation Restructuring", mimeo, UNICEF-Somalia.

—— (1994) "Angola – Peace, Reconstruction, Rehabilitation, Regionalism: Through a Dark Glass Dimly", African Studies Centre Workshop, 21–22 March, Cambridge.

UN Inter-Agency Task Force Africa Recovery Programme/Economic Commission for Africa (1990) *South African Destabilisation: The Economic Cost of Frontline Resistance to Apartheid*, New York.

UNICEF (1987) *Children on The Frontline: The Impact of Apartheid, Destabilization and Warfare on Children in Southern and South Africa*, New York.

—— (1989) *Children on The Frontline: The Impact of Apartheid, Destabilization and Warfare on Children in Southern and South Africa*, update with new section on Namibia (3rd edn), New York.

The Political Economy of Internal War: Asset Transfer, Complex Emergencies and International Aid
Mark Duffield

Introduction

Since the 1980s, an important aspect of the emerging global interdepend-ence has been the increasing frequency of large-scale, complex disasters (Childers and Urquhart, 1991; Borton, 1993). In parts of Latin America, Eastern Europe, the Middle East, Asia and especially Africa, the lives of millions of people are now regularly affected by a variety of disaster agents. Complex emergencies are a characteristic of areas of protracted economic crisis and growing social vulnerability. They are usually highly politicised and are frequently associated with non-conventional warfare, regional in-security or situations of contested governance. The effects of such emer-gencies often cross international boundaries, and, because of official obstruction, they often present aid agencies with major problems of humanitarian access. Moreover, the difficulties in resolving such emergen-cies and relieving the suffering they cause has increasingly highlighted the limitations of the present international humanitarian system.

Political Survival in a Permanent Emergency

Besides sharpening contradictions within the humanitarian system, the present period of rapid political change has called into question the adequacy of much conventional analysis and terminology. In the case of Sudan, for example, outsiders could be forgiven for having difficulty in understanding how governance has survived over the past decade. Since the early 1980s, successive famines have impoverished rural producers in the north; civil war has devastated the peoples and subsistence economies of the south; violence and instability have become widespread; prices for Sudan's staple exports have fallen; official debt has increased; and in recent years there has been a growing antipathy and aid embargo on the part of Western donors. In many respects, Sudan appears to have entered a stage of "permanent emergency" marked by end-to-end relief operations.

However, since the fundamentalist-backed coup of June 1989, the government has not only strengthened its internal political and economic base, but has regained a clear military momentum in the south, survived the negative consequences of its support for Iraq in the Gulf War by realigning itself within the Middle East, and allegedly has sufficient confidence to involve itself in the internal politics of several of its neighbours (Jamal, 1991). Sudan has even been a recent contributor of relief supplies to Somalia. Rather than collapse, in many respects a form of development has taken place.

Governance in Sudan is a good example of what can be termed "political survival in the context of permanent emergency". It is a poorly understood phenomenon, yet both Somalia and the former Yugoslav federation indicate that is not simply an aberration of a single, atypical state. The Sudanese example illustrates the development of a radical form of political economy which can only be partially understood through orthodox forms of analysis (Brown, 1992). As complex disasters continue to develop and reverberate around the world stage, uncovering the nature of this economy has become an important policy issue.

Limitations of conventional analysis

A key proposition in the examination of political survival is that complex emergencies have winners as well as losers. When conflict is involved this is obvious. Although famine in Africa is frequently an effect of conflict, analysis of food security issues has, with some justification, tended to concentrate on the losers. Since the mid-1980s, for example, a growing body of literature has drawn attention to how vulnerable groups attempt to survive growing environmental and economic stress through the development of coping strategies (Longhurst, 1986; de Garine and Harrison, 1988; Swift, 1989). Apart from reducing food consumption, coping strategies can involve labour migration, petty trading, the accumulation of debt, gathering wild foodstuffs and, as a last resort, the sale or pledging of such subsistence assets as livestock, land or jewellery, often at rock-bottom prices.

During the latter part of the 1980s, policy debate was informed by such observations. Within a framework in which famine is usually conceived as a temporary and largely natural phenomenon, various models have been suggested to strengthen the coping strategies of losers as well as providing them with external support. It has been attempted, for example, to establish famine early-warning systems to monitor such phenomena as livestock prices, and initiate market and nutritional support mechanisms as necessary. The main drawback with this approach, however, is that it offers a technical solution for an essentially political problem. It has consequently met with limited practical success.

While the application of research on coping strategies raises some questions, the basic principle that informs it is of vital importance: people are not passive victims but take a proactive response to crisis. Nevertheless, coping strategies have usually been presented one-sidedly in terms of how they operate to support losers. It should not be forgotten that coping strategies, especially in more extreme circumstances, through sale, barter or loan, can involve the loss of assets by those in distress. This negative affect of coping under stress has often been neglected. What is missed is that local merchants and middlemen, for example, stand to make significant gains in such circumstances (Keen, 1991). They can buy such assets at very low prices. Moreover, these winners are often powerful local actors capable, through neglect or even design, of influencing market or political conditions to their advantage. The coping strategies of losers, therefore, can become an important factor in the continued survival of more fortunate groups. From this perspective, asset transfer, while helping some, is also part of a process of active underdevelopment: resource depletion, the spread of absolute poverty and the collapse of social and economic infrastructure.

Towards a political economy of complex emergencies

Prompted by the post-Cold War continuation of internal conflict in many parts of Africa, a new analysis of complex emergencies is emerging. This argues that complex disasters, such as famine in certain parts of Africa, have a distinct political economy structured by relations of power and gender (Downs et al., 1991). Within this framework, it is possible to regard famine as one possible outcome of a process of impoverishment resulting from the transfer of assets from the weak to the politically strong. Equally, large-scale migration, the rapid expansion of urban slums or a refugee exodus, could result. The methods of wresting assets from losers can range from market pressure to violent appropriation. The more direct or coercive the form of transfer, the more likely it is that winners have mobilised ethnic, national or religious sectarianism as justification for their extra-legal activity. In this respect, the cultural genocide that has accompanied armed asset-stripping in the Sudan and Somalia is comparable with the ethnic cleansing that has occurred in the former Yugoslavia. The impotence of the international humanitarian system in the face of such illegitimate activities is increasingly apparent.

By looking at the winners as well as the losers, this chapter will analyse the phenomenon of political survival in a permanent emergency in terms of whether the actions of the state and its internal clients, together with those of the international community, support the weak or the strong in the process of asset transfer. First, however, using examples drawn from the Horn of Africa, it is necessary to describe more fully some of the characteristics of a complex, permanent emergency.

Examples of local asset transfer

Evidence suggests that during the 1980s, as Sudan's formal economy and hence the opportunities for legitimate wealth creation declined, the local transfer of assets from weak to politically strong rural producers and their political allies began to gather momentum. This was not a new phenomenon in Sudan. The earlier expansion of mechanised agriculture in the north, for example, had been accompanied by the state appropriation of nomadic rangelands (Duffield, 1990). While sections of the nomadic population were losers up until the early 1970s, this expansion was linked to the development of an internal market which conferred many benefits on peasant producers (O'Brien, 1985). Since this period, following the increased integration of Sudan within the global economy, these gains have been undermined. By the 1980s, the process of asset transfer began to assume a violent sectarian and inter-ethnic character based upon the direct seizure of moveable property and the forcible eviction of rural subsistence producers from their lands. Its spread is largely associated with the rekindling in 1983 of civil war between the "Arab" north and the "African" south. The scale and extent of this violence has been unseen in Sudan since the nineteenth century. It marks a major, yet little understood, transformation in the regional economy.

In relation to north Sudan's rural producers, initially at least, asset transfer was through state appropriation and the manipulation of the market. In the south and more recently in the north, apart from market pressure created by the deliberate restriction of food aid, violence has been used increasingly as a means of direct appropriation. Some examples of asset transfer will be given before drawing them together in a wider conception of a parallel economy.

A detailed case study examining the relationship between neighbouring Baggara and Dinka of south-west Sudan, has demonstrated that the terrible 1988 famine amongst the Dinka of Bahr al Ghazal was not a result of their poverty or lack of entitlements. To the contrary, it was due to their natural wealth in cattle (Keen, 1991). This wealth was highlighted by the impoverishment of their northern Baggara neighbours as a result of enviro-economic crisis, including the loss of rangelands due to the mechanisation of agriculture. An essential aspect of asset transfer, however, was a long-term process of political marginalisation and the stripping of the Dinka of all legitimation. Without this, the violent appropriation of Dinka cattle during the mid-1980s could not have taken place. In the eyes of the Baggara raiders, the Dinka were not fit to hold such wealth. These observations firmly establish the direct link between famine and the political processes underway at the time.

In north Sudan, the forms of legitimation that have accompanied the emergence of the transfer economy have been the steady re-Islamization of the state and the resurgence of civil war. In the case of the Baggara, enviro-economic decline meant they became ready tools in the government's strategy of arming irregular militias. Since decimating northern Bahr al Ghazal, by the late 1980s the Baggara militias (Murahaleen), in conjunction with Zaghawa raiders, had begun to place pressure on the Fur agriculturalists in central Darfur (Africa Watch, 1990b). Since the beginning of the 1990s, the Murahaleen have also been increasingly active against the Nuba in the Nuba mountains (Africa Watch, 1991b). More recently, forcible eviction by government and militia forces of the Nuba from their homes and agricultural lands has attracted direct comparison with the ethnic cleansing of the former Yugoslavia (Flint, 1993). In this manner, the government's strategy of supporting the militias, established in the mid-1980s and consolidated by the fundamentalist regime of El Bashir, satisfied both the local economic needs of client groups whose economic position has deteriorated in recent years, and the wider political aims of the state in opening south-west Sudan to Arab commercial exploitation.

Asset transfer in the north also has an urban dimension. Since 1990, helped by new legislation which gave sweeping powers to the state, over 500,000 of the squatters and displaced living in Khartoum (the majority of whom come from the south and west of the country), were forced to relocate to agricultural "productive areas" or badly resourced "peace villages" located at some distance from the city. Over the years, despite official resistance, many squatters have managed to secure basic amenities in the areas in which they live. Given Khartoum's rapid urbanisation, this land has become an increasingly valuable asset. Reflecting earlier practices, forced relocation, often carried out with the wilful destruction of shelter and belongings, has been accompanied by scapegoating the victims as criminals and a political fifth column. A new development, however, has been the pledging of the confiscated land and buildings to neighbouring Arab residents, or to client members of the civil service, police or militias (Africa Watch, 1992b).

In south Sudan, the Sudan Peoples Liberation Army (SPLA) has used different forms of legitimation to underpin local asset transfer and so secure its own physical survival. During the latter part of the 1980s, its alliance with the Ethiopian Dergue allowed it to use local opposition to the resettlement and villagisation programme in south-west Ethiopia as a pretext to loot, especially in Illubabor Province (Africa Watch, 1991a). More widely, however, it has relied upon the manipulation of traditional enmities between local ethnic groups through a process of selective arming with modern weapons. In south Sudan, in order to secure a base and provisions near the Uganda border, the SPLA made use of the long-standing hostility between the Acholi and the Madi (Allen, 1989). Since the mid-1980s, the process of selective arming, also engaged in by the Sudanese army, has produced great instability along Sudan's borders with Uganda and Kenya. Local food wars have developed as losers have attempted to make good their loss.

By the end of the 1980s, the SPLA had become an unstable alliance of ethnically polarised groups (Duffield, 1991). In August 1991 the SPLA leadership split. Initially, this was presented as a progressive move against a repressive leadership following destructive policies. It quickly developed, however, into a division between the Nuer and Dinka. The ensuing fighting affected areas of the south which had been spared conflict for some time. Civilians were not only the victims of this violence, but were themselves the perpetrators of tit-for-tat raiding and looting (Johnson, 1992). Besides the loss of Ethiopian support with the fall of the Dergue in May 1991, these events weakened the SPLA and enabled the government to regain the military initiative during 1992 at the cost of further asset-stripping and displacement (de Waal, 1992). This government resurgence was accompanied by continuing ethnically defined conflict between SPLA factions (*Sudan Human Rights Voice*, 1993).

Local asset transfer and the parallel economy

The emergence of a political economy that includes asset transfer is extremely destructive and creates ever-deepening poverty and misery. Moreover, since subsistence assets are a finite resource, once such an economy is established it demands fresh inputs as the wealth of different groups is exhausted. Asset transfer becomes a moving feast on an ethnic table.

Many social groups in Sudan since the 1980s have been seriously weakened or have disappeared altogether in the sense of being distinct and semi-independent socio-economic entities. There is limited, but compelling, evidence (Ryle, 1989), regarding the Dinka, Fur and Nuba noted above, as well as the Maban, Uduk (James, 1992) and Anuak (Duku, 1988) in Upper Nile, the Chai (Africa Watch, 1991a), and the Murle, Toposa and Mundari in Equatoria. Asset transfer, once systemic, becomes synonymous with cultural genocide and the destruction of group rights. The crippling of the subsistence base in this manner has created several million displaced people, left whole populations destitute, robbed of their cultural and economic heritage, and dependent on the uncertainties of international relief assistance.

Despite its destructiveness, it would be a mistake to regard asset transfer as an anarchic process. It should be seen as part of a wider parallel economy. This economy goes beyond simple smuggling or illegal dealing: it is more complex, extensive and established. A better model would be the drug economies of Latin America, which are not only highly lucrative, but integrate producers vertically: entrepreneurs and politicians develop powerful cartels which have had a historic regional and international impact (George, 1992). In the case of Sudan the parallel economy consists of a number of interconnecting levels or systems. Local asset transfer is linked to national level extra-legal mercantile activity. In turn, this articulates with higher-level political and state relations together with regional and international parallel networks which trade in commodities and hard currency. It is this level that provides the initial site for the integration of international aid and relief assistance with the parallel economy. As assets flow upwards and outward, culminating in capital flight, international assistance flows downwards through the same or related systems of power.

An example of regional parallel exchange

This section provides an example of a regional circuit of parallel exchange, indicating how it integrates actors vertically, and how it articulates with international relief assistance. It should be emphasised that asset transfer is not bound by nation-states but is regional in character. An arc of instability and fragmentation now runs from Sudan, through southern Ethiopia to Somalia (Bowden, 1992). It is an area greater than the size of Western Europe yet, apart from sporadic disaster reporting, receives scant attention and even less systematic analysis.

In Sudan the emergence of a hidden foreign-exchange market is an integral component of the parallel economy. During the latter part of the 1980s, some of the illegal dollar remittances of Sudanese workers in the Middle East were being exchanged, via hidden trade links across the war zone of south Sudan, on the coast-to-coast parallel networks of northern Uganda and Zaire. It has been estimated that between 1978 and 1987 capital flight from Sudan amounted to $11 billion dollars, roughly equivalent to the country's entire foreign debt (Brown, 1992). Access to such significant amounts of hard currency has increasingly shaped the antagonistic relations at the centre of northern Sudanese politics (Jamal, 1991). The illegal dollar trade has traditionally been in the hands of a few powerful Khatmiyya merchants. The Khatmiyya is an Islamic sect linked to the Democratic Unionist Party (DUP), which, toward the end of the 1980s, was in a fractious coalition with the Umma Party and the fundamentalist National Islamic Front. Following the fundamentalist coup of June 1989, the internal struggle to control the parallel currency market has become increasingly bitter, resulting in the government dissolving the Khatmiyya sect in September 1992 (Malwal, 1992).

The involvement of army officers in trade within the war zone is also widespread (Africa Watch, 1990a). Most of this trade exploits the shortage of food and basic commodities amongst war-affected populations by using the army's ability to prevent population movement and its monopoly of transport. At best, it is asset transfer through barter, the terms of which are heavily to the advantage of the merchant-officer. During the latter part of the 1980s, one point of entry into the parallel economy for illegal dollars exploited the DUP/Khatmiyya links with the army. The dollar trade went through Juba, the capital of south Sudan. Having cut the overland routes and deterred civilian airlines from landing, the SPLA blockade meant that apart from military transport, the only way anything got in or out of Juba was by periodic donor/NGO airlift of relief food or the irregular army convoys to and from the Ugandan border.

The hard currency flown into Juba by the military was taken by armed convoy to the Ugandan border. That the amounts conveyed were significant can be judged from the fact that the exchange rate on the Ugandan parallel currency market fluctuated according to the timing of the Juba convoy (Meagher, 1990). Within northern Uganda, Sudanese merchants traded these dollars on the Uganda/Zaire parallel market. In a detailed account, Meagher (1990) describes this network as linking Senegal, Guinea Bissau, Zaire, Sudan, Uganda, Kenya and Somalia. In the late 1980s, the chief players were Zairois with gold wanting imported goods, food and fuel; Sudanese with dollars wanting food, clothing and coffee; and Ugandans with imported goods wanting gold and dollars for Kampala's parallel market. This was not barter trade, but took place in hard currency and convertible commodities and was sensitive to international exchange rates.

From Uganda, coffee and other merchant goods were transported, again in convoy, back to Juba. The public reason for these convoys was to bring donor food aid from the border to the war-displaced population in and around Juba. The convoy system proved extremely unreliable in this respect. Toward the end of the 1980s, not only was the route becoming increasingly insecure, but merchant supplies would invariably be substituted for relief food. This is also true of military convoys in other areas of south Sudan (Africa Watch, 1990a).

In Juba, substitution had several implications. Due to the growing SPLA blockade, the price of foodstuffs began to climb steeply leaving many of the town's residents worse off than the displaced population that was eligible for relief (Graham and Borton, 1992). Merchant goods, imported under army auspices, were therefore at a premium and could be used to commercial advantage. The unreliability of the convoy system and the insecurity of the overland routes forced the donors and NGOs providing relief to rely increasingly on expensive, stopgap airlifts of emergency supplies.

The Internationalisation of Public Welfare

In summary, a shrinking resource base and decline in formal economic opportunity have led to the direct transfer of assets from the weak to the politically strong. This local transfer is integrated with a wider regional parallel economy. In the case of Sudan, some aspects of this economy come together in the state, where they are controlled and contested by sectarian political interests. It is an inherently authoritarian, violent and disaster-producing structure. In relation to Somalia, where more than a decade ago the growth of parallel activity was prophesied as leading to breakdown (Miller, 1981; Jamal, 1988), it is possible to interpret the present situation as a division of the country along clan lines, some of which control or contest different aspects of the parallel economy (Africa Watch, 1992a).

This summary, however, is only a partial description of the power relations involved in the structure of permanent emergency. The nature of the humanitarian intervention is itself part of, and a contributing factor to, the complexity of modern emergencies. As the above example of regional parallel exchange indicates, international relief assistance is also involved and articulates with the parallel economy at many points. This analysis differs substantially from conventional approaches, which tend to conceptualise external humanitarian intervention as uncoupled from the dynamics of internal conflict, designed only to ameliorate the effects of conflict-related disasters. The linkage of the internal emergency with the external response is one facet of the increasing globalisation within the world economy, which had become manifest by the mid-1980s in the form of the internationalisation of public welfare. In crude terms, this process has been characterised by NGOs replacing the state in the pro-vision of basic welfare services (Duffield, 1992b).

The end of the Cold War, which in Africa had already run its course by the mid-1980s (Clough, 1992), simultaneously saw NGOs increasingly taking over, or providing afresh, key aspects of public provision. At the same time, the problems of conflict and endemic poverty have grown and spread to regions previously regarded as stable. The system of humanitarian relief that has emerged is symptomatic of a wider post-Cold War re-structuring of North–South relations. The following sections describe the linkage between emergency and international response and how the latter helps fuel the former.

NGOs and the subcontracting of humanitarian relief

During the latter part of the 1980s, Africa became the world's largest regional recipient of food aid and humanitarian assistance. Simultaneously, NGOs became increasingly important in the management and targeting of this aid (Borton and Shoham, 1989). This trend has been encouraged by the increasing willingness of Western donor governments to direct official aid away from Southern states and through NGOs (Clark, 1991). In nett terms, NGOs now collectively transfer more resources to the South than the World Bank.

In Africa, Western intervention has encouraged the emergence of a neo-liberal, two-tier system of public welfare (Duffield, 1992a). From the end of the 1970s, IMF/World Bank structural adjustment programmes have been attempting, with highly debatable consequences, to stimulate market reform and encourage local producers. For those people unable to benefit from these measures, since the mid-1980s an NGO welfare safety net has emerged. IMF/World Bank programmes are currently in operation in thirty African countries; and welfare safety nets, particularly associated with disaster relief, are found in about a dozen. These two measures (currently being modified in relation to Eastern Europe and the former Soviet Union), have coalesced during the 1980s into what amounts to the West's regional policy for Africa.

The safety-net system in Africa divides into compensatory or development programmes and, especially, targeted relief operations. Typical relief programmes involve a contractual relationship between an international bilateral or multilateral donor and an NGO, whereby the latter acts as an implementing agent of the former in an agreed programme of assistance. If present at all, African governments usually play a symbolic role. The growth of official funding channelled through NGOs, reinforced by the high cost of relief work, has given donors a significant measure of influence over welfare priorities as the safety-net system has spread. This trend has changed many NGOs from relatively independent bodies into implementers of donor policy. It has contributed to the politicisation of humanitarian aid and is not without its NGO critics (Borton and Shoham, 1989). As a style of work that can include development as well as relief goals, it is sometimes known as "public service contracting" (Korten, 1990). The scale of this phenomenon is not insubstantial: in Sudan, for example, in the late 1980s, some twenty NGOs working in Sudan were operating safety nets which covered, even if only nominally, several million people.

Relief operations have drawn many types of NGO, including African agencies, into subcontracting relations. Several different forms of organisation can be found. In some cases, a single international NGO has assumed responsibility for emergency provision in a given area. This is especially the case with regard to the large USA-based NGOs. In others, consortia of agencies have developed, comprising a dozen or more NGOs. Usually supported by several donors, these groups can be shaped around a division of labour based either upon geography or function, such as transport, food distribution, medical services or nutritional surveillance (Duffield, 1990). Non-operational NGO consortia are also found which fund local implementing agencies.

Humanitarian relief and the support of the strong

Until the mid-1980s, aid to Africa usually followed a Cold War logic. Regimes inclined to the West received help while those still pursuing a centrally planned alternative were treated less favourably. Towards the end of the 1970s, however, changes were already underway. In 1977, the Carter administration made the receipt of American development aid, although not emergency assistance, conditional on the respect of human rights (Tomasevski, 1989). Although never rigorously applied by the Americans, and ignored by the main European donors, the distinction between development and emergency assistance did have the effect of raising humanitarian relief above politics. It created, for example, a political space which allowed the USA and other Western donors to disregard Ethiopian sovereignty from the mid-1980s and assist those areas of Eritrea and Tigray not under government control. In some respects this can be seen as one of the first hesitant steps toward the present era of humanitarian interventionism (Duffield and Prendergast, forthcoming).

The weakening of sovereignty and loss of revenue that has accompanied the internationalisation of public welfare and the enhanced role of NGOs has had contradictory effects on the African state. In some cases, antagonistic relations have developed between it and the international humanitarian agencies, especially NGOs (Tandon, 1991). Somalia has become an extreme example of this antagonism, which there encompasses the UN and USA (African Rights, 1993a; 1993b). On the other hand, development aid has been declining since the end of the 1980s as a result of recessionary pressures. Western emergency assistance itself has therefore become increasingly important as a form of state support (Borton, 1993). In countries like Sudan, for example, humanitarian relief is practically the only Western aid currently received. While much of this assistance passes through the indirect and parallel system developed by NGOs, the indirect gains that the state is able to achieve from large-scale international relief operations greatly exceeds this potential loss.

State finance

The treasuries of several governments in the Horn of Africa have been major beneficiaries of international humanitarian operations. In Ethiopia and Sudan, the official overvaluing of local currencies relative to hard currency has been the main means of facilitating this. It has had the effect of imposing an unofficial relief tax every time the UN or an NGO needs to exchange hard for local currency to support the relief effort. While much relief expenditure is external to the receiving country, local currency transactions can be significant to cover the costs of office rents, salaries of national employees, fuel, transport, import duties, licences and, importantly, the in-country purchase of food aid.

In 1983, Sudan restricted all aid transactions to an official rate of Ls1.28 to $1. Despite periodic devaluations, from this period the value of the official rate began to deteriorate in relation to the Sudanese pound on the parallel exchange market. By 1988, the official rate stood at Ls4.4 to $1, while its value on the parallel market was more than Ls17 to $1. In effect, the aid community was purchasing Sudanese pounds at a rate of at least four times their real value, with the state keeping the difference. Similarly, in Ethiopia during the 1980s the official exchange rate was pegged at 2.07 Birr to $1, while for most of this time its value on the parallel market was a third of this at 6 or 7 Birr to $1 (Africa Watch, 1991a).

Given the high cost of large-scale relief operations, the financial benefit of overvalued currencies cannot be underestimated. In 1989, for example, the total value of international relief aid in Ethiopia exceeded $1 billion. In the same year in Sudan, it has been speculated that from Operation Lifeline alone, the Sudanese government could have secured the equivalent of half its annual military expenditure (Keen, personal communication). A similar situation currently exists in Iraq. A defecting banker has attested that in 1992 the UN relief operation contributed $250 million to the Iraqi treasury (Vallely, 1993). In the operation of exchange rates, one has a good example of how donor governments and NGOs attempt to ameliorate suffering, yet at the same time indirectly sustaining oppression by providing indirect support for predatory regimes.

Diversion of food aid
In a sectarian asset-transfer economy the control of food aid is of vital strategic importance. In the Horn, the diversion of food aid to feed troops and militia at the same time as denying relief to contested areas has been widespread. In Somalia, the diversion of refugee food was already an established parallel activity in the 1970s (Miller, 1981) and formed an important part of the regional economy (Ryle, 1992). In Ethiopia, relief food was regularly used to feed government troops and especially its unpaid peasant militia. Similar diversions have occurred on both sides of the conflict in south Sudan. Within a large-scale emergency, a 5 per cent leakage of food aid is generally regarded by donors as acceptable. Due to the amounts involved, however, this can still support a lot of people. In the case of Ethiopia, 5 per cent would have fed 300,000–400,000 for several months in the latter part of the 1980s: equivalent to the entire armed forces (Africa Watch, 1991a). Diversions of imported food do not therefore require the disappearance of large proportions of incoming aid.

Another aspect of the diversion of food aid concerns the co-option of NGO subcontractors. In many respects, especially in a situation of internal war or divided governance, NGO relief operations, lacking an international mandate or externally guaranteed access, will almost inevitably be co-opted by one side or another. Indeed, the perceived threat to an NGO's operations by straying from the government's domain has commonly been used to justify nonintervention in contested areas. Few international agencies practice the "active neutrality" of Médecins Sans Frontières, which aims to work on both sides of a conflict (Padt, 1992). In Ethiopia, for example, it has been estimated that during the 1980s more than 90 per cent of all international relief assistance was distributed in government-controlled areas (Africa Watch, 1991a). Until 1989, north Sudan similarly monopolised the international relief programme.

Tacit donor support and the denial of food aid

In Sudan and Ethiopia, the state's denial of international food aid to civilians in contested areas was accomplished by a variety of means ranging from a reluctance to acknowledge emergency conditions, assurances to donors that relief supplies were reaching all the needy, claiming insurmountable security and logistical problems to account for interminable delays, denying access for assessment purposes, through to plain obstruction. During the latter part of the 1980s, government policies of selective food denial (an important aid to asset transfer) were not effectively challenged; nor was an accountable relief system insisted upon (Cutler, 1988; Africa Watch, 1990a, 1991a; Keen, 1991). In Sudan, since 1989 some bilateral donors have become more critical and in some cases have cut development assistance. The UN and many NGOs operating in the north, however, have continued to provide tacit support for predatory government policies, including the forcible relocation of displaced southerners from Khartoum (Africa Watch, 1992b) and Nuba from the Nuba Mountains (Flint, 1993).

Grain speculation

The delays between assessment and the delivery of emergency food aid, together with the increasing demand on the world's emergency stock, has meant that stated emergency requirements have seldom been met in full or on time (Keen, 1991). This has necessitated various stopgap measures, which have created opportunities for speculative and parallel activity.

Local purchase and swap arrangements are two of the main measures. At a time when the world price for coarse grain is depressed, the mechanised production of sorghum in northern Sudan has been assisted by recurrent famine elsewhere in the country. In particular, the need for local purchase by relief agencies has provided a source of speculative earnings for Sudanese merchants, commercial farmers and lorry owners, resulting in the failure of at least one relief operation in northern Sudan, that of the 1988 Western Relief Operation (Cutler and Keen, 1989). Swap arrangements usually involve the securing of local grain against food normally imported on a commercial basis for the urban market. In Sudan, such swaps are notorious for their delays and high rates of exchange. The Islamic banks have a history of grain speculation, having been accused of hoarding during the 1984–85 famine (Cater, 1986). Since being made responsible for managing Sudan's strategic food reserve following the 1989 fundamentalist coup, similar controversy surrounds the export of the strategic reserve during 1989–90 despite evidence of returning famine conditions (Africa Watch, 1990c).

Humanitarian intervention provides a significant amount of political and especially economic support, albeit often indirect, for the dominant political and commercial groups. When these groups are themselves allied in a predatory or sectarian structure that is connected with a process of asset transfer and inter-ethnic conflict, then relief intervention itself can become an organic part of the political economy of internal warfare. Although the logic of the argument may be convincing, it does not yield easy solutions. While diversion and indirect gains flowing to predatory structures are difficult to condone, the effect of withdrawing or restricting aid could be worse. If the parallel gains from the aid and relief circuit were to dry up, it is likely that the position of losers would be made correspondingly worse as the dominant groups attempt to maintain their position.

Humanitarian relief and support of the weak

Given the indirect and appropriated benefits that disaster relief can impart to the politically strong, it is legitimate to ask what the losers, the object of the humanitarian intervention, receive? Where estimates have been made the answer is, broadly speaking, very little. In Darfur during 1984–85, in relatively good operational conditions in the absence of political violence, it has been suggested that the international relief programme supplied no more than 12 per cent of required assistance (de Waal, 1988). In Ethiopia, a figure of 10 per cent has been suggested (Africa Watch, 1991a). While still important to the groups concerned, relief aid should not hide the fact that the remaining 90 per cent of food needs are met by peoples' own coping strategies, including the transfer of assets to more fortunate and powerful groups. Insufficient research has been conducted in conflict-famines to assess the relative role played by food aid in ensuring survival. It might be argued that dependence on food aid is likely to be relatively higher because of the obstacles to implementing survival strategies under conditions of violence. However, given the operational complexities in these contexts and the absolutely low levels of assistance channelled into the majority of conflict situations, it is likely that food aid will continue to contribute only a fraction of survival needs.

For donors, the basic principle of African relief operations is to define, usually according to nutritional status, the most vulnerable groups within a population and target them with the minimum necessary food, water and shelter to sustain life (Borton and Shoham, 1989). The problem in conflict-related famines is that one is not dealing with a temporary emergency, involving a normally robust and self-sustaining population which can eventually resume its former life. A process of sustained asset transfer creates high levels of absolute poverty. Relief operations may, to varying degrees, help keep people alive; but, even at best, this is all they do. The way such programmes are conceived and resourced means they are usually unable to tackle the process of resource depletion, an important factor underlying food insecurity. It is no coincidence that since the role of NGOs has become clearly established (supplying the 10 per cent), vulnerability and impoverishment have continued to grow apace.

It should be noted that the donor/NGO relationship is a contradictory one. As mentioned above, not all NGOs involved in relief work have uncritically embraced a subcontracting role. These tensions, and the manner in which agencies have attempted to align themselves either to the weak or, often by default, to the strong, in the process of asset transfer has effected a rough division between "progressive" and "conservative" NGOs. Progressive NGOs usually attempt to maintain a certain independence in relation to large subcontracting operations. They have also tried to protect subsistence assets using a variety of means. These include cattle-vaccination programmes, credit schemes and the use of food aid as a means of market intervention to support the price of livestock (Stockton, 1986). They have also pressed human-rights issues and have attempted to expose the limitations of the international humanitarian system (Dutch Interchurch Aid, 1992). Despite the enhanced role of NGOs and their frequent cooperation in consortia, however, the sheer scale of impoverishment means that NGOs are overstretched, underresourced and, apart from political obstacles, frequently face major logistical constraints. Subcontracting from individual donors, moreover, makes for fragmentation and poor overall coordination. In almost every respect, the donor/NGO safety net is an inadequate response to the unfolding crisis.

Conclusion: The Challenge of Internal War

The end of the Cold War has revealed a worrying trend, that is, the emergence of protracted and complex emergencies. Using material from the Horn of Africa, this chapter has attempted to define this concept more fully. The notion of permanent emergency is premissed on the collapse and decline of formal economic structures. More particularly, however, it is the process of political survival adopted by the dominant groups and classes within this crisis that gives complex emergencies their special character. Survival has been associated with the spread of parallel and extra-legal activities which themselves promote inter-ethnic tensions, asset transfer, conflict and population displacement. They form an essential part of the political economy of internal war. The internationalisation of public welfare has developed as a consequence of the breakdown of governance and collapse of local public provision. External humanitarian intervention, however, has tended to favour and support the politically strong to the detriment of the weak. By the end of the 1980s, this contradiction had reached crisis point in Africa, with some NGOs openly calling for the limiting of sovereignty and more direct political intervention to support the losers (Oxfam, 1991).

The Gulf War and the creation of a "safe haven" for the Kurds brought this debate into the public domain and resurrected the idea of military humanitarianism (Weiss and Campbell, 1991). Despite some early optimism, direct intervention has created more problems than it has solved. In relation to Somalia (African Rights, 1993a) and the former Yugoslavia (Magas, 1993), in a similar manner to the indirect economic benefits outlined above, international political involvement has compounded the situation and strengthened conservative and predatory forces. Indeed, in Somalia, Angola and the former Yugoslavia a watershed appears to have been reached: the post-Gulf War enthusiasm for military intervention has been dissipated under the conditions of internal war. The crisis facing the (democratic and secular) international community thus lies in its inability to curb the development of predatory and totalitarian social formations which exist beyond the conventional economy, while also protecting the victims of these processes.

The development of humanitarian policy in this situation is difficult. One begins from a weak and conditional position. Realistic policies can only emerge from an adequate understanding of the situation that one wishes to ameliorate. The international community, however, continues to misunderstand the significance of complex emergencies and to disregard the importance of parallel activity. If international intervention is not to continue to fuel a process of active underdevelopment, then a framework of analysis needs to be established. This involves recognition of a number of key issues:

In complex emergencies humanitarian policy can only develop as part of a political process. In the past, aid agencies have often depoliticised policy by reducing it to a technical matter of organisation or good practice. This found acute expression in the former Yugoslavia where humanitarian aid has been deployed consciously as an alternative to political engagement (Traynor, 1993).

Policy must be premissed upon the centrality of indigenous political relations. This demands levels of analysis and local understanding not usual in conventional practice. If predatory local political structures are the determining factor in a complex emergency, it follows that the situation can only be adequately addressed by an alternative indigenous political structure. International trusteeship or permanent refugee status cannot play this role. International efforts must therefore be geared to developing popular and alternative indigenous solutions. If US intervention in Somalia is anything to go by, moves in this direction have been a spectacular failure (African Rights, 1993a).

The internationalisation of public welfare means that an internal emergency and its external response are organically linked. In the past, attempts to maintain political distance or neutrality have hidden this relationship. In practice, the linkage has meant that relief operations have usually provided indirect or tacit support to the politically strong. Humanitarian aid has never been, and will never be, neutral. The challenge to the international community, therefore, is consciously to direct the wide-ranging effects that its assistance has to support the emergence of alternative and popular political structures.

The recognition that the causes of, and responses to, complex emergencies are symptomatic of a historic transformation of North–South relations. This reworking has already begun to take shape in the form of inward-looking Northern economic blocs attempting to manage the crisis in non-bloc regions of the South through the extension, by force if necessary, of the donor/NGO safety-net system. The challenge is to break down these walls, reform humanitarian aid and, in a period in which the nation-state is becoming less significant, define new global roles and responsibilities for regional organisations, governments, political parties, NGOs and peoples.

With the possible exception of Eritrea and northern Ethiopia, a review of current trends would suggest that the prospects for preventing the further consolidation of an asset-transfer economy across the Horn of Africa are not good. There is a danger of disengagement by the main donor governments leaving NGOs and an increasingly financially and politically marginalised UN to pick up the pieces. Declining aid flows will increase dependence on extra-legal and disaster-producing parallel systems. For those in the region who stand to gain from conflict and famine, the lack of clear policy and political will within the international community suggests that the institutions benefiting from permanent emergency will continue to consolidate.

References

Africa Watch (1990a) *Denying the Honour of Living: Sudan: A Human Rights Disaster*, New York, Africa Watch.

———— (1990b) "Sudan: The Forgotten War in Darfur Flares Again", *News From Africa Watch*, 6 April.

———— (1990c) "Sudan, Nationwide Famine: Culpable Negligence in the Management of Food Security, War, and the Use of Food as a Weapon", *News From Africa Watch*, November.

———— (1991a) *Evil Days: 30 Years of War and Famine in Ethiopia*, New York, Africa Watch.

————— (1991b) "Sudan: Destroying Ethnic Identity, The Secret War Against the Nuba", *News From Africa Watch*, 10 December.

————— (1992a) "Somalia, A Fight to the Death?: Leaving Civilians at the Mercy of Terror and Starvation", *News From Africa Watch*, 4 (2).

————— (1992b) "Sudan: Refugees in Their Own Country", *News From Africa Watch*, 4 (10): 1–24.

African Rights (1993a) *Operation Restore Hope: A Preliminary Assessment*, London.

————— (1993b) *Somalia: Human Rights Abuses by the United Nations*, London.

Allen, T. (1989) "Violence and Moral Knowledge: Observing Social Trauma in Sudan and Uganda", *Cambridge Anthropology*, 13 (2): 45–66.

Alvarsson, J. (1989) *Starvation and Peace or Food and War?: Aspects of Armed Conflict in the Lower Omo Valley*. Uppsala: Uppsala Research Reports in Cultural Anthropology.

Borton, J. (1993) "Recent Trends in the International Relief System", *Disasters*, 17 (3): 187–201.

Borton, J. and Shoham, J., eds. (1989). *Experiences of Non-Governmental Organizations in the Targeting of Emergency Food Aid*, London, Relief and Development Institute.

Bowden, M. (1992) "1991: The Year of Missed Opportunities", talk given at Save the Children Fund/London School of Hygiene and Tropical Medicine, Working Meeting on Conflict and International Relief in Contemporary African Famines, Westminster Hall, London, 26 March.

Brown, R. (1992) *Public Debt and Private Wealth: Debt, Capital Flight and the IMF in Sudan*, Basingstoke, Macmillan.

Cater, N. (1986) *Sudan: The Roots of Famine*, Oxford, Oxfam.

Childers, E. and Urquhart, B. (1991) *Strengthening International Response to Humanitarian Emergencies*, Uppsala and New York.

Clark, J. (1991) *Democratizing Development: The Role of Voluntary Organizations*, London, Earthscan Publications.

Clough, M. (1992) *Free at Last?: US Policy Toward Africa and the End of the Cold War*, New York, Council on Foreign Relations.

Cutler, P. (1988) *The Development of the 1983–85 Famine in Northern Ethiopia*, unpublished Ph.D. dissertation, University of London.

Cutler, P. and Keen, D. (1989) *Evaluation of EEC Emergency, Rehabilitation and Food Aid to Sudan: 1985–88*, Institute of Development Studies, University of Sussex.

de Garine, I. and Harrison, G., eds. (1988) *Coping With Uncertainty in Food Supply*, Oxford, Oxford University Press.

de Waal, A. (1988) "Is Famine Relief Irrelevant to Rural People?", *IDS Bulletin*, 20 (2): 63–9.

————— (1992) "Fiddling While Somalia Starves", *Independent*, 14 August.

de Waal, D. (1990) "A Re-assessment of Entitlement Theory in the Light of Recent Famines in Africa", *Development and Change*, 21: 469–90.

Downs, R.E., Kerner, D.O. and Reyna, S., eds. (1991) "The Political Economy of African Famine", *Food and Nutrition in History and Anthropology*, Philadelphia, Gordon and Breach.

Duffield, M. (1990) "Sudan at the Cross Roads: From Emergency Preparedness to Social Security", *Discussion Paper* 275, Institute of Development Studies, University of Sussex.

————— (1991) "War and Famine in Africa", *Oxfam Research Paper No. 5*, Oxford,

Oxfam Publications.

———— (1992a) "The Emergence of Two-Tier Welfare in Africa: Marginalization or an Opportunity for Reform?", *Public Administration and Development*, 12: 139–54.

———— (1992b). "Famine, Conflict and the Internationalisation of Public Welfare", in M. Doornbos et al., eds., *Beyond the Conflict in the Horn: The Prospects for Peace, Recovery and Development in Ethiopia, Somalia, Eritrea and Sudan*, The Hague, Institute of Social Studies, pp. 49–62.

Duffield, M., and Prendergast, J. (forthcoming) *Neutrality and Humanitarian Assistance: The Emergency Relief Desk and the Cross-Border Relief Operation into Eritrea and Tigray.*

Duku, J.J. (1988) *The Anyuak Tragic Situation*, mimeo, Sudan Relief and Rehabilitation Association, Ethiopia.

Dutch Interchurch Aid (1992) *The Right to Humanitarian Assistance in Emergency Situations: Protocol on the Roles and Responsibilities of Non-Governmental Organizations*, Utrecht, Dutch Interchurch Aid.

Flint, J. (1993) "Nuba Rebel Leader Appeals to Britain", *Guardian*, 24 May, p. 7.

George, S. (1992) *The Debt Boomerang: How Third World Debt Harms Us All*, London, Pluto Press.

Graham, R. and Borton, J. (1992) *A Preliminary Review of the Combined Agencies Relief Team (CART), Juba 1986–91*, London, Overseas Development Institute.

Institute of Development Studies (IDS) (1988) *Food Security Study, Phase 1: Report to the Government of Sudan, Ministry of Finance and Economic Planning*, Brighton, University of Sussex.

Jamal, A. (1991) "Funding Fundamentalism: The Political Economy of an Islamist State", *Middle East Report*, 21 (172): 14–17.

Jamal, V. (1988) "Somalia: Survival in a 'Doomed' Economy", *International Labour Review*, 127 (6): 783–812.

James, W. (1992) *Uduk Asylum Seekers in Gambela, 1992: Community Report and Options for Resettlement*, Report for UNHCR, Addis Ababa, UNHCR.

Johnson, D. (1992) *The Southern Sudan: The Root Causes of Recurring Civil War*, mimeo, Oxford.

Keen, D. (1991) "A Disaster For Whom?: Local Interests and International Donors During Famine Among the Dinka of Sudan", *Disasters*, 15 (2): 58–73.

Korten, D.C. (1990) *Getting to the 21st Century: Voluntary Action and the Global Agenda*, Connecticut, Kumarian Press.

Longhurst, R. (1986) "Household Food Strategies in Response to Seasonality and Famine", *IDS Bulletin*, 17: 27–35.

Magaš, B. (1993) *The Destruction of Yugoslavia: Tracking the Break-up 1980–92*, London, Verso.

Malwal, B. (1992) "Regime Dissolves Khatmiya Islamic Sect", *Sudan Democratic Gazette* 29: 6.

Meagher, K. (1990) "The Hidden Economy: Informal and Parallel Trade in North-western Uganda", *Review of African Political Economy*, 47: 64–83.

Miller, N.N. (1981) "The Other Somalia: Part 1 – Illicit Trade and the Hidden Economy", *American Universities Field Staff Reports*, Queen Elizabeth House, Oxford, 29: 1–17.

O'Brien, J. (1985) "Sowing the Seeds of Famine", *Review of African Political Economy*, 33: 23–32.

Oxfam (1991) *UN Response to Humanitarian Emergencies: A Challenge to the International Community*, briefing paper, Oxford, August.

Padt, R. (1992) "The Meaning of Neutrality and Its Consequences: The Médecins Sans Frontières Experience", in G.L. Wackers and C.T.M. Wennekes, eds., *Violation of Medical Neutrality*, Amsterdam, Thesis Publishers, pp. 48–54.

Ryle, J. (1989) *Displaced Southern Sudanese in Northern Sudan with Special Reference to Southern Darfur and Kordofan*, London, mimeo, Save the Children Fund.

——— (1992) *Where There is no Border: Repatriation of Somali Refugees from Ethiopia, The Implications for SCF Programmes in Harerghe and Somaliland*, mimeo, London, Save the Children Fund.

Sen, A.K. (1981) *Poverty and Famines*, Oxford, Oxford University Press.

Sudan Human Rights Voice (1993) "Dinka and Lokoro Tribes Face New Perils", 2 (6): 6.

Stockton, N. (1986) *South Sudan Programme, November 1984–July 1986*, Juba, Oxfam.

Swift, J. (1989) "Why are Rural People Vulnerable to Famine?", *IDS Bulletin*, 20 (2): 8–15.

Tandon, Y. (1991) "Foreign NGOs, Uses and Abuses: An African Perspective", *ifda dossier*, 81: 68–78.

Tomasevski, K. (1989) *Development Aid and Human Rights*, London, Pinter Publishers.

Traynor, I. (1993) "Why Mercy Fails to Bring Relief", *Guardian*, 13 April.

Turton, D. (1989) "Warfare Vulnerability and Survival: A Case From Southern Ethiopia", *Cambridge Anthropology*, 13 (2): 67–85.

Vallely, P. (1993) "How He is Getting His Cash", *Daily Telegraph*, 25 August, p. 15.

Weiss, T.G. and Campbell, K.M. (1991) "Military Humanism", *Survival*, 33 (5): 451–65.

Human Rights and Wars of Starvation
Katerina Tomasevski

Human-Rights Protection against Purposeful Starvation

Wars of starvation cannot be reconciled with human rights: it is impossible to imagine a government or a rebel movement that respects human rights imposing starvation on the population under its control. However, to say that government and opposition groups which wage wars of starvation are violating human rights does not make anybody any wiser; nor does it constitute an effective deterrent, evidenced by the fact that wars of starvation continue.

International action against gross, systematic and irreversible human-rights abuses can result in their condemnation, but cannot effectively stop them. What can be done is to assist victims, with or without condemnation of those responsible. Because saving human lives in practice takes precedence over establishing accountability for their jeopardy, human rights are neither the first nor the most important source of international standards applicable to wars of starvation. Three different legal sources – human rights, humanitarian law, refugee law – contain norms which should inform international responses to wars of starvation. These constitute a complex and fragmented range of instruments rather than a coherent system. Moreover, international action to prevent starvation cuts across the mandates of a multitude of international agencies: in the absence of clear leadership in this field, a variety of responses to wars of starvation have occurred.

Attempts to codify international principles of assistance to prevent starvation predate human rights by at least two centuries. An indicative view from the middle of the eighteenth century summarises the rationale as follows: "If a nation is suffering from famine, all those who have provisions to spare should assist it in its need ... To give assistance in such dire straits is so instinctive an act of humanity that hardly any civilized nation is to be found which would refuse absolutely to do so" (Toman, 1989). This view has been affirmed by the current development of international human-rights law: there is a paucity of norms, even proposals, on what governments should do to implement the human right to food, but full consensus on what governments should *not* do. Because human-rights prohibitions are not self-executing, less attention has been paid to telling governments not to starve people to death and more to legitimising international responses to prevent death by starvation.

The right to food: uncertain entitlements

The establishment of the right to food, like other economic, social and cultural rights, has resulted only in empty promises, raised expectations and widespread frustration. To say that everybody *has* the right to food, which the decisive wording of international human-rights instruments implies, is obviously false. The millions of people dying because of the lack of food belie the existence of anything resembling a human right to food, in the sense of an effective entitlement.

Attempts to define the contents of the human right to food have largely been confined to scholarly writings and nongovernmental advocacy. These followed the adoption, in 1966, and entry into force, ten years later, of the International Covenant on Economic, Social and Cultural Rights (Netherlands Institute of Human Rights, 1984; Alston and Tomasevski, 1984; Eide et al., 1984). The right to food was defined in its full scope by Asbjorn Eide, the United Nations Special Rapporteur, as follows:

> Everyone requires access to food which is (a) sufficient, balanced and safe to satisfy nutritional requirements, (b) culturally acceptable, and (c) accessible in a manner which does not destroy one's dignity as human beings. (Eide, 1989)

His report was, however, not followed up, and the right to food has virtually disappeared from the United Nations human-rights agenda.

Significantly, the 1993 Vienna Conference on Human Rights did not mention the right to food. In a convoluted listing of "gross and systematic violations and situations that constitute serious obstacles to the full enjoyment of all human rights", it included "poverty, hunger and other denials of economic, social and cultural rights" (United Nations, 1993a). The Conference further reaffirmed "that food should not be used as a tool for political pressure" (ibid., para. 31). If it did not help to clarify what the right to food means, it did take note of famines and urged "the defence and protection of children, in particular ... children victims of famine and drought and other emergencies" (ibid., paras 21, 25). The 1992 International Conference on Nutrition had reaffirmed the obligation "to protect and respect the needs for nutritionally adequate food ... for civilian populations situated in the zones of conflict", the prohibition of the use of food "as a tool for political pressure", and added that "food aid must not be denied because of political affiliation, geographic location, gender, age, ethnic, tribal or religious identity"(Food and Agricultural Organisation/World Health Organisation, 1992, para. 15).

The failure of the international human-rights bodies to transform the universally recognised right to food into a set of effective entitlements and corresponding governmental obligations has been described many times. This raises a question: is there a rights-based solution to challenges to food security? One should not be misled by the United Nations' change of terminology, whereby food and agricultural "problems" were redesignated food and agricultural "development", thus implying that problems had been solved (United Nations, 1992a). Rhetoric had to accommodate reality and the United Nations kept on the agenda "the response to world food and hunger problems" (United Nations, 1992b). Human rights, however, are notoriously unsuitable for tackling structural problems, and ineffective unless legal remedies are available to individuals to protect and enforce their rights and freedoms. Human rights entail corresponding obligations. These corollaries to the right to food have not been specified in most countries, hence individual claims remain unenforceable; violations can be exposed, but not effectively opposed. The contents of governmental obligations are, however, fairly clear. Governments have a general obligation to enable people to provide food for themselves and exceptionally to provide food to those unable to do so. There is as yet no remedy for the numerous cases of purposeful starvation, even where these can be attributed to a government and factual evidence furnished. Because governmental obligations have not been specified, nor individuals given the right to remedy if they deem their rights violated, purposeful starvation belongs to what Osita Eze (1990) calls "nonjusticiable violations".

The history of human rights, short as it is, demonstrates that advocacy emerges in response to perceived violations; and, indeed, agreement exists concerning the fact that government-made famines deny human rights. Human Rights Watch (1992), an independent human-rights organisation, while not accepting that there is such a thing as the human right to food, argues that "a callous indifference to human suffering and human rights by those in power is the essential prerequisite for a famine", adding that "every single major famine in modern history has been caused, at least in significant part, by systematic abuse of human rights" (p. 1). The ongoing disagreements about the status of the human right to food do not negate the link between human rights and man-made famines. This link is evident from the multitude of international instruments (binding and non-binding, legal and political, human rights and humanitarian) which lay down what governments should and should not do. There are 120 international instruments, adopted between 1921 and 1986, which deal with this link between human rights and food (Tomasevski, 1987).

Prohibition on imposing starvation

International formulations of the right to food revolve around freedom from hunger as the minimum level that should be secured for all. This minimum is derived from the primacy attached to the right to life. The corollary governmental obligations are, first, not to starve people purposefully, and, second, to provide food to those who are in danger of starving.

The right to life comes first in any listing of human rights, and governments are prohibited from killing, torturing or starving their populations. Norms of international humanitarian law extend this prohibition to armed conflicts and outlaw starvation of civilians as a means of warfare. Exposing people to death by starvation obviously negates their right to life. The Human Rights Committee, the supervisory body for the International Covenant on Civil and Political Rights, interpreted the obligations of governments emanating from the right to life as including measures to eliminate malnutrition, thereby stretching governmental obligations beyond a mere prohibition of purposeful starvation (Human Rights Committee, 1982). When denial of access to food jeopardises life, the status of the right to food becomes irrelevant because the right to life is at stake. This is reinforced by norms of humanitarian and refugee law where the obligation to provide food – and the prohibition of purposeful starvation – figures prominently. International humanitarian law prohibits the starvation of civilians as a means of warfare and destruction of objects indispensable for the civilian population, including food, agricultural areas for food production, crops and livestock (Protocol Additional to the Geneva Conventions Relating to International Armed Conflicts, Article 54; Protocol Additional to the Geneva Conventions Relating to Non-international Armed Conflicts, Articles 69 and 70). The protection of civilian populations requires the occupying power to secure food supplies for the civilians, and "bring in necessary foodstuffs ... if the resources of the occupied territory are inadequate"(The Geneva Convention 1949, Article 55). While the substantive norms specifying what governments should and should not do are many and detailed, international law is silent regarding the standing and entitlements of victims of purposeful starvation.

In order to prevent abuses of power, rules of conduct for governments have to be accepted by the governments themselves and depend on self-policing. Some form of international supervision is necessary to prevent governments (and indeed rebel forces) from determining whether they are complying with human-rights norms and thus being judges in their own case. Such supervisory bodies are necessarily intergovernmental and lack an enforcement machinery – self-policing by governments has yet to be supplemented by some form of international policing. It is a truism that it is much easier to criticise the international human-rights system for not functioning than to make it function.

Safeguards against abuses of (armed) force

Human rights aim to put into practice safeguards against abuses of power by the state against its own population. Preservation of human life ranks the highest, as its loss is irreversible, hence the focus on the use of armed force. The prohibition on killing is therefore continuously broadened and reinforced. States of emergency were added to the human-rights agenda in 1977 (Questiaux, 1982), and disappearances in 1980 (United Nations, 1981). Summary and arbitrary executions were placed on the agenda in 1983, and found to take place most often in armed conflicts and through excessive use of (armed) force. Governments are urged to ensure that arbitrary or abusive use of force is punished as a criminal offence, and to apply safeguards in situations of "internal political instability or any other public emergency" (United Nations, 1990a, paras. 7–8, at 121).

The decade of the 1980s was marked by attempts to induce the United Nations to recognise that human rights continue to apply in armed conflicts, and to articulate basic norms for their protection. Human rights apply fully in peacetime, while a much narrower protection, codified in humanitarian law, applies in warfare. Human-rights treaties typically include derogation clauses whereby states may suspend their human-rights obligations in emergencies. Neither peace researchers nor human-rights lawyers have managed to elaborate a term that would encompass the infinite variety of emergencies: the problem is not natural but man-made disasters.

International humanitarian law is far better developed for international than internal wars. Armed conflicts within national borders often remain beyond both human-rights and humanitarian law. Much attention in the 1980s focused, therefore, on this grey area between peace and war, where the government typically derogates from its human-rights obligations, while warfare remains below the threshold of international humanitarian law. A considerable number of efforts to extend human-rights norms in order to curb the use of armed force in emergencies was made in the 1980s: the 1984 Siracusa Principles on the Limitation and Derogation Provisions in the International Covenant on Civil and Political Rights (International Commission of Jurists, 1985); the 1984 Paris Minimum Standards of Human Rights Norms in a State of Emergency (International Law Association, 1984); the 1987 Oslo Statement on Norms and Procedures in Times of Public Emergency or Internal Violence; the 1990 Declaration of Minimum Humanitarian Standards (Institute of Human Rights, 1990). The General Assembly shied away from affirming that human rights continue to apply in warfare, but made pronouncements relating to specific country situations, urging observance of *both* human rights and humanitarian norms.

Common principles of human-rights and humanitarian law form the core of protection accorded by law to every human being under any circumstances. Fundamental human rights – the right to life, freedom of conscience, prohibition of torture, prohibition of slavery, prohibition of retroactivity of criminal law, and the application of nondiscrimination – are exempt from derogation and also form part of humanitarian law.

Gaps in protection

An inverse protection law describes international human-rights protection in a nutshell: gaps are the greatest where the needs are the most desperate. A 1992 United Nations study on the internally displaced concluded that

> applicable international law is a patchwork of customary and conventional standards: some of it is applicable to all persons, some of it is applicable only to certain subgroups ... and parts of it may not be applicable at all in certain situations, such as an emergency threatening the life of the nation, or, on the contrary, may be applicable only during certain situations, such as a state of emergency. (Commission on Human Rights, 1992, para. 103)

The internally displaced illustrate existing gaps in international protection: if they cross the border, they become refugees and are entitled to international protection and assistance; this is not the case if they remain within their own country. It is sufficient to recall Cambodia, where most international action had focused on assisting Cambodian refugees in camps along the Thai border, and provided them with resettlement aid to return to their country. The internally displaced were "discovered" late and assisted much less.

The United Nations Commission on Human Rights noted in 1991 "the lack of humanitarian assistance" to the internally displaced and urged "the protection of human rights and the needs of internally displaced persons" (United Nations, 1991a, preamble and para.2). The 1993 Vienna Conference on Human Rights emphasised "the importance of and the need for humanitarian assistance to victims of all natural and government-made disasters"(United Nations, 1993a, para. 23). This paradox has been partially redressed by international relief actions to assist the internally displaced victims of armed conflicts. These actions, however, did not and cannot change the lack of an *entitlement* to international protection and assistance, or standing to seek it. The existing law represents a patchwork where entitlements depend on the type of conflict people find themselves in (armed/unarmed, international/internal) and the category they are classified into (combatants/civilians, refugees/internally displaced). Moreover, even such diverse entitlements are, to a large extent, rhetorical because procedural means to exercise them are lacking or beyond the reach of victims of conflict.

The key to controversies surrounding international human rights and humanitarian intervention is the lack of agreement as to when and how the functions of government should be taken over to prevent conflict-related famines when the existing government is unwilling to perform them. Such unwillingness is conveniently cloaked under the notion of sovereignty, which enables governments to preclude international action aimed at preventing them from starving their own population. The notion of sovereignty was, and remains, an obstacle to much human-rights work. In practice, the defence of sovereignty has been to a large extent overcome in investigating past human-rights violations, but remains an obstacle to preventing violations. In theory, sovereignty can be deemed to pertain to the state, the government or the people: where the general international law opted for the first and human-rights scholars argue for the latter. Abdullahi Ahmed An-Na'im defined sovereignty as the "means to achieving the substance of self-determination" (Ferris, 1992). Such an approach was followed in the Bellagio Statement, which emphasised the contents of self-determination relating to victims: "the first step of all humanitarian programs should be to strengthen the ability of the beneficiaries to provide for their own futures" (Refugee Policy Group, 1992).

International Policy: Relief, Development and Human Rights

Human rights and the corollary obligations in development have become a new global battlefield, much resembling the previous East–West confrontation, except that the dividing line has changed to North–South. "Development" has been added to the global human-rights agenda against much opposition. Demands for the recognition of entitlements for those deprived of opportunities for survival, let alone development, have not been successful. Efforts to affirm entitlements under the umbrella notion of the right to development first succeeded at the 1993 Vienna Conference on Human Rights. Seven years after the Declaration on the Rights to Development had been adopted by the General Assembly of the United Nations, Western governments finally agreed that there was such a thing as the right to development. However, accompanying this rhetorical agreement was a warning that such right by no means entails any entitlements for individuals or countries.

Human-rights conditionality and international aid

Current international responses to man-made famines are marked by two paradoxes: first, the linkage between aid and human rights is dominantly punitive, in that people whose government is violating their rights are likely to get additionally victimised by the withdrawal of aid (Tomasevski, 1993); second, when aid is aimed at promoting human rights, priority is attached to conventional notions of democratisation rather than the protection of social, economic and cultural rights, including the right to food.

Development aid is increasingly subject to conditions on human rights. While this new interest in human rights might be seen to respond to past criticisms that the international community was providing implicit support to oppressive regimes, many cynics suggest that donors adopted the language of their critics, but not their arguments. At best, human rights were added as yet another layer to multiple conditionalities. Jan Pronk, the Minister of Development Cooperation in the Netherlands, who argued in favour of introducing human rights into aid as early as the 1970s, expressed his concern twenty years later about "an overload of conditionalities" (Shepherd, 1992). The relative importance attached to each conditionality is evidenced by the effort expended to secure compliance. To nobody's surprise, human rights rank low.

Aid flows reflect donor priorities through support for elections at the expense of freedom from hunger. That this is not a pessimist's speculation is demonstrated by the September 1992 elections in Angola:

> The international community seems to be giving priority to democracy rather than to the survival of people in developing countries. Angola had no difficulty in getting the needed foreign support for the recently held elections. But response to the appeals for relief aid has been modest, and this in turn may endanger the peace process. (*Development Today*, 1992)

Responding to man-made famines

International action to prevent purposeful starvation can aim at defending human rights (enforcement in the narrowest sense of the word), punishing the government, or alleviating consequences by providing relief to victims. The third aim dominates humanitarian action, and is construed around the notion of solidarity. Solidarity has been, however, relegated to the "third generation" of human rights and it is not an operative principle or an enforceable right. The General Assembly of the United Nations noted that "the severe suffering of innumerable human beings through the world ... calls for the strengthening of a common sense of human solidarity" (United Nations, 1989). Common sense would argue that preventing disasters – particularly humanitarian crises resulting from governmental policy (which are inherently preventable) – would prevent human suffering. A shared sense of human solidarity constitutes the basis for the multitude of private citizens' nongovernmental activities; these range from fund-raising for development projects to challenges to the official policies and practices in the North which undermine development in the South. The human-rights rationale permeates many consciousness-raising campaigns:

> As the nature of the misery is forcefully presented to the general public, the possibility of politically ignoring the question becomes, to that extent, unviable.... More exposure has led to more awareness, and that seems to have led to more concern and to a sense of obligation which many people have felt they had to act on. (Sen, 1986)

In the 1980s, international action focused on alleviating the effects of man-made disasters. No matter how swiftly and effectively victims can be reached and helped, action remains within the realm of consequences. *The Economist* (11 May 1991) summed it up well: "Private charity may alleviate the consequences of bad government. To eradicate its causes, public action is needed." Such action is, however, apparently incompatible with international law. The authority of international law is not based on an international capacity to govern, but on the willingness of states to abide by the rule of law. Forcible action to mould the conduct of states to make them conform to legal rules has been envisaged only when international peace and security are threatened. In those situations where the rule of law has collapsed, there is the need to create an international right to intervene to protect the rights of the civilian population. It might be suggested that when law collapses force has to come to the rescue. Because governments cannot be *forced* to observe human rights and humanitarian law, or any law for that matter, assistance to people victimised by the rule of force emerged as a specific type of *enforcement*.

During the Cold War, armed intervention, known as the Reagan Doctrine, was promoted as a means to assist "democratic self-determination", described by Louis Henkin as "a claim of the right to intervene by force in another state to preserve or impose democracy" (Henkin, 1989). The 1991 *Human Development Report* acknowledges that the previous East–West bipolarity may have been replaced by a different dividing line: "The rising tension between the Islamic and the non-Islamic world, aggravated by large discrepancies in wealth, threatens to replace the tensions of the Cold War, both between and within nations" (UNDP, 1991: 81–3). Much discussion has focused on the fact that targets of international enforcement are indeed Islamic countries (Muzzafar, 1993).

Preventing Purposeful Starvation

Different meanings of "emergency"

Differences in the meaning attributed to "emergency" illustrate the obstacles to the application of human rights to prevent wars of starvation: the same emergency that triggers off international relief action is the very emergency that the government invokes to limit its human-rights obligations. Arguing human rights in situations where governments have derogated from their human-rights obligations cannot be easy, and attempts to nudge the international community into applying human-rights safeguards against wars of starvation have thus far failed. While the primacy of sovereignty was overcome in investigating gross, systematic and widespread human-rights violations, sovereignty remains an obstacle to the provision of humanitarian assistance.

The term "emergency" means different things to different people. In assistance to refugees, emergency is "the period during which mortality rates are higher that those experienced prior to displacement" (Toole and Waldman, 1990). In international human-rights law it denotes the right of a state to derogate its human-rights obligations. Thus, providers of (emergency) assistance may operate in (emergency) conditions of severely reduced human-rights protection both for themselves and for those they came to help. The silence of relief agencies about human-rights violations they unavoidably witness is explained as a condition of providing material assistance to the needy population. However, recent soul-searching has challenged this dissociation between assistance and protection; for example, the UNHCR has asked "whether it can provide effective protection to persons in their countries of origin without assuming more of a role in monitoring and reporting on human rights conditions" (Cohen, 1993).

International human-rights law recognises the right of governments to derogate from their human-rights obligations in the case of "a public emergency which threatens the life of the nation" (International Covenant on Civil and Political Rights, Article 4). An emergency is frequently declared in unnatural disasters and institutionalises the denial of human rights. Declarations of emergencies constitute a threat to human rights because of their widespread use: eighty countries – almost half of the countries in the world – have had an emergency since 1985 (Sub-Commission on Prevention of Discrimination and Protection of Minorities, 1992).

An illustrative sample of what is subsumed under "emergency assistance" is provided in resolutions which the General Assembly of the United Nations adopts every year. These relate to both natural and man-made disasters. In 1992, the Assembly decided on emergency assistance to war-stricken countries (Afghanistan, Somalia, Sudan), at the same time adopting resolutions on human rights in Afghanistan and Sudan (United Nations, 1992c). In the former, the Assembly expressed its concern about continued armed confrontations and human-rights violations (United Nations, 1992d); in the latter, it stressed "that access by the civilian population to humanitarian assistance is being impeded" (ibid.). The two, parallel, agendas continue.

Droit d'ingérence

Prevention of starvation obviously constitutes one of the main purposes of humanitarian action. However, access *of* victims to foreign or international aid does not have clear-cut human-rights norms to rely upon. Efforts are made instead to affirm a right of access *to* victims of starvation for the international community and/or humanitarian organisations. International standard-setting thus focused on the rights of providers of

aid. *Droit d'ingérence*, a right to interfere and/or intervene, was proposed as
an operative principle for international humanitarian action.

The right to intervene is in a way a revival of the traditional humanitarian intervention, which had been recognised in international law long
before human-rights legislation emerged. States were allowed to intervene
to rescue their own nationals who were in peril on the territory of another
state. In the 1980s, its purpose was to assist citizens of the very state
where the intervention took place, thus challenging the ultimate power of
the state over its citizens. Its legitimacy derives from the universality of
human rights: rights of people anywhere represent a legitimate concern
for people everywhere. International action to alleviate human suffering
and to prevent starvation necessitates access to victims to be able to help
them. The proposal for an international recognition of such a right origi-
nated from Médecins Sans Frontières, and posited that no government
should be allowed to prevent or obstruct the delivery of humanitarian
assistance to its population.

In 1988, the General Assembly made a move towards eliminating the
obstacle of sovereignty in granting access to humanitarian agencies. It
stated that access to victims of natural disasters and similar emergency
situations could be demanded as a right by organisations providing humanitarian assistance (United Nations, 1988). What was meant by "similar
emergency situations" was, for obvious reasons, left undefined. Nevertheless, the Assembly reiterated "that it is up to each State first and foremost
to take care of the victims" (ibid., preamble). While not mentioning that
refusal of governments to "take care of victims" prompted its action, the
Assembly departed from its previous adherence to sovereignty as *the*
obstacle to humanitarian action. Humanitarian action was kept separate
from human rights because it was thought that the needs of victims should
take precedence over investigating whether a disaster was "unnatural",
that is, man-made. However, the defence of sovereignty returned in 1991.
The lengthy General Assembly resolution which reformed the United
Nations humanitarian emergency assistance said: "humanitarian assistance
should be provided with the consent of the affected country and in
principle on the basis of an appeal by the affected country" (United
Nations, 1991b).

The main proponents of *droit d'ingérence* admit that their objective has
been to strengthen the right to assist people (primarily to save their lives)
and to increase the efficiency of humanitarian programmes (Bettati and
Kouchner, 1987). Its main purpose is to overcome the unwillingness of
national or local authorities to allow access to victims. The lively debates
that ensued changed the proposed terminology, and departed from claiming a right to intervene to postulating that there is a duty, even an obligation, to intervene, deriving from solidarity with people in dire need of
assistance (Federation Internationale des Ligues des Droits de l'Homme,

1993). The ICRC commented, however, that this right of interference is "seen as a means of manifesting active solidarity ... [and] comes more into the politico-military sphere than into the humanitarian field, since it also encapsulates the notion of the possible use of force" (United Nations, 1993b, para. 18).

Rights of victims?

Recognition of a right to intervene for the benefit of people victimised by man-made disasters challenges international human-rights law: people are defined as *objects* of assistance rather than *subjects* of rights. International human-rights law does not treat victims as a subject of rights either. The rule is that only individuals may submit complaints for violations of rights, because rights are conferred on individuals. This precludes the recognition of victims as a collective entity. One of the stumbling blocks to developing remedies for widespread and institutionalised violations, particularly those committed in the grey area between peace and war, is that victims have standing only as individuals, even in conditions of mass victimisation. The procedure developed for gross and systematic human-rights violations enables individuals to bring cases to the attention of the United Nations, but the complainant is only an informant, not a party to the procedure.

The United Nations instruments dealing with victims of abuse of power have come the closest to recognising that victims are entitled – collectively – to redress, but this has not yet been consolidated. The Declaration of Basic Principles of Justice for Victims of Crime and Abuse of Power laid down the basic norms using the notion of "criminal abuse of power" (United Nations, 1985). This process had been initiated to give standing to victims of crime; thus private, and not public, misdeeds had been the target. Had the main target been victims of abuse of power by governments, the Declaration would probably never have been adopted.

There is a multitude of proposals arguing that there should be a right to assistance for those victimised by wars of starvation, but few have argued that there already is such a right. The XVIIth Round Table of the International Institute of Humanitarian Law concluded that international humanitarian law "could be interpreted as implying a right to humanitarian assistance" (*International Review of the Red Cross*, 1992). The Vienna Conference on Human Rights formulated such a right as "the right of the victims to be assisted by humanitarian organizations, as set forth in the Geneva Conventions of 1949 and other relevant instruments of international humanitarian law", and it called for "the safe and timely access for such assistance" (United Nations, 1993a). These proposals demonstrate that pressure towards the recognition of such a right is getting stronger as they advance from nongovernmental to inter-governmental conferences.

Humanitarian action accordingly does not – as yet – operate on the basis of rights. In 1991, the United Nations Commission for Refugees (UNHCR) argued that the three legal pillars of international protection, namely human-rights law, humanitarian law and refugee law, "should ideally permit the individual to assert a claim not only against his or her own country, but against the international community as a whole – a claim to its direct involvement on humanitarian grounds" (UNHCR, 1991, para. 56). This suggestion aims to restore balance: giving individuals the standing to seek international protection and assistance runs in the opposite direction to the current demands that humanitarian agencies be granted rights of access and protection.

The General Assembly recognised the link between human-rights violations and humanitarian action in saying that "human rights violations are one of the multiple and complex factors causing mass exoduses of refugees and displaced persons", and this enabled it to introduce human rights into its humanitarian agenda (United Nations, 1990b, preamble). It also recognised "that unresolved humanitarian problems may impede the effective realization of human rights and even lead to violations of these rights" (United Nations, 1990c, preamble). Further standard-setting may, however, make things worse:

> It would risk weakening the progress so far achieved over the years in providing humanitarian assistance. In particular, since it is assumed that the concept of national sovereignty as interpreted by some might reinforce the insistence of Governments on the non-interference in their internal affairs and thus render a convention counterproductive. (United Nations, 1990d, paras. 43–4)

This incapacity to change rules prompted changes in practice.

Stretching the Limits of Human Rights: Which Way?

Reconciling "human" and "humanitarian"

Because the United Nations system can only act in response to information it has received, the initiative of victims of human-rights violations, or on their behalf, is the first step. Thus the right of victims to seek international protection and assistance is crucial. But this has been recognised as a right to seek, but not necessarily to obtain, either. Indeed, activities of especially established bodies for disappearances, torture and summary executions are explicitly termed *humanitarian*. One can easily understand that such an apolitical term as "humanitarian" is used by human-rights bodies to make their work acceptable to targeted governments. What is more difficult to understand – or justify – is the current practice of merging humanitarian action with inherently controversial military intervention, particularly when military intervention victimises the intended beneficiaries of humanitarian assistance.

The language of human rights and governmental obligations is absent from humanitarian action. Nevertheless, in practice, human-rights problems emerge with a vengeance: "There is no such thing as just feeding the hungry, if what's keeping them from eating is not crop failure but vandalism and thuggery" (Krauthammer, 1993). The rationale for making human rights explicit is clear:

> One basis for inquiry into the relevance of human rights to relief actions is the fact that most humanitarian emergencies have a significant government-made component. From recognition of the role of the human agency in disaster situations, with the ready power to prevent or alleviate suffering, arises the question of responsibility for the plight of the victim. (McAlister-Smith, 1985, p. 63)

Agencies involved in humanitarian action tend to get more blame for human-rights problems than governments that created them. In the case of Sudan in 1990, the General Assembly referred to "the principle of safe access for personnel providing relief for all in need" as an accepted principle of United Nations emergency programmes in conflict situations. When this principle is breached, the Assembly has sometimes blamed the operational failings of international relief agencies themselves, rather than the national governments responsible for protecting them. A cynical explanation would be that national governments are voting in the General Assembly while relief agencies are not.

Preventing multiple victimisation

The sole method of overcoming the unwillingness of a government to allow assistance necessary to prevent starvation is the involvement of the Security Council, which can – and does – override the requirement of its consent. This method was applied in March 1992 in the case of northern Iraq, in December 1992 in Somalia, and most recently in Bosnia and Herzegovina. These relief actions exposed the existing normative deficiencies, but did little to solve underlying problems. Moreover, by blurring the distinction between assistance and enforcement, they compounded the existing and unsolved problems.

Much criticism had focused in the 1980s on humanitarian action limited to the delivery of assistance, which disregarded protection. The use of armed force to secure the delivery of humanitarian aid emerged apparently as a response to such critiques. The Security Council, referring to Somalia, stressed in December 1992 "the urgent need for the quick delivery of humanitarian assistance in the whole country", and authorised military intervention to establish a secure environment for the delivery of humanitarian assistance (United Nations, 1992f).

The legal basis for humanitarian action to prevent the starvation of civilians is explicitly recognised in Article 59 of the Fourth Geneva

Convention of 1949. Its legitimacy is seen in "the inherently benign character of the objective" (Helton, 1992). The loss of such an "inherently benign character", when armed force is used to deliver aid, obviously questions this assumed legitimacy. The problem gets even more complicated when humanitarian relief is merged with peacemaking. While the General Assembly declared that "programmes of impartially-provided humanitarian assistance and peace-keeping operations can be mutually supportive" (United Nations, 1992g, Section V, preamble), the UNHCR lamented the erosion of "the distinction between humanitarian assistance and humanitarian intervention" (UNHCR, 1992).

The precedent was set in April 1991 with the armed humanitarian intervention in Iraq. This intervention combined a multitude of unusual features. The Security Council authorised a United Nations humanitarian action, without mentioning a military action accompanying it. No consensus could be reached, hence "a murky compromise was cobbled together" (Friedman, 1991). Humanitarian assistance was organised and delivered to internally displaced Kurds, accompanied by allied armed forces to ensure delivery to the recipients and their safety. The idea of creating safe havens for displaced Kurds was publicly announced by John Major, the British prime minister, on 8 April 1991. His idea was that these safe havens should be sponsored by the United Nations; thus the plan was to replace the allied forces with the deployment of a small United Nations armed contingent, this presumably complying with the Security Council resolution 687 to terminate the military presence in Iraq of "the Member States cooperating with Kuwait" (United Nations, 1991c). Two days later, on 10 April, the relief operation started with an airlift of relief supplies, and was secured by imposing an exclusion zone for the Iraqi military presence.

The explicit aim of this safe haven was to meet the humanitarian needs of the internally displaced people. A precedent was made in the agreement between Iraq and the United Nations "that humanitarian assistance is impartial and that all civilians in need, wherever they are located, are entitled to receive it" (*International Legal Materials*, 1991). Thus the right to assistance was affirmed for the first time. Another aim was to facilitate the return of the displaced by ensuring their safety, within the general objective of restoring peace and security in the area (United Nations, 1990f). Another stated purpose was to alleviate the consequences of repression, namely human suffering and threats to security of neighbouring countries.

The Security Council resolution 688, adopted on 5 April 1991, was thus another precedent: until that point the Council primarily concerned itself with issues of international security, rather than those of human rights and humanitarian affairs. The Council expressed its concern regarding "the repression of the Iraqi civilian population", condemned it, and added that it was "deeply disturbed by the magnitude of the human suffering involved". It requested the Secretary-General to "pursue his humanitarian efforts in Iraq [and] use all the resources at his disposal ... to address urgently the critical needs of the refugees and displaced Iraqi population", and demanded "that Iraq allow immediate access by international humanitarian organizations to all those in need of assistance in all parts of Iraq". Besides authorising international action to alleviate the consequences of repression, the Security Council demanded that Iraq eliminate causes, that is, to "immediately end this repression", and "to ensure that the human and political rights of all Iraqi citizens are respected" (United Nations, 1991d).

The intervention of April 1991 raised much debate about its compatibility with international law. There is no right of armed intervention on the grounds of human-rights violations. The International Court of Justice affirmed in 1986 that the "use of force could not be the appropriate method to monitor or ensure" respect of human rights. Moreover, in the case of Iraq, it was more than armed force that jeopardised human rights, namely the enforcement of international sanctions.

The case of Iraq vividly illustrated the need for safeguards against multiple victimisation: in August 1991 the Sub-Commission on Prevention of Discrimination and Protection of Minorities had to acknowledge the suffering of the population and appealed to all governments and international organisations to "take urgent measures to prevent the death of thousands of innocent persons, in particular of children, and to ensure that their needs for food and health care were met" (ibid.). This followed its 1990 call "to all those participating in sanctions against Iraq not to prevent the delivery of necessary food and medicine" (Sub-Commission on Prevention of Discrimination and Protection of Minorities, 1990).

The facts seemed beyond dispute: people were deprived of access to food and health care, exposing the apparent conflict between sanctions applied to Iraq and the human rights of those victimised by sanctions (Government of Iraq, 1993). The tricky question of whose responsibility it is to prevent starvation as a consequence of sanctions against a government was addressed by Max van der Stoel, the then United Nations Special Rapporteur on Human Rights in Iraq. He described the parallel existence of economic sanctions, which apply to the entire territory of Iraq, and the "internal blockade on the import of food, fuel and medicine for the Kurdish region". Those doubly victimised had no entity responsible for their human rights: Iraq did not seem willing, and the United Nations was not able, to protect their rights, at least to ensure freedom from hunger and disease. The Special Rapporteur noted "this apparent vacuum of responsibility", which should be filled by the "residual obligation on the international community to fulfil the humanitarian needs of the affected population" (Commission on Human Rights, 1993). International action, ostensibly launched to prevent the starvation of the Kurdish minority, made them the principal victims: "In Iraq, those worst hit are the Kurds, who are subject to a double embargo from the international community and the Iraqi government" (Guest, 1993).

Conclusion and Summary

This chapter has reviewed the possibilities and limitations of using human-rights law to respond to man-made humanitarian crises. The right to food appears as the first and most obvious weapon in arguing the human-rights case against wars of starvation. Nevertheless, it is a blunt one because neither individual entitlements nor corresponding governmental obligations have been specified clearly. This chapter therefore considered other parts of international human-rights and humanitarian law that could be invoked to protect people against purposeful starvation.

The primacy of the right to life, and the numerous safeguards against abuse of power, particularly those that cut across human-rights and humanitarian law, have been taken as the starting point. The minimum level of the right to food, termed here the *right not to be starved*, is derived from the protection of human life and operationalised through numerous safeguards against abuses of power.

The counterpart of the right not be starved to death is the legitimacy of international action to prevent purposeful starvation. Emergency assistance, provided directly or indirectly by the international donor community, implicitly recognises that international action is necessary and legitimate to save human lives, even where the action of national governments potentially threatens those lives. This chapter has emphasised the need for *protection* for communities threatened by human-rights abuses, in addition to the existing focus on material assistance. To date, issues of protection have largely emphasised the protection of relief personnel, not the protection of victims of human-rights abuses.

The bulk of this chapter discussed the confused and confusing practice of responding to famines, especially in situations of conflict. The interplay of human rights and humanitarian considerations have in practice merged an inherently political activity, exposing and opposing human-rights violations with the postulated apolitical provision of humanitarian aid. The much discussed *droit d'ingérence* has further politicised humanitarian aid. Contrary to what appears from the use of human-rights language, this "right to interfere and/or intervene" posits, in the name of efficiency, access *to* victims but disregards the rights *of* victims. Moreover, the disappearance of a dividing line between humanitarian assistance and armed intervention necessitates asking whether the current international response to wars of starvation has become part of the problem rather than the solution.

References

Alston, P. and Tomasevski, K., eds. (1984) *The Right to Food*, Dortrecht, Martinus Nijhoff.

Bettati, M. and Kouchner, B. (1987) *Le devoir d'ingérence*, Paris, Denoël.

Cohen, R. (1993) "Human Rights and Humanitarian Action Go Hand-in-Hand", *Refugees*, 92: 4.

Commission on Human Rights (1992) *Analytical Report of the Secretary-General on Internally Displaced Persons*, UN Doc. E/CN.4/1992/23.

——— (1993) *Report on the Situation of Human Rights in Iraq*, prepared by Max van der Stoel, Special Rapporteur of the Commission on Human Rights, UN Doc. E/CN.4/1993/45.

Development Today (1992) "Angola: Assistance for Democracy Forthcoming – But Not for Further Survival", 2 (17) .

The Economist (1991) "Disasters Galore", 11 May.

Eide, A. (1989) *Right to Adequate Food as a Human Right*, New York, United Nations, E.89.XIV.2.

Eide, A., et al., eds. (1984) *Food as a Human Right*, Tokyo, The United Nations University.

Eze, O. (1990) "Human Rights Issues and Violations: The African Experience", in G.W. Shepherd and M.O.C. Anikpo, eds., *Emerging Human Rights. The African Political Economy Context*, Westport, Conn., Greenwood Press.

Federation Internationale des Ligues des Droits de l'Homme (1993) "Droits et devoir d'ingérence: vers une réforme de la Charte de l'ONU?", *La Lettre Hebdomadaire de la FIDH*, 501/502, September.

Ferris, E.G., ed. (1992) *The Challenge to Intervene: A New Role for the United Nations?*, Uppsala, Life and Peace Institute, Conference Report 2.

Food and Agricultural Organisation/World Health Organisation (1992) *The World Declaration on Nutrition*, International Conference on Nutrition, Rome, 11 November.

Friedman, T. (1991) "Nations at War with Themselves: Today's Threat to Peace is the Guy Down the Street", *New York Times*, 2 June.

Government of Iraq (1993) "Note verbale of 19 February 1993 from the Permanent Mission of Iraq to the United Nations Office at Geneva" addressed to the Centre of Human Rights, UN Doc. E/CN.4/1993/99 of 25 February.

Guest, I. (1993) "Peace-keeping at War – the U.N. Dilemma", *Terra Viva*, 15 June, p. 6.

Helton, A.C. (1992) "The Legality of Providing Humanitarian Assistance without the Consent of the Sovereign", *International Journal of Refugee Law*, 4 (3): 375.

Henkin, L. (1989) "The Use of Force: Law and U.S. Policy", in L. Henkin et al., *Right v. Might: International Law and the Use of Force*, New York and London, Council on Foreign Relations Press.

Human Rights Committee (1982) General Comment 6 (16) to Article 6, UN Doc. A/37/40.

Human Rights Watch (1992) *Indivisible Human Rights. The Relationship of Political and Civil Rights to Survival, Subsistence and Poverty*, New York, September.

International Commission of Jurists (1985) "Siracusa Principles on the Limitation and Derogation Provisions in the International Covenant on Civil and Political Rights", *Review of the International Commission of Jurists*, 36: 47–56.

International Court of Justice (1986) *Military and Paramilitary Activities in and against Nicaragua, Nicaragua v. United States of America, Merits*, ICJ Report.

International Law Association (1984) "The Paris Minimum Standards of Human Rights Norms in a State of Emergency", *Report of the Sixty-first Conference*, pp. 58–76.

International Legal Materials (1991) "Memorandum of Understanding, signed on 18 April", 30: 861.

International Review of the Red Cross (1992) "XVIIth Round Table of the International Institute of Humanitarian Law", 32 (291): 600.

Institute of Human Rights (1990) *Declaration of Minimum Humanitarian Standards* 2, Abo Akademi University, December.

Krauthammer, C. (1993) "The Immaculate Intervention", *Time*, 26 July, p. 52.

MacAlister-Smith, P. (1985) *International Humanitarian Assistance. Disaster Relief Actions in International Law and Organization*, Dortrecht, Martinus Nijhoff.

Muzaffar, C. (1993) *Human Rights and the New World Order*, Penang, Just World Trust.

Netherlands Institute of Human Rights (1984) "The Right to Food: From Soft to Hard Law", Right to Food Project, Utrecht.

Oslo Statement on Norms and Procedures in Times of Public Emergency or Internal Violence (1987), *International Review of the Red Cross*, 28 (262) 1988: 66–76.

Questiaux, N. (1982) *Study of the Implications for Human Rights of Recent Developments Concerning Situations Known as States of Siege or Emergency*, UN Doc. E/CN.4/Sub.2/1982/15.

Refugee Policy Group (1992) *The Belaggio Statement on Humanitarian Action in the Post Cold War Era*, Bellagio, May, pp. 9–10.

Sen, A. (1986) "Famine and Fraternity", *London Review of Books*, 8 (12) 3 July, p. 6.

Shepherd, A. (1992) "From Adjustment to Development. Interview with Jan Pronk", *Africa Report*, July/August, p. 67.

Sub-Commission on Prevention of Discrimination and Protection of Minorities (1990) *Appeal Concerning the Situation in the Gulf*, decision 1990/109 of 24 August.

——— (1991) *Appeal Concerning the Civilian Population in Iraq*, decision 1991/108 of 29 August.

——— (1992) *Fifth annual report and list of States which, since 1 January 1985, have proclaimed, extended or terminated a state of emergency*, presented by Leandro Despouy, Special Rapporteur, UN Doc. E/CN.4/Sub.2/1992/23 of 1992.

Toman, J. (1989) "Towards a Disaster Relief Law", in F. Kalshoven, ed., *Assisting the Victims of Armed Conflict and Other Disasters*, Dortrecht, Martinus Nijhoff, pp. 181–2.

Tomasevski, K. (1987) *The Right to Food. Guide through Applicable International Law*, Dortrecht, Martinus Nijhoff.

——— (1993) "Punishment for the Sins of their Rulers", in *Development Aid and Human Rights Revisited*, Pinter Publishers, London, pp. 95–121.

Toole, M.J. and Waldman, R.J. (1990) "Prevention of Excess Mortality in Refugee and Displaced Populations in Developing Countries", *Journal of American Medical Association*, 263 (24): 3296.

United Nations (UN) (1981) *Report of the Working Group on Enforced or Involuntary Disappearances*, UN Doc. E/CN.4/1435.

—— (1985) *Declaration of Basic Principles of Justice for Victims of Crime and Abuse of Power*, Annex to General Assembly resolution 40/34 of 29 November.

—— (1988) *Humanitarian Assistance to Victims of Natural Disasters and Similar Emergency Situations*, General Assembly resolution 43/131 of 8 December.

—— (1989) "Human Rights Based on Solidarity", General Assembly resolution 44/148 of 15 December.

—— (1990a) "Basic Principles on the Use of Force and Firearms by Law Enforcement Officials", Annex to resolution 2, *Report of the Eighth United Nations Congress on the Prevention of Crime and the Treatment of Offenders*, Havana, Cuba, 27 August–7 September 1990, UN Doc. A/CONF.144/28 of 5 October.

—— (1990b) – *Human Rights and Mass Exoduses*, General Assembly resolution 45/153 of 18 December.

—— (1990c) *Promotion of International Co-operation in the Humanitarian Field*, General Assembly resolution 45/102 of 14 December.

—— (1990d) *Humanitarian Assistance to Victims of Natural Disasters and Similar Emergency Situations*, Report of the Secretary-General, UN Doc. A/45/587 of 24 October.

—— (1990e) *Operation Lifeline Sudan*, General Assembly resolution 45/226 of 21 December.

—— (1990f) Security Council resolution 678 of 29 November.

—— (1991a) "Internally Displaced Persons", resolution 1991/25 of the Commission on Human Rights of 5 March, preamble and para. 2.

—— (1991b) *Strengthening of the Coordination of Humanitarian Emergency Assistance of the United Nations*, General Assembly resolution 46/182 of 19 December, Annex: Guiding Principles, para. 2.

—— (1991c) Security Council resolution 687 of 3 April, part B.

—— (1991d) Security Council resolution 688 of 5 April.

—— (1992a) *Food and Agricultural Development*, resolution 47/149 of 18 December.

—— (1992b) *Strengthening the United Nations Response to World Food and Hunger Problems*, resolution 47/150 of 18 December.

—— (1992c) *Emergency International Assistance for the Reconstruction of War Stricken Afghanistan, Emergency Assistance for Humanitarian Relief and the Economic and Social Rehabilitation of Somalia, and Emergency Assistance to Sudan*, General Assembly resolutions 47/119, 47/160 and 47/162 of 18 December.

—— (1992d) *Situation of Human Rights in Afghanistan*, General Assembly resolution 47/141 of 18 December.

—— (1992e) *The Situation in Sudan*, General Assembly resolution 47/142 of 18 December.

—— (1992f) Security Council resolution 794 of 3 December.

—— (1992g) *An Agenda for Peace: Preventive Diplomacy and Related Matters*, resolution 47/120 of 18 December.

—— (1993a) *Vienna Declaration and Programme of Action*, UN Doc. A/CONF.157/23 of 12 July 1993, para. 30.

—— (1993b) *Contribution from the International Committee of the Red Cross*, UN Doc.

A/CONF.157/PC/62/Add.7 of 8 April.

United Nations Development Programme (UNDP) (1991) *Human Development Report 1991*, Oxford and New York, Oxford University Press.

United Nations High Commissioner for Refugees (UNHCR) (1991) "Note on International Protection".

—— (1992) *Report to the XVIIth Round Table on Current Problems of Humanitarian Law*, San Remo, 2–4 September, mimeo, p. 2.

PART II

Five African Case Studies

Angola: Surviving against Rollback and Petrodollars

David Sogge

Introduction

In mid-May 1991 the people of Angola began experiencing something most of them had never known: the absence of war. A suspension of armed action was a relative matter, however, as ruined bridges continued to block relief to isolated villages and explosive mines continued to tear off legs. But even that "peace" proved unsustainable. After about five hundred days, fighting resumed. In the year that followed, in what came to be called "the worst war in the world", an estimated hundred thousand people died and several million Angolans found themselves in even greater depths of hunger and wretchedness (*Africa Confidential*, 1993).

There has been no peace in Angola since 1961, when Portuguese overrule, and a nationalist project to end it, led to open conflict. Scarcely had that ended in 1974 when a post-colonial war began. Armed hostilities continue and look certain to drag on into the mid-1990s. Compounding their destructive force have been massive economic upheaval and malfeasance. Externally, their primary impetus was drawn from the American-led project to "roll back" communism on the world's periphery.

By almost any measure, Angola's war has been catastrophic. From 1975 to mid-1991, an estimated 120,000 people died, most of them combatants as a direct result of armed action. Up to six times as many noncombatants, most of them children, probably died from indirect causes. Only Angola and Mozambique had the odious distinction of being countries where a child's chances of survival were thought to have decisively worsened in the 1980s (UNICEF, 1992a). The chief cause was the "malnutrition–infection complex", a significant cause of global childhood mortality and morbidity (World Bank, 1993). Available data on three important indicators of protein-energy malnutrition, stunting (weight-for-age), wasting (weight-for-height), and incidence of low-birth-weight babies, confirm that Angolans were hit hard. Most of the blows were localised and temporary; there is evidence of strong capacity to survive. Angola has never been a land of walking skeletons.

What accounts for this resilience? Food aid and other forms of foreign help have been of negligible importance for most Angolans, and government efforts on behalf of the rural poor have been intermittent and weak. Nor can wartime survival be ascribed to a system of basic health care, adequate water supply and means to preserve public hygiene, since these have largely collapsed. As described elsewhere (see, for example, Wilson, 1992) poor people's resilience is better explained by their own means of coping: utilising social ties, productive techniques and ingenuity. Yet those Angolans or foreigners in positions to design and implement remedies generally failed to consider local coping strategies as starting points for their interventions. As a result, such interventions have been of uneven impact and were frequently unsustainable. However, coping strategies have never afforded iron-clad guarantees of survival. Their limitations, and the vulnerabilities of the Angolan population, should be seen against a history of distorted growth and development. A highly productive agrarian system was put under increasing stress and was ultimately devastated by forces shifting the economy to outwardly-oriented enclaves "disarticulated" from the (largely unregistered) general economy (see De Janvry, 1981 for a discussion of "articulation" and "disarticulation" in the Latin American context). The first part of this chapter looks at the shift of the economy's centre of gravity from "onshore" to "offshore". The second part considers responses to the crisis.

Origins of Vulnerability

Unlike its neighbours in southern Africa, Angola has been largely exempt from widespread natural disasters. Rather, human agency has played the foremost role, with armed aggression a continual counterpoint in the rhythms of Angolan history.

In such a well-endowed land, hunger may seem paradoxical. Suitable land is abundant. Soils and rainfall patterns give most of western Angola moderate to high farming potentials. It has southern Africa's greatest potentials for irrigation (FAO, 1984; Serrano and Carter, 1991). A sophisticated agrarian system was the main motor of accumulation until the early 1970s. Angola was a nett exporter of food, importing only wheat, olive oil and dried codfish to meet Portuguese tastes. These food surpluses came mainly from African smallholders, not the settlers, a fact apparently overlooked by post-colonial policy-makers and their advisors (see, for example, Bhagavan, 1986).

Key to the system was the interlinking or *articulation* of land and labour, city and countryside. Its strength and complexity developed as farmers adopted higher-output technologies and responded to commercial incentives. An abundance of cattle in Angola's southern provinces made possible introduction of the plough in the central highlands, or Planalto, where farming came to pivot around maize and beans. By 1973, nine out of ten farming households in this "breadbasket" zone, comprising about half the rural population of the time, made use of the plough (Robinson, 1987).

It was an exploitative system, extracting surpluses under the whip of taxation, and through a well-calibrated flow of incentive goods (cheap Portuguese wine, bicycles), wage goods (textiles, foodstuffs) and producer goods (hoes, oxen, carts). A tightly woven network of trading posts, railway, bus and trucking services supported the system. No fewer than twenty thousand petty traders and transporters ran it. Angola's "shopkeeper colonialism" was thus many times denser than that of Mozambique, where around six thousand settlers ran the commercial system for a larger population.

Backward and forward linkages to industry also developed. Having overcome the prohibitions on import-substituting industry in the African colonies which were promoted under Salazar (the dictatorial Portuguese prime minister from 1932 to 1968), local manufacturers began meeting the needs of farmers for goods as well as services such as milling. Chemical fertilisers entered the mix of inputs in market-oriented African farms.

The system's main vulnerabilities can be traced to the limits that settler power imposed on African control over land, labour-power, commerce, and the means to gain political leverage.

The emergence of "traditional" African farming

Actively encouraged by the Portuguese state, which derived significant revenues from Angola's coffee and cotton exports, settlers began arriving in large numbers in the late 1940s. Among them were some of the poorest and least skilled of Portugal's population. Confiscation of the lands of African cash-croppers proceeded apace. At the end of the colonial period, settlers had laid claim to 41 per cent of all surveyed farm and ranch lands, most of which they never actually used. With the establishment of forest and game reserves, more land was barred from farmers and pastoralists. Demographic and political pressures meant that Angolan farmers used what lands they retained more intensively, with shorter fallow periods, so exhausting soils.

Complementing the competition for farmland in this land-rich country was the system's need to mobilise labour cheaply without wholly under-cutting its capacity to reproduce itself, especially with food. Semi-proletarianisation, generated by hiring on settler farms and plantations, was promoted. By the end of the colonial era, one-third of the economi-cally active population worked for wages or had been forced into labour gangs by the authorities. Most rural households faced no option but to exchange commodities to get basic foodstuffs such as cooking oil, sugar and salt, as well as tools to grow food.

A new African agrarian system emerged, which the colonisers labelled "traditional" agriculture. Yet only some households could fully support themselves by farming. Increasingly, off-farm labour was the better option. To sustain everyone, rural women and girls had to work harder for poorer returns. Stratification set in between households with just enough land and those with too little land to provision themselves (Pössinger, 1973). Malnutrition and disease afflicted the most vulnerable: those land-, labour- and oxen-poor rural households dependent on unstable or migrant low-wage employment.

Pressures on African labour and land intensified in the 1960s as settler apprehensions rose. Jolted by rural revolts and alarmed by transitions to formal black rule elsewhere in Africa, the authorities introduced reforms and coercive measures in 1961 under terms of *Reordenamento Rural* (rural reorganisation). Africans were forced into labour reserves, culminating in "protected villages" under military surveillance. By the early 1970s these measures had uprooted over a million Angolans, nearly a quarter of the rural population.

Skewed accumulation and the emergence of the enclave economy

A bimodal pattern common to southern African farming systems emerged in Angola. Large-scale mechanised agriculture crowded out and subjugated small-scale, non-mechanised farming. But Angola's bimodalism stood in contrast to that found in South Africa and Southern Rhodesia, where most African farming atrophied. In Angola, a significant minority of African farmers succeeded. Portuguese settlers, although they paid and otherwise subsidised themselves well, could not match aggregate food output by Africans. Settler limitations, in numbers, skills, capital, and even political clout, meant that many African petty producers could gain footholds in the market even where the rules were against them.

The agrarian system was, however, ultimately self-limiting: through unfavourable city–countryside terms of trade, low purchasing power among Africans, the denial of scientific knowledge, and sheer repression, the colonial order blocked further transformation of the African mode. Despite last-minute Portuguese efforts to create one, there emerged no significant stratum of African farmers with larger land holdings and permanent labour forces. As a result, only one of Angola's three nationalist parties (the FNLA) was rooted among rural producers with ambitions to accumulate, and those roots were meagre.

Agrarian-based accumulation was limited to the Portuguese settlers. Yet most of their financial surpluses went not toward agriculture, but to proprietors resident in Europe and to the better-off residents of Angola's booming cities. Luanda's tower blocks and motorways were built on the strength of coffee revenues. Import-intensive industries served settler wants and tastes. After 1968, petroleum and diamonds shifted the focus of accumulation "offshore" into enclaves with little to do with Angolan daily life. The agrarian system, already under stress, was eclipsed. Pressed on all sides by land-hungry settlers and their politico-military interests, by rising landlessness and stratification, and by ecological decline, African smallholder agriculture entered a period of crisis even before colonial rule ended. Rising numbers of households lacked food security.

The agrarian system denied Africans control over its crucial nonfarm underpinnings: commercial and transport networks, processing industries, input supplies, technical support services, and finance. The energy and business acumen of Angolan farmers could not compensate for their lack of basic literacy and numeracy, as well as of political leverage. Confined to subordinate roles and largely ignored as a base for anti-colonial mobilisation, the Angolan rural strata could neither evolve, nor gain political leverage. Collapse followed. The period after 1974, usually termed "post-colonial", may be as meaningfully termed "post-agrarian".

Breakdown and Descent into Widespread War

Struggles around the supply of food have marked urban–rural relations, Angola's interaction with the global system, and the domestic economy of every Angolan household. Since 1975, tensions beset each of these spheres. One historian suggested that food was the first and perhaps most abiding problem of that period (Birmingham, 1992). Most decisive was the collapse of commercial circuits. Settler shopkeepers, wholesale merchants and transporters departed en masse in the period 1974–76. Commercial capital left the country or went up in smoke as foreign-backed armies laid waste to small towns. Only one cargo vehicle in five registered in 1974 was still operating in 1976. Products could no longer get to market. The flows of goods and services for rural households began to dry up as distribution systems collapsed and factory output and imports fell. This was the beginning of the "goods famine" in Angola's countryside, a condition persisting to the present. Its chief effect has been to cut real returns in directly productive activities, making service employment more attractive.

Factories and plantations also shut down, abruptly ending wages for hundreds of thousands of workers. Migrants working in northern coffee zones were forcibly expelled; they returned to a depleted and disorganised *Planalto* with few prospects. Overall purchasing power dropped further as both lowered real output and crippled distribution systems drove up food prices.

These processes were driven by war. Playing on the ambitions and fears of Angola's three rival nationalist movements, the FNLA, MPLA and UNITA, successive United States administrations promoted destabilisation in collusion with its regional clients, South Africa and Zaire.

As in Central America, Afghanistan and Indochina, the name of the game was "rollback", the displacement of the Cold War to the Third World. And while Angola saw deployment of aircraft, tanks and other forms of capital-intensive warfare between 1975 and 1991, the central thrust was mutual attrition through insurgency and counterinsurgency action.

For the UNITA guerrillas and their backers, major aims were to raise costs to their opponents by choking off lines of transport, communication and electricity. Coercion of local populations was standard operating procedure for both sides, but UNITA never shrank from applying terror in its operations. To a much greater degree than government forces, it used food as a point of leverage. It planted land mines on roads and rural pathways. Lacking the logistical advantages and oil revenues of its government opponents, it extracted tribute in labour and food from local households, and encouraged family members to accompany soldiers during long sieges so that they could raise food crops. UNITA's economy was in principle cashless; markets were suppressed. It set up its own farms near its rear bases, but most provisions in the 1980s came from South Africa (Minter, 1990; Africa Watch, 1991; Toussie, 1989).

State responses

Having beaten back armed invasions and secured, from the top down, its grip on formal power, the new MPLA leadership in 1976 faced the task of feeding officialdom, the armed forces, factory and plantation workers, and city residents at large. Those groups' claims were strong, yet the government had few human and organisational capacities to meet them. The Portuguese had blocked Angolan advancement in schooling and responsibility to such a degree that even jobs such as ticket collectors in buses and market hawkers had been set aside for settlers, many of whom were illiterate. Angola's pool of human resources was thus very shallow indeed. When the settlers left, a void appeared.

Crucial for the MPLA was its early, and in many ways unavoidable, step: a strategic alliance with multinational oil corporations. This formed the main material and financial basis on which Angola's military and economic projects depended. The agrarian system was undermined in favour of the enclave-based economy: in the event, the urgency and logic of spending oil revenues to balance the food equation was overpowering. Reviving rural–urban circuits and smallholder production could wait. Yet the leadership did have options. Much of the agrarian system was still intact. Foreign-exchange and debt problems were practically nonexistent. It could have opted for an "onshore" solution premissed on rebuilding an internal market, while meeting immediate food needs temporarily through imports. But that option was not taken, and its prospects have dimmed further since.

Thus began Angola's ties to world grain merchants and other food suppliers abroad. By the late 1970s, a quarter of Angola's import bill went toward foodstuffs. A decade later, commercial purchases (18 per cent of the import bill in 1989) and donations accounted for 20 to 30 per cent of all staple food available to Angolans (RPA/Agricultura, 1992).

The mainstream media portrayed Angola as a renegade Marxist state ostracised by all but the Eastern Bloc. In fact, with the important exception of the United States, Western powers established ties rather promptly; for them there could be no time for ideological posturing while potentially rich business pickings were at stake. Consulates and embassies opened, salesmen and consultants began arriving, and air links with Europe multiplied.

The flow of petrodollars, and the political buffer against "onshore" claimants which they conferred on Angola's elite, led to technocratic optimism. The leadership could apply its policy motto, "make agriculture the base and industry the decisive factor", without having to look seriously at the workings of the former agrarian system. Even in agriculture the engineering approach prevailed: the messy and politically risky business of mobilising poor people was an unattractive option where "development" could instead be purchased "off the shelf".

The MPLA contracted Eastern Bloc and Western agribusiness firms to revive abandoned plantations, manage crop and livestock schemes conceived by the Portuguese, and to start new large-scale ventures, such as the cultivation of pineapples and farming of European breeds of dairy cattle. Even cassava, smallholder crop *par excellence*, could not be entrusted to peasant farmers: two state farms were tasked with mechanised cassava cultivation under a $4 million contract with a Brazilian agribusiness firm. The scheme failed.

By 1980 the Ministry of Agriculture had thirty-five big agricultural projects on the drawing board: their total value exceeded $132 million (RPA/Agricultura, 1982). Other state bodies, especially the armed forces, also made farming investments. These efforts absorbed the lion's share of farm inputs: between 1978 and 1980 some 2,200 tractors were imported, almost all of them for state farms. They also put further claims on the state, which was obliged to print money to meet the payrolls of overstaffed and undermanaged enterprises, and then to back up those payments with more imported wage goods, especially foodstuffs.

In its first ten years, the government spent 5 per cent of its foreign exchange on agriculture. Most of this, as President Dos Santos acknowledged in 1986, yielded nothing (RPA, 1986). Losses suffered by state farms totalled $114 million for the year 1980 alone. Budgets of state enterprises were notoriously "soft": the average state farm in 1980 spent three times what it earned (RPA/Agricultura, 1982). Their output of food was derisory. In 1977 state farms were said to have met only 12 per cent of urban food needs; as their food output fell, and city populations rose after that year, their contribution declined further.

Optimism about the factory-in-the-field model went with the received wisdom of state socialism. These helped close off other options. Angola's new leaders saw rural producers as politically hostile or at best unreliable, and they were not keen to see the reappearance of the hated class of merchant-transporters. This stance rested on pessimistic views of small farmer capacities and futures, and on fears that rural producers would pose a threat to the state socialist project. Agostinho Neto, first president of independent Angola and MPLA icon, held that the peasant farmer contained "the germ of the capitalist". All this fitted well with other prejudices about the semi-proletarian farming peoples of the *Planalto*, home to the UNITA. Unsurprisingly, a survey of MPLA membership in 1980 revealed that less than 2 per cent were small farmers, a social category comprising at least three-quarters of Angola's population at the time.

State policy toward small-scale farming fluctuated between benign neglect and half-hearted support, depending on trends in politics and especially the balance of payments. In the early years the accent lay on drawing farmers into systems of state-supervised producer cooperatives. But after 1979, the Treasury was again flush with oil revenues and the defence and food-import burdens were relatively light; policy-makers turned to "modern" models. In 1986, with the collapse of oil prices, UNITA military advances, and growing numbers to feed in the army and the cities, the leadership shifted position, announcing a peasant-friendly stance and launching a new system of rural extension.

However, actual support to rural producers hardly flourished after 1986. The supply of inputs continually fell short of farmers' needs. Overall in the 1980s, the government met less than half estimated requirements for hoes, less than one-third the requirement for ploughs (even less for plough parts, which are crucial), and about 10 to 15 per cent of the requirements for maize seed. In a rare 1988 survey of constraints facing rural households in Huíla Province, which was militarily stable and relatively well-supplied at the time, lack of farm tools was second on the list, just after clothing.

Official retailing took place through a hierarchy of shops, with access determined politically. In the 1980s there were at least four types of shops, for common citizens, lower-level bureaucrats, and for lower and upper levels of the *nomenklatura*. Other shops catered for those with dollars, mainly foreign residents. Lacking a ration card, which represented an entitlement to buy basic goods, a small farmer had almost no status in this system. But even if she had such entitlements, the supply was meagre: national distribution plans routinely allocated only 10 to 40 per cent of basic goods to small town and rural outlets, where the bulk of the population resided (UNDP/Plano, 1986).

A common phenomenon in any wartime economy, and in any state-socialist "resource-constrained" economy, is unregistered trade (see Post and Wright, 1989). In Angola this "parallel market" came to dwarf the official market (Frigyes and Bessa, 1989). Rural producers naturally took their goods to parallel markets, where they could fetch ten to fifty times more in cash or in bartered items. Thus the state managed officially to buy only small fractions of total output: in the period 1985–90, for example, it took in about 4 per cent of estimated output of maize, 3 per cent of sorghum and millet, 7 per cent of sweet potato, and less than 1 per cent of cassava (RPA/Agricultura, 1991). And most of what the state acquired came from units under its own supervision, the state farms and co-operatives, although such units themselves had to trade on parallel markets to survive.

A few hundred large-scale commercial farmers continued to farm in Angola. Information about them is hard to obtain, but anecdotal evidence suggests that most of them made strategic alliances with party officials and other institutions, such as Churches, to survive. For example, food parcels destined for the *nomenklatura* in Luanda and elsewhere went regularly from the 25,000-hectare estate of a settler family in the southern province of Huíla. In return, that commercial ranch received an allocation of foreign currency and other privileges (*South*, 1986).

Officials worked hard to make valid estimates of farm output, but in contested areas data on hectarage cultivated and yields remained informed guesswork. Some hint of how far off official estimates could be came in Huíla Province in 1987, when the provincial government earmarked a million dollars' worth of goods, cloth, blankets, second-hand clothing, bicycles and tools for sale to farmers at (low) official prices against (low) official purchase prices for their farm produce. The result was spectacular: nearly 30,000 tons of maize flooded into state warehouses where they had captured a mere 200 tons two years before, under similar climatic and military conditions. Official underestimation of smallholder capacity has been gross and pervasive.

Households

For most households the food crisis meant longer hours of reproductive work. Trade in goods, services, and US dollars became a means of direct procurement of food and of gaining cash income. Those caught up in "forced commerce" were the foot soldiers of *candonga*, the parallel market, a phenomenon which a seasoned Angolan anthropologist has cited as evidence of people's "astonishing and adequate" capacity for creativity in the face of "officially-established inviability" (de Carvalho, 1992).

A household's capacity to cope was strongly conditioned by who and how many managed to survive the tides of war and the related fear, coercion and opportunity. Those who could do so stayed at home, but this was probably true of less than half of Angola's rural population (totalling about five million in 1975). By 1991, just before the 500-day "peace" began, about 900,000 were officially considered displaced inside the country, with 400,000 more as refugees in neighbouring countries. At least twice that number, a third of the population, were thought to have been uprooted by mid-1993. However, the truly massive displacements were not to rural encampments but to towns and cities. In 1970 urban settlements accounted for 850,000 people, about 15 per cent of the total population; by 1990 they accounted for at least 4.7 million people, nearly half the total population (UNICEF, 1992a). Even after discounting natural urban growth, these estimates confirm the extent of flight as a survival strategy and urban areas as the main sanctuaries.

Recruitment into rival armed forces drew away significant numbers of young people. In 1990 as many as a quarter of a million people, around 7 per cent of the economically active population, were tied up directly or indirectly in military occupations (Morel, 1990; Bender and Hunt, 1991a). The nett result in farming zones was a labour shortage of massive proportions. A 1988 survey in villages in Malange Province found that up to two-thirds of all men and two-fifths of all women had departed and never returned (Curtis, 1991).

Beyond shortages of human energy, the drying up of circuits supplying oxen reduced farm household capacities to work the land, transport goods and manure the soil. "Plough farmers" became "hoe farmers" in great numbers, yet animal traction may have still accounted for 10 to 20 per cent of basic land preparation (as against a third or more in the early 1970s). The government persisted, however, in sinking millions into tractors, whereas they accounted for less than 1 per cent of all land preparation (Robinson, 1987).

Access to farmland was an even more fundamental problem. Beyond the dispossession of the colonial era, war tactics limited access to land still further as belligerents on both sides planted anti-personnel mines on pathways. At least one Angolan in 470 is an amputee because of mines (Africa Watch, 1993). The result: vast abandoned tracts where fields and homesteads once stood. A relief official directing a farmer support programme in the central highlands in the late 1980s wrote:

> On the *Planalto* the main factors limiting production are: the availability of cultivable land which is limited by the hazards of the war, the mines and the size of the security perimeter ...; the lack of compost which can be related to manpower shortage and the higher mine risks prevailing in the large grassland areas laying beyond the security perimeter; last but not least a comprehensible lack of enthusiasm to grow a crop which might again be stolen. (König, 1989)

Whatever the actual hectarage-per-person ratios may be (official estimates of land use and population are ambiguous), the war cut farmers off from their most vital asset. Lacking a massive mine-clearing operation, that access may remain blocked for generations.

How did people cope?

When it becomes possible to assemble a full picture of people's survival strategies, it is likely to include the following:

People used accessible land more intensively. In some cities tiny gardens, some no bigger than a bed sheet, covered marginal pieces of ground. In peri-urban zones, where struggles for land and water were intense, there was strong market-driven growth in vegetable gardening, small livestock and fuelwood. In moist depressions, called *olonaka* in the central highlands, gardening intensified, involving sophisticated local systems of intercropping and water management (Serrano and Carter, 1991).

Farmers spread risks over wider crop varieties and other sources of food. Reliance on small grains, namely sorghum and millet, moved northward; cassava advanced southward, probably boosting output above prewar levels. The sweet potato, groundnuts, bananas and other fruit literally gained ground. Where they could, rural people took up hunting of wild game and especially fishing with greater intensity.

Storing food, where possible in secret caches, was a common tactic especially where theft and pillage were rampant. But hiding food was no guarantee of security; a traditional leader in the central highlands told a visiting journalist, "It did not matter where we hid our food or other things because the guerrillas are our own sons and they know where we keep things."

Rural people revived *mutual aid labour practices,* such as *onduluca* in Huíla Province. Displaced persons became casual workers for local residents, becoming a major source of cheap labour.

Petty activities multiplied, from car washing to hair plaiting, to traditional healing. However, households in Luanda spend less time in income-generating activities than do households in comparable cities elsewhere in the world. This is perhaps explained by the sheer scarcity of food and other commodities, and by the constraints on low-income markets created by grossly skewed income distribution, resulting in better-off consumers buying abroad, not locally (Bender and Hunt, 1991a).

Prostitution and soft drug dealing became common; more serious was the rise of both petty theft and armed robbery. An active trade developed in firearms and explosive devices.

Old crafts, notably blacksmithing, tinkering and ceramics, were revived. By making or repairing farm tools, Angola's blacksmiths have made the difference between survival and atrophy of farming in many zones. However, petty producers were denied access to Angola's rich repositories of metallic junk (mainly damaged vehicles), which has become one of the country's foremost foreign-exchange earners.

Survival often meant *overcoming social taboos and personal pride.* When, for example, herdsmen in southern provinces began setting up roadside butcheries, they first had to overcome their disdain for trade. Among Angola's survival strategists, people living in the harsh, semi-desert rangelands of the south may have done best of all: surveys revealed that, even months after a searing drought, rates of malnutrition were low and the average granary well-stocked (CARE International, 1990; RPA/Plano-Gabinete de Planificacao Regional, 1991).

Innovation. In districts where truckers could not, or dared not, transport goods because of blown bridges and mined highways, local inventors began making their own cargo vehicle: the *trotineta*, a heavy wooden scooter capable of handling up to 200 kg, mainly grain and firewood. In Kwanza Sul Province, local people set up scooter transport routes, repair depots and spare-part systems. On busy days police had to cope with traffic jams when dozens of scooters converged on major market towns.

The limits of coping

The most common way of surviving, to flee, also put people in jeopardy. Much depended on one's chances of tapping social networks and gaining an economic toehold in petty trade or services. For women with dependents, the majority of the uprooted, this meant longer working hours. For their children it meant an end to schooling. In extreme cases family units dissolved completely; many children and old people were simply abandoned and consigned to orphanages and institutions for the elderly.

Sanctuary in an official settlement was attractive where the authorities could supply food and make land available for farming. But food entitlements in such settlements expired six months after one's arrival, and the prospects for farming could be nil where others, including self-settled refugees, had prior claims.

Surveys of areas with many displaced persons commonly showed high levels of malnutrition. A 1990 survey in Kwanza Sul Province indicated rates of malnutrition four times higher among displaced persons than among local residents (RPA/Saude, 1991). Surveys in UNITA-held areas of Kuando-Kubango province, where many hundreds of thousands were displaced (some of them forcibly), suggested catastrophic levels of malnutrition among children in the late 1980s (RPA/Saude, 1992). Where breakdowns in distribution systems had isolated many, as in Kwanza Sul, Moxico, Kuando Kubango and Uige provinces, data showed consistently poor levels of nutrition. Malnutrition also reached peaks where drought had compounded the effects of war, as in the southern reaches of the *Planalto* in the farming season 1989–90.

In official settlements, improvement depended on the reliability of food supply and just good luck – such as ending up in a settlement with good leadership. But most people did not meet such good fortune, and had to keep moving. Official settlements were more like streams than pools of people.

Although urban zones were favoured from the first hour, for the urban poor the supply of food was inadequate. A 1991 survey in Luanda showed that the daily calorie intake in nearly 70 per cent of households was less than adequate; the intake of 44 per cent of all households was less than two-thirds of basic requirements (Bender and Hunt, 1991a). A 1987 dietary study of poor households in the city of Lubango, an island of relative stability and of better-than-average food supply, showed that adults consumed an average of 1,472 calories and their children 1,664 calories daily; members of better-off households in the same city consumed a daily average of 2,020 calories (UNDP/Plano, 1987).

The nutritional crisis often expressed itself in illness and heightened risks of death. Where broken-down water and sanitation systems of cities were burdened with wartime populations five to eight times the size for which they were built, the collapse of public hygiene was inevitable. The presence of open cesspools and filth was so widespread in Luanda that poor and rich ran almost equal risks of falling ill (Devereux and Hunt, 1991). Diarrhoeal disease (including recurrent outbreaks of cholera), acute respiratory infections, and malaria were the chief killers, and children the chief victims.

The response from abroad

Minimalism and opportunism best describe the outside world's response to the crisis in Angola. Aid flows were meagre, ranging from a mere $7 to $15 per capita and between 1 and 2 per cent of GDP, lower than to most middle-income oil exporters in Africa (World Bank, 1989). With the exceptions of the early and sustained programmes of help from Sweden and (up to 1990) Cuba, technical assistance for development has been modest.

Donor interest has been lukewarm because of low disbursement rates and high risks of failure. "The experiences gained by external donor agencies in Angola", says one recent report, "have so far been largely negative" (Tarp, 1992). United Nations-backed appeals met feeble responses year after year. Shortcomings in organisation and management have been formidable barriers. But war, politics and petrodollars have been the most significant.

The history of foreign aid in Angola reveals many discontinuities. Following the failed *putsch* in 1977, for example, many *cooperantes* were sent home, as they were presumed to hold left-wing "populist" views associated with the *putsch*'s backers. Then, as military spending rose and oil revenues abruptly fell in the mid-1980s, the door swung wide to allow in a variety of donors, not least of which were the IMF and the European Community's Lomé facilities. Although the donors' hand grew stronger in the latter half of the 1980s, the MPLA leadership continued to call the shots. But once political barriers to relief and development aid began to fall, new impediments arose. These were both political and military. For example, relief programmes of the United Nations and International Committee of the Red Cross had to be suspended at various times when government or UNITA fears arose about who would benefit or claim credit for food deliveries. Aid flows stopped when armed action, or the threat of it, simply made delivery too dangerous.

Internal obstacles and donor reluctance meant that relief aid was limited. In the 1980s Angola received, on average, only half of the food aid it had requested. The government purchased far more food on the world market than Angola received in "gifts". Of estimated staple foods available in the period 1988–91, the peak period for food aid, commercial imports accounted for 15 per cent, food aid 9 per cent, and local production (probably underestimated) 76 per cent. This overall supply of staples is thought to have met only 82 per cent of total nutritional needs during those four years, one of which saw drought-induced famine in south-central zones (RPA/Agricultura, 1992).

However, the quantity of aid has been less problematic than its end uses. City dwellers have been the main beneficiaries. Luanda and other coastal cities became quasi-enclaves fed from abroad. In them, food subsidies indeed helped the poor to survive, but within grossly regressive systems in which the nonpoor extracted greater absolute benefits (Bender and Hunt, 1991b). Distribution of food aid did not differ much from patterns set by larger streams of commercial imports. In the late 1980s about half of all food aid went into normal government sales channels, and another 10 per cent went toward projects meant to stabilise labour forces in key enterprises. The bulk of food aid thus went to urban populations, beginning with the privileged segments of the labour force. The remaining two-fifths was earmarked for "emergency" distribution, via Churches and the government's overburdened social affairs department (SEAS), which was tasked with care for the elderly, disabled and orphaned, as well as war- and drought-affected displaced persons.

Leakage of foodstuffs and other goods was common to all these channels. Pilferage on docks, at railway sidings and in warehouses occurred; but with such losses running between 5 and 15 per cent, they were never as serious as in other countries. Rather more important leakage, however, took the form of in-kind payments to staff members, transporters and officials. Such payments greased the system. For bodies such as the Catholic Church, which had been dispossessed and sidelined by the MPLA until the mid-1980s, the food relief pipeline was vital to institutional survival, and restoration of influence. As with state and party bodies, control of food conferred the power of patronage. Leakage and regressive patterns of distribution were also repeated in nongovernmental channels, but these food aid' flows became politically significant where they began to undermine state/party monopolies over this vital currency of clientalist politics.

As elsewhere, self-provisioning, the major means of survival, was never high on the foreign-aid agenda. Foreign-supported measures to boost output among poor farmers, including displaced persons and peri-urban dwellers, were astonishingly few and far between. And their results were uneven at best, disastrous at worst. In one case in the late 1980s, a foreign-supported programme promoted hybrid maize seed, requiring moist soils and fertilizer, to local farmers who duly planted them at the urging of "experts". An ensuing drought, however, meant total crop failure. Famine for many tens of thousands of people resulted. Some projects have focused on seed varieties and farming systems actually in use, but these have been exceptional.

However, most Angolan officials, the *nomenklatura,* and their foreign supporters have shown little interest, and sometimes outright contempt, for such things. While a few donors may have been frustrated by elitist policies and funding proposals (the health-care system is grossly skewed toward urban hospital-based curative services, for example), the donor mainstream has been, at bottom, concerned chiefly to defend or seize commercial advantage. During the 500-day hiatus in the war,

> at the corporate and bilateral level ... states and companies [were] tripping over themselves for a share of contracts or a pledge of rehabilitation aid.... But this flurry of *bonhomie*, as one analyst pointed out, is just "dressing up oil deals in terms of aid deals". There are well-founded fears that donors and traders are equally guilty of playing upon the political insecurities of government to win contracts which, over the medium-term, will ransom larger and larger amounts of the country's oil production to debt repayments. (Griffin, 1992)

Conclusion

Peace will be a distant prospect even when the shooting stops again in Angola. The ground is saturated with explosive mines, and countless thousands of firearms still circulate in a land whose young people know only a violent past and an impoverished future: a war of sorts will continue. Yet there are grounds for hope, and much human energy is yet to be tapped. Ordinary Angolans have demonstrated resilience and capacities to rise to new tasks. Events of the 500-day "peace" betoken the potential for organised collective action. Among these was the 1992 election process: with a mere 800-odd foreigners (UN officials and others) looking on, Angolans registered 4.7 million of their fellow citizens and then organised voting at 5,800 polling stations, an impressive display of local capacities under daunting circumstances. In Cambodia, for the same number of voters, more than 22,000 UN troops and officials ran the electoral process involving 1,500 polling stations.

It cannot be repeated too often: Angolans have shown great resourcefulness and stamina against heavy odds. But this heroism of daily life is not inexhaustible. Its limits arise where interests of powerful outsiders have the upper hand. To recapitulate:

First, the colonial order dispossessed large numbers of rural people, blocked Africans' access to productive assets and skills, set in motion forces which atomised society, and precluded a tradition of organised, active resistance.

Second, the post- or neo-colonial political economy of Angola has become one of economic enclaves and social islands of privilege in seas of poverty. Petrodollars and elite preferences generated strategies which largely insulated politicians from the economic and political consequences of their malfeasance. Petrodollars made possible the Babylonian projects, the capital-intensive war, and the cohesion and continuation of the power bloc "without, basically, needing the production of the population" (Messiant, 1992).

Indifferent at best to the re-emergence of a productive agrarian system and a flourishing internally oriented market, the leadership looked abroad, and took the course of import-based survival. In the countryside this meant further abasement in living conditions, further gains by a rurally rooted insurgency, and massive flight to the towns and cities. Here people were captive in a rapacious "free" market twinned with a regressive system of distribution linked to gradations of social privilege.

The population surviving under UNITA, where life was much more militarised, were not dissimilar. UNITA exercised power not only through the barrel of the gun, but also through its control over the supply of food. In the end, it was their fear of UNITA's barbarism and totalitarianism that led many voters to overcome their low opinion of the governing bloc and grant the MPLA victory in the country's first free elections in September 1992.

Third, the hand of foreign stakeholders loomed largest of all. Rollback war was the thumb; merchants of arms, food, loans and "development" were the fingers – Angola's leadership was caught in a fearsome grip. Overshadowed by business interests, and constrained both by unfavourable operating conditions and minimal budgets, most foreign agencies have kept playing their minor set parts in integrating Angola's enclave-centred economy still further in the world system. A few cultivated alliances with that small number of Angolan policy-makers who had sought alternatives in meeting the crisis and in adopting an "onshore" development path. Those dissidents remained marginalised and bereft of any significant support from abroad. As endgames in South Africa and Zaire begin to choke off supplies and as exhaustion sets in, possibly provoking a sudden and decisive change in UNITA, the shooting war will wind down. The issue then will be how to relax the grip of an order that still holds Angolans fast.

References

Africa Confidential (1993) "Angola: The Worst War in the World", 27 August.

Africa Watch (1991) *Angola: Civilians Devastated by 15 Years of War*, Washington.

———— (1993) "Land Mines in Angola", London.

Beaudet, P., et al. (1991) *Angola: Rebuilding a Country*, Montreal, CIDMAA.

Bender, W. and Hunt, S. (1991a) "Poverty and Food Insecurity in Luanda", Min. do Plano/Unicef/Oxford Food Studies Group (the Luanda Household Budget and Nutrition Survey, Working Paper No. 1).

———— (1991b) "Options for Streamlining Consumer Subsidies", Min. do Plano/Unicef/Oxford Food Studies Group (the Luanda Household Budget and Nutrition Survey, Working Paper No. 3).

Bernadino, D. (1988) "Contribuição para a Luta Contra a Desnutrição", 1, A antropometria nutricional, mimeo, INSP, Huambo.

Bhagavan, M.R. (1986) *Angola's Political Economy 1975–1985*, Uppsala.

Birmingham, D. (1992) *Frontline Nationalism in Angola and Mozambique*, London, James Currey.

CARE International (1990) "Needs Assessment Survey: Cunene Province", mimeo.

Curtis, V. (1991) "Angola: The Effects on Women and Children", in B. Turok, ed., *Witness from the Frontline*, London, Institute of African Alternatives.

de Carvalho, R.D. (1992) "Angola: A Crise e o Desafio Democrátic", mimeo, Luanda.

de Janvry, A. (1981) *The Agrarian Question and Reformism in Latin America*, Baltimore, Johns Hopkins University Press.

de Morais, J. and Pacheco, F. (1991) "Diagnostico das Associações de Camponeses em Angola", Provincias da Huíla, Huambo e Malanje, Acord/Adra, Luanda.

Devereux, S. and Hunt, S. (1991) "Strategic Options for Health Service Provision in Luanda", Min. do Plano/Unicef/Oxford Food Studies Group (the Luanda Household Budget and Nutrition Survey, Working Paper No. 5).

FAO (1984) *SADCC Agriculture: Toward 2000*, Rome, Food and Agriculture Organisation.

Frigyes E. and Bessa J. (1989) "O mercado parallelo de Luanda", mimeo, Luanda.

Griffin, M. (1992) "Angola", *The African Review 1992*, London.

Hunt, S. (1991) "The Reorganisation of Public Sector Employment in Luanda: Options and Implications for Poverty", Min. do Plano/Unicef/Oxford Food Studies Group (the Luanda Household Budget and Nutrition Survey, Working Paper No. 4).

Kaplan, I., ed. (1979) *Angola: A Country Study*, American University, Washington D.C.

Konig, E. (1989) "Seed Distribution Programme: 1985–1990", ICRC, Huambo, typescript.

Messiant, C. (1992) "Social and Political Background to the Democratization and the Peace Process in Angola", in *Proceedings, Seminar on Democratization in Angola*, African Studies Centre and Eduardo Mondlane Foundation, Leiden, 18 September.

Minter, B. (1990) "UNITA as Described by Ex-Participants and Foreign Visitors", research report to SIDA, Washington D.C.

Morel, A. (1990) "Formação para o Trablho no Sector 'Informal'", consultant's report to ILO, Luanda.

Pössinger, H. (1973) "Interrelations between Economic and Social Change in Rural Africa: The Case of the Ovimbundu of Angola", in F.-W. Heimer, ed., *Social change in Angola*, Munich, Weltforum Verlag, pp. 32–51.

Post, K. and Wright, P. (1989) *Socialism and Underdevelopment*, London, Routledge.

RPA (1984) Sintese do Cumprimento das Orientacoes Fundamentais do Primeiro Congresso Extraordinario do MPLA-PT, Luanda, June.

—— (1986) Speech Delivered by President Jose Eduardo Dos Santos at the First National Meeting on Development Prospects of the Agrarian Sector, Luanda, 6 June.

RPA/Agricultura (1982) "Relatorio sobre a Actividade do Sector Agrario em 1981", Luanda, May.

—— (1991) "Agropecuária de Angola em Cifras", Luanda.

—— (1992) *Food Security Bulletin*, January–March.

RPA/Plano (1989) "Social Institutions, Health, Reconstruction Programme for the Province of Huíla, Namibe and Cunene", sectoral studies 2c, Luanda.

—— (1990) "Famílias e Aldeias do Sul de Angola: Análise dum Inquérito Socio-Economico-Demográfico nas Zonas Rurais da Régião Sul-Sudoeste", Luanda.

RPA/Plano-Gabinete de Planificacao Regional (1991) "Inquerito Nutricional Regiao Sul de Angola, Huile-Kunene-Namibe, Lubango", typescript.

RPA/Saude (1991) *Boletim de Vigilancia Nutricional*, September.

—— (1992) *Boletim de Vigilancia Nutritional*, March.

Robinson, G. (1987) "Animal Traction in Angola", consultant's report to FAO, Luanda.

Serrano V. and Carter, R. (1991) "Small Scale Irrigation in Angola: Potential and Promise", *Outlook on Agriculture*, 20 (3): 175–81.

Sogge, D. (1992) *Sustainable Peace: Angola's Recovery*, Harare, SARDC.

South (1986). "Third Generation Success", November, p. 93.

Tarp, F. (1992) *Angola: Background Report and Possibilities for Danish Development Assistance*, Copenhagen, Danida.

Toussie, S.R. (1989) "War and Survival in Southern Angola: The UNITA Assessment Mission", International Rescue Committee, New York.

UNICEF (1987) *Children on the Front Line. The Impact of Apartheid, Destabilization and*

Warfare on children in Southern and South Africa, New York.
——— (1992a) "Annual Report, Area Office Angola", Luanda.
——— (1992b) *The State of the World's Children 1992*, Oxford, Oxford University Press.
UNDP/Plano (1986) "Trade and Marketing, Reconstruction Programme for the Provinces of Huíla, Namibe and Cunene", Sectoral Studies 2g, Consultant's Report, New York, March.
——— (1987) "Health in Reconstruction Programme for the Provinces of Huíla, Namibe and Cuene", Sectoral Studies 2c, Consultant's report, New York, November.
Wilson, K.B. (1992) "Internally Displaced, Refugees and Returnees from and in Mozambique", SIDA Studies on Emergencies and Disaster Relief, Refugee Studies Programme, Queen Elizabeth House, University of Oxford.
World Bank (1989) "African Economic and Financial Data", Washington D.C.
——— (1993) *World Development Report 1993 Investing in Health*, New York, Oxford University Press.

The Functions of Famine in Southwestern Sudan: Implications for Relief
David Keen

Introduction

The policy implications of any given account of famine will depend on whether the goal of policy-makers is to relieve famine, or to promote it.[1] Michel Foucault argued, in relation to the imprisonment of dissidents in the Soviet Union, that, "The problem of causes must not be dissociated from that of function: what use is the Gulag, what functions does it assure, in what strategies is it integrated?" (Foucault, 1988). The same questions may be usefully asked about famine.

This account focuses on the famine which gathered force in northern Bahr el Ghazal, Sudan, between 1983 and 1988, spilling over into southern Kordofan and southern Darfur. At the peak of the suffering in 1988, death rates among (mostly Dinka) famine victims in Bahr el Ghazal were among the highest ever recorded anywhere in the world. According to a report by Médecins Sans Frontières (18 August), in the camp for famine migrants at Meiram, southern Kordofan, an average of 7.1 per cent of the population were dying *every week* in a nine-week period from the end of June to mid-August. By comparison, in Korem, at the height of the Ethiopian famine in late 1984, an average of 1.6 per cent of the displaced were dying every week (King, 1986). The Sudanese famine, quite clearly, was a famine of exceptional severity.

Whereas the Indian economist and philosopher Amartya Sen has emphasised that famine is "an economic disaster" (Sen, 1981), it may be more helpful to follow the lead of the Indian sociologist Amrita Rangasami, who has argued that "the famine process cannot be defined with reference to the victims of starvation alone. It is a process in which benefits accrue in one section of the community while losses flow to the other" (Rangasami, 1985). In the Sudanese case, famine promised and to some extent delivered important economic and military benefits. The famine was also linked with sexual oppression and religious indoctrination.

Sudan's second civil war began in 1983. The rebel Sudan People's Liberation Army (SPLA) drew support from many groups in the south, most notably the Dinka. It sought to remedy the economic neglect and exploitation of the south, whilst at the same time advocating the creation of a "new Sudan" which would yield economic justice and cultural and religious tolerance for all groups within Sudan, in the north as well as the south. The SPLA attempted to enlarge the areas of rural southern Sudan under its control and to wrest control of strategic southern towns from government garrisons. The manipulation of hunger was to prove an important tactic for both sides in the civil war. In August 1991, the so-called "Nasir faction" of the SPLA split away from the mainstream SPLA headed by John Garang. The Nasir faction was more amenable than the mainstream SPLA to the idea of separating the south from the north.

A Combination of Exploitative Processes

The famine can most usefully be seen as a combination of four exploitative processes. First, raiding (often in combination with scorched-earth army tactics) created large-scale disruption of economic life and left communities without the cattle and grain stores with which they had traditionally resisted natural adversity (Africa Watch, 1990; Aweil Rice Development Project, 1987).

Second, famine victims sought to sell assets (including labour) and to buy grain, encouraging sharp price movements in these markets which further exacerbated famine. These price movements were shaped by the exercise of various kinds of force – from raiding to intimidation and collusion in the marketplace, to the blocking of relief. In this sense, it was "forced markets" rather than "market forces" which served to deepen the famine.

Third, non-market strategies – such as collecting wild foods and moving to areas where relatives lived – were artificially restricted, notably by government soldiers and officials and by government-supported militias. The importance of such strategies in ameliorating famine has been convincingly demonstrated by de Waal (1989) in his study of famine in Darfur, western Sudan, in 1984–85.

Fourth, relief deliveries were inadequate in relation to the very severe needs. Indeed, relief was blocked by a variety of politically influential groups with vested interests in allowing the processes of famine to proceed untrammelled.

Although famine developed principally as a result of raiding and growing insecurity from 1983–85 onwards (see, for example, Africa Watch, 1990; Keen, 1994), major quantities of relief grain were not delivered to Bahr el Ghazal until 1989 – after the worst of the famine mortality. At the end of August 1988, in the context of wholly inadequate general rations, Médecins Sans Frontières-France described its own medical and supplementary feeding work in Meiram as an "ugly charade" (MSF-France, 1988a).

International donors (of which the most important were the US Agency for International Development, the European Community and the United Nations) regarded the train south from Babanousa, the rail nexus of Kordofan, as the key to providing relief to government-held areas of Bahr el Ghazal. Yet there was no more than a trickle of relief on these trains. Donors were promised in May 1987 that 324 wagons a month would be sent from Babanousa railway station, loaded primarily with relief goods (letter from UNDP Resident Representative Joachim von Braunmuhl to Prime Minister Sadiq el Mahdi, 24 June 1987). The rebel Sudan People's Liberation Army (SPLA) had a policy of blockading government garrison towns in the south. But it did not have a strong presence in Bahr el Ghazal for 1986 and much of 1987, and despite this only ten trains left for Aweil between March 1986 and March 1988, carrying *a total* of just thirty-two wagons of relief food. This is clear from records obtained by the writer at Babanousa railway station. There were no subsequent trains until January 1989. In the summer of 1988, twenty-three wagons of grain consigned to Aweil were "discovered" in Babanousa railyard. Ten had been waiting there for a year, and eight for two or more years (Concern, 1988).

Critically, the four processes driving the famine were actively promoted by groups who stood to benefit from them in important respects. For central government, the processes of famine served a number of related functions. By 1983, central government was faced with a dangerous combination of continuing restlessness among the increasingly well-armed Baggara of western Sudan (Allen, 1986; see also Africa Watch, 1990), renewed rebellion in the south, and escalating international debt and balance-of-payments problems. The SPLA was preventing access to newly discovered oil, a potential balm for the government's financial problems.

The combination of political, strategic and economic pressures on central government encouraged Nimeiri and subsequent heads of state to enlist the Baggara militias in organised attacks on the Dinka and other southern groups – providing arms, ammunition, intelligence and effective immunity from prosecution (Amnesty International, 1989; Africa Watch, 1990). The militia strategy offered a cheap and politically acceptable means of debilitating the Dinka, principal supporters of the SPLA (Mahmud and Baldo, 1987), offering the prospect of gaining access to unexploited oil (Johnson, 1988) and at the same time channelling Baggara frustrations against the south.

The use of famine as a cheap counterinsurgency tactic was a technique of long standing in Sudan, as was the device of buying the loyalty of potentially rebellious groups (like the Baggara) by granting them a licence to plunder. Both techniques had been used in the early years of the British condominium administration, as colonial officials sought, on the basis of meagre central-government resources, to bring Sudanese civil society under control (Collins, 1971; Warburg, 1971; Hargey, 1981; Henderson, 1939).

The inadequacy of relief in the 1980s famine also appears to have served an important function in minimising the unwanted side effects of famine, notably by discouraging famine migrants (with associated health, economic and security threats) from coming to particular areas in the north (Keen, 1994). The militia raiding, associated price movements, and the neglect of relief also performed important economic functions for many Baggara, livestock merchants and army personnel.

The Baggara – victims of long-term neglect by a Sudanese state that was dominated by *riverain* elites in the centre-east (Karam, 1980; Saeed, 1982) – had suffered severe loss of cattle during the drought of 1984–85 (de Waal, 1989) as well as growing labour shortages as Sudan's second civil war reduced the flows of Dinka labour from 1983 (Africa Watch, 1990). Meanwhile, merchants and army officers who had benefited from a lucrative trade in Dinka cattle during the 1970s found this trade increasingly under threat, first, from Dinka who were largely excluded from these benefits (Niamir et al., 1983) and, second, after 1983, from the civil war itself.

The transfer of livestock resources from the south to the north between 1984 and 1988 was very great. Between 1984 and the spring of 1986, an estimated 340,000 head of cattle had been stolen from people in the eastern part of Bahr el Ghazal (*New York Times*, 4 May 1986). This was *before* the worst of the raiding. In addition to their function in securing livestock and labour (both directly through capture of slaves and indirectly through their effect on markets), the raids offered the prospect of driving the Dinka away from the often-contested pastures surrounding the Bahr el Arab river (Johnson, 1988; Africa Watch, 1990; Keen, 1994).

Traders and army personnel benefited significantly from the flow of cattle into the north – whether these cattle were captured or sold by Dinka migrants. The terms of trade in livestock and grain markets distorted by famine and intimidation were very favourable for those buying cattle and selling grain. Indeed, during July and August 1987 the terms of trade for those in this position were some twenty-seven times more favourable in the famine-hit town of Abyei than in the major market town of El Obeid in northern Kordofan (Interagency Situation Report, 1988; Ministry of Agriculture, 1987). It is clear that livestock traders provided finance for many of the militia raids (Mahmud and Baldo, 1987).

The army, often acting in collusion with merchants, was involved in the grain trade in all garrison towns, including Abyei and Aweil (Africa Watch, 1990). Officials in one major donor-funded development project in the Aweil area noted that such involvement had given the army a powerful incentive to restrict grain supplies to Aweil (Aweil Rice Development Project, 1987). In Aweil in the summer of 1988, sorghum was priced as high as Ls 3,000 per sack (donor/NGO Technical Coordination Committee meeting minutes, 5 September 1988), roughly ten times the price obtaining in Babanousa. Price movements constituted not only a major *cause* of famine (as highlighted in Sen, 1981), but also a major *function* of famine. A variety of official restrictions on the gathering of wild foods and on free movement by famine victims (Africa Watch, 1990) inevitably increased the economic benefits derived from such "famine" prices – whether in grain, livestock or labour markets – by depriving famine victims of alternatives to exploitative market transactions.

Given adequate relief (combined, ideally, with a strong donor and NGO presence in areas where exploitation was taking place), it is reasonable to surmise that all these economic benefits of famine – like the political benefits – would have been substantially reduced. Raiding would have been more politically embarrassing. And distress sales and purchases would have been greatly diminished by ameliorating the distress.

There is evidence that, when substantial relief did arrive in key centres of famine, grain prices fell dramatically. When, after belated donor pressure, significant relief reached Meiram in September 1988, prices fell suddenly from Ls 600 to Ls 120 per sack. Merchants, who had been holding substantial stores, were caught out and had to bring substantial quantities of grain *out of* the town, taking advantage of prices that were now higher in Muglad town to the north (MSF-France, 1988b; see also Africa Watch, 1990).

The connections between continued exploitation and a lack of adequate relief were apparently well understood. For example, there were reports that merchants had paid bribes to railway workers so that they would not load relief onto trains at Babanousa (*Africa Report*, July–August 1989; see also Wannop, 1989). As far as labour markets were concerned, there were many complaints that relief was removing "incentives" to work. For example, local farmers in the Meiram area complained that relief distributions at Meiram were depriving them of Dinka labour (UNICEF, 1987; interviews by the author in Meiram market, November 1988).

Critically, the same groups benefiting from "famine" prices also possessed substantial control over the delivery and local distribution of relief. In addition to the bribing of railway workers by merchants, the army possessed an effective veto on rail deliveries to Aweil and Meiram. Given the lack of any relief agreements with the SPLA, the trains to Aweil required military escorts. The army's extreme slowness in providing these was a key reason for the lack of relief deliveries (Aweil Rice Development Project, 1987). As far as relief by train to Meiram was concerned, delays of up to six weeks in dispatch were defended on the grounds that military escorts were not available – despite the absence of SPLA activity within a hundred miles of Meiram. Meanwhile, military supplies ran unimpeded along the rails that bisect the town (Africa Watch, 1990).

When trains were despatched to Aweil, army staff and merchants between them controlled their contents: the majority of wagons were reserved for army supplies and merchants' goods, leaving very little room for relief (interviews with railway workers, December 1988). Local reports said the January 1989 trains to Aweil carried fifty-four wagons of goods for the army, along with six relief wagons (*Sudan Times*, 23 January 1989).

While local distribution in Bahr el Ghazal was principally in army hands, local distribution in southern Kordofan was largely controlled by a combination of army officers and Baggara (Africa Watch, 1990), both of which groups were benefiting from "famine" prices. There is evidence that relief was diverted from the intended Dinka beneficiaries on a major scale (US Congress, 1989; see also *Guiding Star*, 3 November 1988; Africa Watch, 1990). Western aid agencies, which might have pressed for a fairer distribution and might have mitigated the worst forms of intimidation, were kept out of Abyei by the Sudanese government – until after the worst of the crisis (Africa Watch, 1990).

Donors' Limited Agendas and their "Room for Manoeuvre"

Despite the considerable obstacles to effective relief in the context of a civil war, there was significant "room for manoeuvre" (Clay and Schaffer, 1984) towards improved relief outcomes which remained largely unexplored by the major international donors – until after the peak of famine mortality in 1988 and associated media coverage.

Before 1989, donors' relief agendas had three main limitations. In the context of the active promotion of famine and the blocking of relief by indigenous groups, these limited agendas helped to produce the severe famine under discussion.

Neglecting the causes of famine

The first limitation was that donors did not concern themselves with tackling the underlying processes of famine, concentrating instead on reacting, with nutritional interventions, to the final stage of famine when mortality was severe.

One way of addressing underlying processes was through political pressure on the Sudanese government. The opportunity to exert such pressure – whether to check raiding and associated human-rights abuses, or to advance peace negotiations – undoubtedly existed. Western donors were providing roughly half of the recurrent government expenditure in Sudan in the winter of 1988–89 (*Financial Times*, 24 February 1989). Yet no linkage between continued aid and reducing conflict was made until the winter of 1988/89, with donors also eschewing public criticism of the Sudanese government until this time. Donors did not publicly highlight the processes of raiding that were creating famine, nor the government's role in these. As late as November 1988, the key UN document that purported to address the issue of the displaced made only one reference to the militias in 164 pages (UNOEA, 1988). Donors downplayed the militias' links with the Sudanese government (Africa Watch, 1990) and stressed their defensive role (US Congress, 1988); yet research available to donors showed clear links between the Baggara militias and the government, and demonstrated the militias' aggressive role (Mahmud and Baldo, 1987).

Despite frequent donor references to the importance of preserving the "sovereignty" of the Sudan, there is evidence to suggest that such concerns could be dropped when donors so chose. In July 1988, at close to the height of the famine, USAID spelled out for the Sudanese government the likely consequences in terms of various aid programmes of the government's pursuing, or not pursuing, favoured economic reforms (Koehring, 1988). Infringements of sovereignty in the name of IMF/World Bank packages are of long standing in Sudan and elsewhere.

Donors' tackling of the underlying processes of famine would also have been assisted by early interventions. Providing more substantial relief to the south in the early years of developing famine would have helped people to remain in their home areas and cultivate (Sudan Council of Churches, 1986), and would have reduced the sale of livestock and labour at "famine" prices by those fleeing north. Yet famine was defined in such a way as to encourage, and legitimise, interventions late in the famine process. For example, the reports of USAID's Famine Early Warning System (FEWS) used a methodology in which "Four stages of vulnerability (to famine) are identified: vulnerable, at-risk, nutritional emergency, and famine" (USAID, 1989). Thus, by definition, famine could only occur after a nutritional emergency.

Mass migration – such as that to Ethiopia peaking in late 1987 – was also taken by USAID as an indicator of forthcoming famine (USAID, 1988), just as British officials in turn-of-the-century India had defined "unusual wandering of people" as a "premonitory symptom of distress", a "warning" of famine (Government of India, 1901).

Turning to relief for those who migrated to Kordofan in the north, allocations of relief grain within this region for 1988 were made jointly by donors and the regional government, largely according to the varying severity of drought in 1987. Abyei area council – which was to experience by far the most severe famine mortality in Kordofan – received the lowest allocation of relief grain (Ministry of Finance and Economy, 1988). When a major relief effort to Abyei was eventually made, in late 1988, this was presented by US officials as a prompt response to news of crisis in Abyei. Such a presentation was underpinned by a definition of the famine crisis in terms of "daily death rates" (US Congress, 1989), rather than, for example, the major distress sales of livestock in Abyei in 1987. In effect, only the final stage in an extended process of famine – the stage of mass mortality – was defined as famine (cf. Rangasami, 1985).

The issue of "accessibility"

The second major limitation in donors' agendas was their concern with getting relief to "accessible" areas, largely accepting government definitions of what these were.

The government's expulsion of the UN's Special Representative Winston Prattley in 1986, which drew scant protest from the major donors, had put an end to donor attempts to reach beyond the government garrison towns. The incident also convinced most private relief agencies that channelling relief to rebel-held areas of the Sudan would not be tolerated by the Sudanese government, nor be supported by donors (Bonner, 1989). Yet there were precedents – in Nigeria and Ethiopia – for donors assisting rebel-held areas without the consent of a sovereign government (see, for example, Wiseberg, 1974).

In Sudan, the NGO-controlled operations of CART (Combined Agencies Relief Team) in 1986 had offered a possible springboard for relief operations that would reach rebel areas. However, as SPLA control of southern Sudan increased and in the absence of firm donor support for CART's operations, CART yielded to government pressures for military escorts, for increasing government control, and for the confining of relief to government-held areas. Noting the end of any semblance of neutrality from December 1986, one experienced CART worker commented: "We are now likely to be regarded by them (the SPLA) as under the control of the government and we must therefore expect to be treated accordingly" (Almond, 1987).

Donors elected to leave responsibility for relieving rebel-held areas to the International Committee of the Red Cross (ICRC), which began negotiations with both sides of the conflict in February 1988. As a result of obstruction by first the government and then the SPLA, the ICRC proved unable to deliver any relief until small quantities were airlifted in December 1988 (Bonner, 1989). Donors repeatedly projected misplaced optimism that ICRC negotiations were about to bear fruit (for example, US Congress, 1988), despite clear evidence (including unambiguous statements from the US Embassy in Khartoum) that the government was determined to obstruct relief efforts (ibid.).

The areas deemed "inaccessible" were not confined to those held by rebels. For example, Aweil was sometimes placed in this category (Interdonor memorandum, 1988). While it is true that the increasing control of Bahr el Ghazal by the SPLA was adding to the difficulties of delivery, the arrival of several trains in Aweil between March 1986 and March 1988 indicated that Aweil was generally reachable; the biggest problems lay in the infrequency of trains, and in their composition. In fact, the composition of the Aweil trains was doubly problematic, for the SPLA justified its threat to the trains on the grounds (to a large extent accurate) that they were being used to carry military supplies, rather than food for civilians (*Sudan Times*, 29 November, 1988; 12 January, 1989). "Inaccessibility" could also be overcome with relief flights – such as those made to Aweil, Meiram and Abyei after the worst of the famine mortality in these towns. In general, a focus on easily accessible areas combined with a focus on the final stages of famine to help delay major interventions until the stage of mass mortality.

Failing to ensure receipt of relief

The third major limitation in donors' relief agendas may be characterised as a concern with allocating relief but not with taking steps to ensure that it was actually received by famine victims.

Donors kept a public silence in the face of the misuse of "relief" trains from Aweil. In July 1988, State Department officials blamed relief failures on a wide variety of logistical factors but made no mention of the attitude of government officials to relief for the South (US Congress, 1988). In October 1988, the State Department blamed the SPLA for relief hold-ups (Bonner, 1989). Meanwhile, the UN, in its November 1988 relief appeal, recommended a six million dollar upgrading of technical facilities at Babanousa, but made no mention of the problem of government priorities that had hampered, and would continue to hamper, relief dispatch from the railhead (UNOEA, 1988).

A second major component of the donors' apparent lack of interest in ensuring that allocated food was actually received lay in the weak support given to those elements of the Sudanese administration, notably the Relief and Rehabilitation Commission (RRC), which had a brief for relief. Whereas there had been over sixty expatriate managers/advisers involved in relief before the RRC took over relief-coordinating responsibilities from the UN in late 1986, by April 1988 there were fewer than ten. The RRC was described by donors at this time as "overstretched with limited staff and insufficient operational resources" (Interdonor memorandum, 1988). By the time of Operation Lifeline in 1989, after the worst of the famine, there were fully 175 personnel from the UN alone assigned to the operation, with the US providing additional resources to strengthen the RRC (Minear, 1991).

Some functions of donors' limited agendas

If the limited agendas of donors contributed to the severity of the famine in southwestern Sudan, these were not simply "mistakes". Like the famine itself, they were in some sense "functional". In particular, adhering to these limited agendas – neglecting the underlying processes of famine, neglecting to channel relief to politically-sensitive areas, and neglecting to ensure that relief reached the intended beneficiaries – allowed donors to present an image of successful relief operations and maintain relatively good diplomatic relations with a Sudanese government that was actually promoting the famine.

Sudan was an important strategic ally for the West. The *New York Times* reported in March 1989:

> American diplomats acknowledge that the lack of public criticism of Mr Mahdi's prosecution of the civil war and his failure last year to provide food to famine victims stemmed from a desire not to push him into the arms of next-door Libya. (14 March 1989)

Donors' limited agendas probably also served a function in helping to protect existing aid projects in northern Sudan against government retribution (see *New York Times*, 28 October 1988; Minear, 1991).

A shift in the donors' stance

Widespread press coverage of famine mortality in the autumn of 1988 significantly changed the balance of risks for donors. As Peter Cutler has argued in relation to donors' shifting response to famine in Ethiopia in particular, the advent of widespread publicity on the famine meant it was now more risky to do nothing than to take vigorous action. Bryan Wannop, then UNDP's Resident Representative, said:

> The press blew the whistle [on the famine]. If it hadn't been for this international public exposure, nothing would have happened... There was a feeling that the world would condemn the UN if there was a repetition. (Bryan Wannop, interview with the author, UNDP, New York, 24 August 1990)

The existence of famine was now incontrovertible – even according to unhelpful definitions that equated famine with the last, fatal stage in the famine process. Meanwhile, an easing of Cold War tensions was apparently reducing the perceived benefits of shielding a "friendly" Sudanese government from criticism. In late 1988 and 1989, donors' relief agendas began to broaden in ways that significantly improved the efficacy of relief, although Sudanese government obstruction was again to reassert itself by late 1989. For a brief period, donors significantly broadened the areas deemed "accessible" and took a more active interest in whether allocated grain was actually received. The Dutch and later the Canadian government linked continued aid with progress on peace (*Sudan Times*, 30 January 1989; Minear, 1991). In January 1989, the US announced an intention to supply aid to SPLA-held areas, and the UN echoed these proposals within a week. It was clear that relief to rebel areas would go ahead with or without the Sudan government's consent. The US also called for progress on peace and on obstacles to relief (Africa Watch, 1990).

There were also new pressures for improved relief and for peace from within Sudan, with the army having suffered a series of military setbacks, and the Democratic Unionist Party, the second biggest party, having reached a peace agreement with the SPLA. The new international and domestic pressures effectively forced Prime Minister Sadiq el Mahdi to agree to the proposed "Operation Lifeline" for the south (Africa Watch, 1990). At the same time, there was an increased readiness on the part of the SPLA to reach agreements on relief.

Relief shipments – to both government- and SPLA-held areas in the south – were unescorted and unarmed, with UN flags and monitors. UN representatives took direct personal responsibility for getting relief trains moving to Aweil and travelled with the trains (Wannop, 1989). The new push to get relief delivered embraced substantial payments to railway workers for delivering the food (ibid.). Meanwhile, the large number of monitors in Lifeline as a whole appears significantly to have reduced "leakage" (Minear, 1991). Most importantly, the relative peace in the south accompanying the relief deliveries allowed some semblance of normal economic activity there.

Concluding Remarks

Notwithstanding Sen's emphasis on the links between "poverty and famines" (1981), it was not so much the poverty of victim groups that exposed them to famine as their increasing inability to secure effective representation within the Sudanese state (Keen, 1994). Indeed, in many respects, it was precisely the assets controlled by southern Sudanese groups (notably the Dinka) – for example, their land, livestock and newly discovered oil – which exposed them, in the context of extreme political powerlessness, to exploitative processes that created and constituted famine. This underlines the need for international donors to exert pressure on behalf of groups lacking political representation within their own societies. Since famine may promise and yield a number of benefits, those seeking to relieve famine need to take account of, and counter, the interests of famine's beneficiaries when designing their interventions.

Unless donors address themselves to the underlying processes creating famine, to the local power structures that shape famine and famine relief, their interventions may serve merely to reinforce these power structures and exacerbate famine. For example, relief shipments may be manipulated for military purposes. Relief may be used to control the movements of populations. And host governments may use the existence of international relief efforts to argue that they are not hostile to their own people.

The need for donors to adopt a more "holistic" approach to the famine process – moving away from a concentration on allocating relief to "accessible" areas once famine mortality occurs – is particularly evident in the context of a civil war, when normal power inequalities are likely to be exacerbated. But the need for such an approach is not confined to war contexts. In 1974, Sheets and Morris (1974) argued, in relation to the drought-led Sahel famine of the early 1970s, that donors had failed to intervene until the crisis had reached catastrophic proportions, and that they had paid inadequate attention to whether food actually reached the intended beneficiaries. These authors pointed to the pressing need for a political advisory system for international relief operations, a system that would draw attention to political or social problems that might hinder relief. These concerns remain as pressing today as they were some twenty years ago.

Note

1. This chapter is a reworking of D. Keen, "A Disaster for Whom? Local Interests and International Donors During Famine Among the Dinka of Sudan", *Disasters*, 15 (2) 1991: 150–65.

References

Africa Watch (1990) *Denying the "Honor of Living": Sudan, A Human Rights Disaster*, New York, Washington, London.

Africa Report (1989) July–August, New York.

Allen, T. (1986) *Full Circle?: An Overview of Sudan's "Southern Problem" since Independence*, Manchester Discussion Papers in Development Studies, 8604, University of Manchester.

Almond M. (1987) memorandum, Oxfam, 31 August.

Amnesty International (1989) *Sudan: Human Rights Violations in the Context of Civil War*, London, Amnesty International, December.

Aweil Rice Development Project (1987) *Report on the Food Situation in Aweil*, 25 April.

Bonner, R. (1989) "A Reporter at Large: Famine", *New Yorker*, 13 March.

Brown, R. (1992) *Public Debt and Private Wealth: Debt, Capital Flight and the IMF in Sudan*, Basingstoke, Macmillan.

Clay, E. and Schaffer B. (1984) *Room for Manoeuvre: An Exploration of Public Policy in Agriculture and Rural Development*, London, Heinemann Educational Books.

Collins, R. (1971) *Land Beyond the Rivers: The Southern Sudan, 1889–1918*, New Haven and London, Yale University Press.

Concern (1988) *Situation Report on Relief Operations*, Khartoum.

Cutler, P. (1989) "The Development of the 1983–85 Famine in Northern Ethiopia", Ph.D. thesis, University of London.

de Waal, A. (1989) *Famine that Kills: Darfur, Sudan, 1984–1985*, Oxford, Oxford University Press.

Foucault, M. (1988) *Power/Knowledge: Selected Interviews and Other Writings, 1972–1977*, edited by C. Gordon, Brighton, The Harvester Press.

Government of India (1901) *Report of the Indian Famine Commission*, Nainital, NWP and Oudh Government Press.

Guiding Star (1988) 3 November, Khartoum.

Hargey, T. (1981) "The Suppression of Slavery in the Sudan, 1898–1939", D.Phil. thesis, Oxford University.

Henderson, K. (1939) "A Note on the Migration of the Messiria Tribe into South West Kordofan", *Sudan Notes and Records*, XXII, part 1.

Interagency Situation Report (1988) South Kordofan, June.

Interdonor memorandum (1988) *Displaced Persons in Sudan: Food Needs and Related Issues*, 29 April.

Johnson, D. (1988) *The Southern Sudan*, report no. 78, London, Minority Rights Group.

Karam, K. (1980) "Dispute Settlement among Pastoral Nomads in the Sudan", M. Soc. Sci. dissertation, Birmingham University.

Keen, D. (1994) *The Benefits of Famine: A Political Economy of Famine and Relief in Southwestern Sudan, 1983–89*, Princeton University Press.

King, P. (1986) *An African Winter*, Harmondsworth, Penguin.

Koehring, J. (1988) Mission Director, USAID, letter to Abu Zid Mohammed Salih, First Under-Secretary, Ministry of Finance and Economic Planning, 17 July.

Mahmud, U. and Baldo, S. (1987) *Al Daien Massacre: Slavery in the Sudan*, Human Rights Violations in the Sudan, Khartoum.

Minear, L. (1991) *Humanitarianism under Siege: A Critical Review of Operation Lifeline Sudan*, Trenton, Red Sea Press, and Washington, Bread for the World.

Ministry of Agriculture (1987) *Agricultural Situation and Outlook*, 3 (5), August Report, Department of Agricultural Economics, Khartoum.

Ministry of Finance and Economy (1988) *Food Aid Administration, Kordofan Region: Distribution Plan*, 11 February.

Médecins Sans Frontières-France (MSF-France) (1988a) *Memorandum for Record*, El Meiram, Southern Kordofan, 27 August.

——— (1988b) *El Meiram Situation Brief*, 22 September.

Niamir, M., Huntington, R. and Cole, D. (1983) *Ngok Dinka Cattle Migrations and Marketings: A Missing Piece of the Sudan Mosaic*, Development Discussion Paper No. 155, Harvard Institute for International Development, Cambridge, Mass.

Rangasami, A. (1985) "Failure of Exchange Entitlements" Theory of Famine: A Response, *Economic and Political Weekly*, XX (41) 12 and 19 October.

Saeed, A. (1982) "The State and Socioeconomic Transformation in the Sudan: The Case of Social Conflict in Southwest Kordofan", Ph.D. thesis, University of Connecticut.

Sen, A. (1981) *Poverty and Famines: An Essay on Entitlement and Deprivation*, Oxford, Oxford University Press.

Sheets, H. and Morris, R. (1974) *Disaster in the Desert: Failures of International Relief in the West Africa Drought*, Special Report, Humanitarian Policy Studies, The Carnegie Endowment for International Peace.

Sudan Council of Churches (1986) *Regional Situations: Especial Report on South Sudan*, Khartoum, February.

UNICEF (1987) *Note for the record, visit to El Meiram, 27–28 October 1987*, Khartoum.

UNOEA (United Nations Office for Emergencies in Africa) (1988) *The Emergency*

Situation in Sudan: Urgent Humanitarian Requirements, November.

USAID (1988) *Sudan: Vulnerability Assessment*, FEWS Country Report, Price, Williams and Associates, Washington D.C.

—— (1989) *Sudan: Vulnerability Assessment*, FEWS Country Report, Price, Williams and Associates, Washington D.C.

US Congress (1988) *Ethiopia and Sudan: Warfare, Politics and Famine*, Hearing before the Select Committee on Hunger, House of Representatives, serial no. 100–30, Washington, 14 July.

—— (1989) *Politics of Hunger in the Sudan*, Joint Hearing before the Select Committee on Hunger and the Subcommittee on Africa of the Committee on Foreign Affairs, House of Representatives, serial no. 101–1, Washington, 2 March.

Wannop, B. (1989) *Report on the First Muglad–Aweil Relief Train, May 20 to May 28*, UNDP, Khartoum, June.

Warburg, G. (1971) *The Sudan Under Wingate: Administration in the Anglo-Egyptian Sudan, 1899–1916*, London, Frank Cass.

Wiseberg, L. (1974) Humanitarian Intervention: Lessons from the Nigerian Civil War, *Revue des Droits de l'Homme, Human Rights Journal*, March.

Relief Aid behind the Lines:
The Cross-Border Operation in Tigray
Barbara Hendrie

Introduction

In 1985, a Dutch aid worker described the Tigrayan people as being caught in a "multi-disaster" (Kettle, 1985). This term aptly describes the combination of factors that affected Tigray region, northern Ethiopia, from approximately 1975 to 1991. These include drought in a region heavily dependent on rain-fed agriculture for food supply, and a war between the central Ethiopian government of Mengistu Haile Mariam and an insurgent movement, the Tigray People's Liberation Front (TPLF). The combined effect of these two phenomena reached a peak in the highly publicised famine disaster of 1984/85, considered by many Tigrayans to be the worst calamity in living memory (Hendrie, 1985). After 1985, localised famines continued to occur until the end of the war, when a coalition of forces led by the TPLF entered the Ethiopian capital, Addis Ababa, in May 1991.

As in other countries experiencing internal conflict, the nature of the famine-disaster in Tigray was complex. In particular, a highly destructive form of counterinsurgency warfare, superimposed on a drought-induced collapse in food production, had disastrous consequences for an already impoverished rural population. Moreover, mechanisms for delivering international relief aid to this population were rendered both logistically difficult and politically controversial as a consequence of the war. By early 1985, for example, Tigray had been divided militarily into two distinct sectors: those areas controlled by the Ethiopian army, consisting mainly of the large towns, and those areas controlled by the TPLF, including most of the countryside (Wright, 1983; Smith, 1987). In parallel to this division of the region along military lines, a division emerged within the international response to the crisis, between an "official" relief operation based in Addis Ababa, serving populations on the government side of the conflict, and an "unofficial" cross-border operation based in eastern Sudan, supporting people in TPLF-controlled zones.

Hence, initial problems of drought and harvest failure were grossly complicated for Tigrayan households by a series of effects linked directly to the character of the war. The aim of this chapter is to consider some of these effects, with a focus on events during the mid-1980s.

Context of the Cross-Border Operation

Drought in the 1980s

Chronic food shortages and periodic famine have a long history in Tigray. Approximately 90 per cent of an estimated 4.82 million people in the region are subsistence producers (REST, 1991), many of whom barely manage the precarious balance between survival and disaster from year to year. A legacy of environmental degradation, exploitation and neglect by central Ethiopian governments, and periodic drought have all contributed to placing Tigrayans on this knife edge.

Agricultural practices have changed little over many centuries, and centre on a system of ox-plough cereal cropping during the main rainy season from June to September. Even during periods of optimal rainfall, however, crop production in Tigray is a high-risk enterprise, with yields rarely providing a full season's food supply. As a consequence, Tigrayan peasants have developed diverse strategies to fill the food gap, including animal husbandry, petty trade, sales of assets, and migration in the dry season (de Waal, 1990a). Mobility, as well as the robustness of local markets, are key to the success or failure of such strategies.

During the last decade, there have been two periods of region-wide drought in Tigray. The first of these began in 1980, when rains failed in the densely populated central highlands and parts of the east. From 1980 to 1984, rains failed successively in these areas; in 1985, they also failed in the normally surplus-producing western lowlands, plunging Tigray into a food-production crisis. Aside from food shortages among individual households, the drought of the early 1980s produced two effects in the region. First, it triggered a widespread decapitalisation of the rural population, as peasants sold assets in exchange for food at increasingly unfavourable terms. Second, it led to a dramatic escalation in the numbers of people involved in "distress" migrations in search of casual labour or food. By late 1984, these migrations involved some 500,000 people moving in search of food both within Tigray and to adjacent regions (REST, 1985).

In a nonwar context, however, it is unlikely that drought alone would have produced frank starvation of the scale that occurred during the famine-disaster of 1984/85. Rather, it was the combination of war and drought that produced a crisis of such intensity, and specifically the fact that conflict either destroyed or curtailed people's options for physical survival. Further, the government's use of counterinsurgency warfare, including direct attacks against the civilian population in rural areas, also acted as a catalyst for the decline of the countryside to starvation, and starvation-associated deaths.

Counterinsurgency warfare

The TPLF was formed in 1975 as a movement aimed at ending the military dictatorship of Mengistu Haile Mariam, who had governed Ethiopia since the overthrow of Emperor Haile Selassie in 1974. By late 1984, TPLF forces controlled up to three-quarters of the rural areas of Tigray (*The Times*, 1985). In areas under its control, the TPLF established a de facto government, administered by "civilian" departments. Land redistribution, the provision of basic health and education services, and new rights for women and minorities were among the more popular reforms initiated by the Front in these areas. In addition, a system of participatory local government was established, through the direct election by villages of an executive committee, or *baito*, responsible for administration and security at *woreda* or district level (Smith, 1983). The *baitos* played a key role during the war years, functioning as both the smallest administrative unit of government in "liberated" areas, and as the main implementers of the relief operation at local level.

TPLF forces were able to move easily through the countryside, and periodically to attack government garrisons situated in major towns. Ethiopian forces, however, had no such clear-cut military targets. Instead, aside from instances when the TPLF army could be engaged directly, the population and economy of the rural areas became key military targets for the state. According to one human rights group:

> There [was] a specific aim of killing civilians believed to be sympathetic to rebel movements, disrupting their economic life, preventing food relief from reaching them, wreaking revenge for defeats by rebel armies, and instilling fear. (Africa Watch, 1990)

This strategy was implemented by the government through a series of major ground offensives, launched across wide areas of the countryside during critical months in the agricultural cycle, as well as an intensive and sustained bombing campaign throughout the war against villages, market-places, and relief centres (Smith, 1987).

The impact of the war

Although there are no statistics available, it is possible to speculate that the combination of ground and air offensives launched by the Ethiopian government caused a significant amount of damage to the rural economy, through the direct destruction of assets such as livestock, crops, houses and storage facilities. At the same time, the indirect effect of the war on the rural economy proved far more damaging, to the extent that survival strategies traditionally pursued by peasants in times of food shortage could no longer operate. This occurred in a number of ways. First, commercial and trading activities suffered a dramatic decline beginning in the late 1970s, when an entire class of professional merchants withdrew from trading in Tigray, especially in bulk grain, as a result of the uncertain business climate created by the war (de Waal, 1990b). During the same period, state farms at Setit were closed due to fighting in border areas, thereby cutting off a source of income for migrant workers (ibid.). More significantly, however, from approximately 1979 until 1989, Tigray was divided into unequal sectors as a result of the war. These comprised the towns and paved roads controlled by the government, and the rural areas controlled by TPLF.

In the "government" sector, urban economies shifted from exchange relations with rural areas to dependence on products supplied by the government. Many of these products, including grain, were brought to Tigray in truck convoys with military escorts from regions in the south of the country. Although some smuggling across military lines did occur, strict controls on mobility and heavy penalties for smuggling discouraged most entrepreneurs (ibid.). The most profitable sectors of the urban economy became employment with the government and the provision of services to army garrisons, including bars and prostitution. Hence, towns that had once been important market centres were dislocated from trade with the countryside. Rural people who normally attended these markets became afraid to do so, for fear of being identified as TPLF sympathisers (Hendrie, 1990).

Meanwhile, rebel-held areas were left with virtually no major centres for economic exchange. Trade was limited to the much smaller markets located in TPLF zones. Moreover, the persistent bombing of markets by government fighter-bomber aircraft accelerated the process of economic fragmentation by forcing all exchange activity to be carried out at night. In this context, markets shrunk greatly in size, and lost their attractiveness as social events.

The nett effect of these factors was to cause severe fragmentation of an already poorly integrated market system, with profound consequences for drought-affected peasants increasingly dependent on the market for access to food. For example, grain surpluses that were produced in parts of western Tigray and northern Gondar every year from 1980 to 1984 were not moved to deficit regions in the central highlands, resulting in an absolute shortage of food in some places (de Waal, 1990b). In this context, the only means for many households to gain access to food became that of migration toward grain-producing areas.

Migration as a coping strategy was widely employed during the drought years. An important direction of these migrations was westward, toward the surplus-producing regions of Shire and Wolkeit. However, the capacity of the western lowlands to absorb migrants in the first half of the 1980s was greatly hampered by the area's position as a prime target for ground offensives by the government. Two of the most destructive offensives, those of 1983 and 1985, occurred during the height of the drought, and included the destruction or confiscation of crops and livestock, as well as the displacement of tens of thousands of households (Wright, 1983; Hendrie, 1985).

The effect of these offensives was partially to collapse the agricultural economy of the western lowlands, and hence limit the capacity of peasants from the worst drought-affected central and eastern regions to sell their labour or obtain food in this area. In turn, this collapse was an important contributing factor to the exodus of nearly 200,000 drought migrants across the border, to refugee camps in eastern Sudan (Hendrie, 1991).

Food as a weapon of war

Migrations "of last resort" to centres of international relief distribution in the major towns were being directly affected by the conduct of the war. There is substantial evidence to suggest that the Ethiopian government made deliberate use of food aid as a weapon in its arsenal of counter-insurgency warfare (Africa Watch, 1991), including the deliberate starvation or forced removal of populations in the conflict zones. This was done in a number of ways.

According to interviews with Tigrayan refugees in Sudan, the government used the promise of relief distributions to encourage peasants from insurgent-controlled areas to cross military lines and enter the towns under its control (Clay and Holcombe, 1985). Once inside the towns, people were then rounded up for resettlement on state farms in Wollega and other regions to the south of the country. Although the resettlement programme was presented to the international community as a means of responding to the famine in the north, many Tigrayans viewed it as a military operation aimed at depopulating the countryside in order to weaken popular support for the TPLF (REST, 1985). In several instances witnessed by international observers, resettlement southward from staging points in Makele, the regional capital, was conducted at gunpoint by the Ethiopian army. Frequently, heads of households were taken, while other family members remaining in villages had no knowledge of their whereabouts (see Clay and Holcombe, 1985; Smith, 1985).

From the point of view of households involved in distress migrations, fear of resettlement was a key reason for avoiding the towns under government control in late 1984/early 1985. Thus, one of the effects of the programme was to influence the direction of distress migrations, as people feared crossing military lines in order to obtain food. In some cases, households living only a three- or four-hour walk from distribution centres in urban areas opted instead for the four- to five-week walk to eastern Sudan (Hendrie, 1985).

Diplomatic activities by government officials in Addis Ababa were also influencing the strategic use of international relief assistance. From approximately 1983 until 1990, the Ethiopian government refused to consider proposals forwarded by the UN, the International Committee of the Red Cross (ICRC) and other international entities for the "safe passage" of relief supplies into Tigray (Hendrie, 1990). Such an agreement would have enabled international relief transports to travel out from towns under government control, across military lines, to the worst-affected rural areas. From the government's point of view, this would entail de facto recognition of the TPLF's control of large parts of the countryside, in direct contradiction of its own official statements that all famine victims in the north of the country were accessible for the purposes of relief distributions through government channels alone (Jansson et al., 1987). Thus, the possibility that food supplies could be delivered to the conflict-zones through "official" channels, utilising established logistical networks, was effectively blocked by the government's rejection of a "safe passage" agreement. Instead, people from TPLF areas were expected to enter the towns to receive dry ration distributions; indeed, many aid officials based in Addis Ababa believed that a majority of people from conflict areas were being fed this way during the height of the crisis (Hendrie, 1990). However, where households from TPLF areas did attempt to enter towns, they were often either harassed or prevented from proceeding by soldiers requesting to see their government identity cards (Clay and Holcombe, 1985). Consequently, the government was effectively able to deny food aid to rebel areas by restricting the geographic scope of the official relief operation.

The Cross-Border Operation: 1984–85

The scope of the "unofficial" relief operation to Tigray was virtually unknown to organisations working exclusively on the government side of the conflict in this period. In contrast to the well-resourced but geographically limited feeding programme based in the towns, the "cross-border operation" from Sudan was geographically broad in its ability to access rural populations, but very poorly resourced throughout 1984/85.

The operation began in 1978 with the formation of the indigenous Relief Society of Tigray (REST). Acting as the sole implementing body for the transport and distribution of relief assistance to civilians in TPLF areas, REST began receiving small amounts of external assistance in the early 1980s, mainly in the form of sorghum purchased in eastern Sudan and trucked across the border at night to avoid attacks by the Ethiopian air force. The primary conduit for this assistance was a consortium of European and American Church-based NGOs, called the Emergency Relief Desk (ERD), led by Norwegian Church Aid, and headquartered in Khartoum. (A cross-border operation to Eritrea from Sudan was also begun at this time, managed by the indigenous Eritrean Relief Association (ERA), and supported by many of the same international NGOs that were assisting REST. ERA operated exclusively in the war zones controlled by the Eritrean People's Liberation Front.)

The identity of NGOs comprising the ERD consortium was kept confidential; it thus acted as a discreet "buffer" which major donors could use to support relief programmes in the war zones, without endangering other programmes already established on the government side. The location of ERD's headquarters in Khartoum enabled it to carry out a regular, independent monitoring programme of donations to REST, from Sudan to final distribution at village level. In addition to ERD, the Tigray Transport and Agricultural Consortium (TTAC), based in London, provided assistance to REST after 1983.

In mid-1984, crop failure in eastern Sudan made it impossible to continue local grain purchases. The first major consignment of external food aid channelled through ERD was received in the form of 5,000 MT of wheat from USAID late in that year. It is likely that fear of the destabilising effect of Ethiopian refugees on Sudan, an important US ally in the region at that time, influenced the American government's initial decision to support the cross-border operation. In subsequent months, threats of increased support to the cross-border programme were used by US officials in Addis Ababa as part of a carrot-and-stick approach toward the Mengistu regime, in an attempt to expand operations from the government side into conflict zones in the north (Smith, 1987). Additional consignments of food aid were subsequently received from Canada and Europe. The increase in external commodities necessitated the establishment of a warehouse facility in Port Sudan, where shipments were stored pending onward transport by REST trucks.

The main obstacle to increasing food distributions via the cross-border operation during the 1984/85 disaster was trucking capacity. By mid-1984, the small number of trucks in REST's fleet were unable to cope with the escalating requirements for food in TPLF zones, and particularly in the migrant-saturated western lowlands. Responding to urgent appeals for additional trucks was highly problematic for major donors, however, because of their perceived potential for military use. Similarly, appeals for additional shipments of food and other forms of assistance forwarded to bilateral, multilateral and NGO donors were met with extreme caution, due to the political sensitivity of supporting operations in TPLF zones.

Thus, although the small amount of aid available from NGOs enabled REST to distribute some food during the height of the disaster, it was grossly insufficient to prevent the exodus of several hundred thousand people across the border to Sudan. It was not until late 1985, after the peak of famine deaths had already occurred, that external support to the cross-border operation began to catch up with food aid requirements in TPLF zones, as well as the organisational capacity of REST. The refugee influx to Sudan in turn triggered a large-scale emergency operation along the border, coordinated by the United Nations High Commissioner for Refugees (UNHCR) and the Sudan Office of the Commissioner of Refugees (COR). By 1987, some 170,000 of the original 200,000 Tigrayans to arrive in 1985 returned home under the auspices of REST (Hendrie, 1991).

"Sovereignty" and the politics of aid

A key reason why the cross-border operation was so poorly supported during the height of the famine-disaster was the Ethiopian government's success in directing not only the flow of aid resources, but also the flow of information, to its side of the conflict. This was done by exploiting diplomatic prerogatives inherent in the notion of state sovereignty, including the right of a government to direct the overall character of relief operations on its territory to its citizens. In the case of Tigray, the notion of state sovereignty, and the corollary of noninterference in a state's internal affairs, was invoked many times by major donors as a reason for not challenging the government more strongly on sensitive questions concerning the relationship between food aid and warfare in the region.

More specifically, throughout the 1984/85 disaster, the Ethiopian government refused to acknowledge the existence of a war in the north of the country. This refusal, in turn, presented a dilemma for major donors, and particularly the various bodies of the United Nations, who could not be seen to contradict government statements. Instead of an openly declared conflict scenario, with two protagonists engaged in armed combat, the international community was encouraged by the government to consider conditions in the north as constituting a security problem only. This view was in fact adopted by many international donors based in Addis Ababa: in nearly all public reports by agencies working solely on the government side during the crisis period, references to the existence or practical implications of warfare in the famine zones is lacking.

Bilateral donors were also cautious in publicly raising awkward questions about conflict in the north, for fear of angering a government with whom they were forced to cooperate on a relief effort of unprecedented size and international profile. Many large international NGOs were also cautious on this point. According to a senior official of a British NGO: "It's really a matter of respecting a country's sovereignty ... It's sad we cannot help these victims, but we do not consider present cross-border operations very effective" (*Christian Science Monitor*, 1985).

The government's success in controlling international perceptions about conditions in Tigray had a number of immediate consequences. First, the crucial question of access to populations in the war zones, and the ways in which military realities on the ground were affecting the flow of relief food, was never specifically addressed in public fora or media reports. Similarly, the existence of the cross-border operation from Sudan was never publicly acknowledged as a means of direct access to rural areas that could complement town-based feeding programmes mounted from the government side. Indeed, many aid officials based in Addis Ababa were unaware of its existence. Instead, the bulk of relief inputs provided to Ethiopia during the 1984/85 disaster were donated through "official" channels, either bilaterally to the government's Relief and Rehabilitation Commission, or through multilateral organisations, international NGOs, and Church networks based in the national capital. For example, between November 1984 and October 1985, the government of Ethiopia received 975,000 tonnes of food, enough to feed the drought-affected population in the north, while REST and ERA together received only 80,000 tonnes (Silkin and Hughes, 1992). This occurred despite the fact that a significant proportion of the famine-affected population in Tigray could not be reached through these channels alone. A confidential Ethiopian government report confirmed that more than three-quarters of the people in Tigray were failing to receive food aid (*The Times*, 25 February 1985). In addition, Leon de Reidmattan, delegate of the International Committee of the Red Cross in Addis Ababa, noted in mid-June of that year that the famine had grown much worse due to the inability of relief workers to access populations in "grey areas" (*New York Times*, 15 June 1985).

For UN agencies in particular, organisational sanctions on working with "non-recognised entities" in situations where partner governments do not acknowledge the existence of such entities meant that throughout the war years the UN employed what amounted to a "hands off" policy vis-à-vis the cross-border operation. Many UN officials remained ignorant of the extent of cross-border activities until virtually the end of the war. Hence, when relief operations from the government side were curtailed in 1989, after government forces withdrew from the region, it was assumed by at least one official of the World Food Programme that Tigray had become "inaccessible to relief transports" (*Guardian*, 5 October 1989).

The relief society of Tigray

The reluctance of major donors to support cross-border activities during the 1984/85 disaster was in direct contrast to the operational assets that existed for delivering such assistance. Foremost among these was a highly effective system of indigenous disaster management in TPLF-controlled areas that incorporated the participation of people at village level, through the *baitos*.

According to one TPLF member, famine was considered to be the main threat to the Tigrayan revolution from approximately 1983 onward (Hendrie, 1991). In that year, a Drought Commission was formed, comprising the relevant departments of TPLF, REST and the *baitos*, with explicit responsibility for managing the famine crisis. While REST carried out the tasks of receiving, transporting and distributing relief goods, the *baitos* were delegated responsibility for identifying potential beneficiaries in each village, and for ensuring that limited aid resources were targeted toward the neediest members of the community. TPLF Departments, in turn, provided security for distribution centres, as well as infrastructural work such as new road construction. According to the REST Field Director:

> One of the most important aspects of this partnership was that both REST and the TPLF were able, through the *baitos*, to consult rural communities throughout Tigray on their views at each critical stage in the escalating crisis. From these consultations, policy decisions were taken that fully integrated the experiences and concerns of those who were directly affected by the disaster. In this way ... an operational framework was created where people were able to participate in the decisions that affected their lives. (Assefaw, 1993)

The existence of the *baito* system enabled REST to decentralise the management of food distributions. *Baito* members took responsibility for ensuring that targeted households came forward to receive supplies at distribution sites, and for organising onward transport of commodities back to villages. Further, the fact that numbers of beneficiaries were continually updated through the *baito* structure allowed for a high degree of operational flexibility in response to changing needs. For example, REST could quickly redirect relief commodities en route from Sudan to alternative distribution sites in order to accommodate newly displaced groups. This flexibility, in turn, also ensured that the war did not unduly disrupt the conduct of the operation, as new distribution sites could be opened or closed depending on the security situation at any given time. During the 1985 government offensive, for example, REST's transport operation was interrupted for a period of two months when government forces cut the route linking western and central Tigray. In response, TPLF drew off government forces with a series of diversionary attacks along the main highway, while REST reopened a new route to the south.

The capacity of REST to implement an effective relief programme "in the field", and the accessibility of this programme to independent monitoring, led to an increasing level of trust on the part of international NGOs participating in the cross-border operation. This trust was manifested in a gradual shift away from the provision of commodities only, to the provision of both cash and commodities from late 1985 onwards. By the end of 1986, ERD was granting cash reimbursements directly to REST for internal transport costs on its truck fleet, based on a calculated rate per tonne, as well as supplying cash grants for the purchase and distribution of rehabilitation inputs, such as seed and oxen, in TPLF-controlled zones.

Growth of the operation: late 1985 to 1989

In mid-1985, after seven months of deliberation, USAID and the United States Office of Foreign Disaster Assistance (OFDA) approved a grant for the purchase of seventy-five trucks to be added to the REST fleet. Although these trucks arrived too late to increase the volume of food aid across the border in that year, the grant nevertheless signalled the US government's willingness to support the operation with more substantial assistance than had previously been the case.

By early 1986, when it became apparent that safe-passage agreements for the war zones would not materialise, and as migrations to Sudan indicated the limitations of the town-based feeding programme, other major donors and international NGOs began to increase food-aid shipments to the cross-border operation. These shipments were either committed directly to REST, or more often channelled through ERD or TTAC. Further, donations of cash for the "internal purchase" of grain surpluses in western Tigray enabled REST to distribute additional tonnages to deficit areas.

Having proved itself capable of handling larger volumes of relief assistance, the cross-border operation continued to receive steady support from major donors in Europe and the United States throughout 1986 and 1987. In early 1988, when rain failure again threatened the region with famine, a second large increase in the volume of donated commodities and grants for the purchase of additional trucks occurred, so that, by the end of that year, REST had transported some 85,000 tonnes of external food aid from Sudan, and distributed over 4,000 tonnes of internally purchased grain and pulses (REST, 1988). This level of operation was approximately equivalent in size to that conducted in Tigray from the government side (Hendrie, 1988).

The 1987/88 famine, unlike the disaster of 1984/85, occurred in the context of a shift in the military situation in the region, where potential areas of access from the government side were greatly reduced as a consequence of TPLF advances. Major donors, having learned from the experiences of the previous famine, were privately relying on the cross-border operation to support two-thirds of the affected population in Tigray (Don Krumm, Bureau of Refugee Affairs, Department of State, Washington D.C., personal comment to the author, September 1989). By assisting the operation early, and with adequate inputs of food and additional trucks, the refugee influx to Sudan widely predicted in early 1988 failed to materialise. Instead, drought-migrants were supported at REST distribution sites in the western lowlands, or at newly established centres at the base of the central highlands.

Conclusion

In recent years, relief operations to address disasters linked to internal warfare have incorporated a degree of flexibility in dealing with different parties to these conflicts. Operation Lifeline Sudan is one example of an international response in which there has been at least explicit recognition of "non-government" entities as legitimate parties to negotiation concerning aid operations in contested areas.

In the case of Tigray, such flexibility on the part of the international community was lacking. This was due in part to a widely publicised view of the disaster that minimised the impact of warfare and maximised the drought as the sole cause of famine in the region. At the same time, the particular, complex politics that emerged around relief operations in the north led major donors to avoid almost entirely either cooperation or dialogue with the TPLF. Instead, the main channel of external aid to Tigray was through a handful of international NGOs. Although in many respects well-suited to this task by virtue of their flexibility, cross-border NGOs nevertheless lacked the protection of UN affiliation to underline the humanitarian legitimacy of their working relationships with REST, and especially TPLF. Consequently, a number of constraints on the operation arose precisely because NGOs were obliged to fill the gaps left by multi-lateral and bilateral donors, who were either unable or unwilling to cooperate directly with a liberation front.

Foremost among these constraints was the lack of any formalised channel of communication between relief managers involved in the cross-border programme, and those implementing similar programmes from Addis Ababa. In particular, the UN Office of Emergency Operations in Ethiopia (OEOE) operated exclusively in government-held areas, and its self-imposed restriction against any of its personnel travelling to Tigray from Sudan meant that no acceptable means existed for disseminating information about conditions in TPLF-controlled areas. Instead, needs assessments and programme reports circulated by the OEOE within the international community were virtually limited to data that could be gathered from the government side. Hence, key figures that affected allocation of resources, such as the number of people served by food distributions on respective sides of the conflict, were never reconciled in direct discussion between sides. The political unwillingness of the UN in particular to establish discreet but formal channels of communication between both parties to the conflict thus created a potentially life-threatening distortion in both the perception and planning of the relief programme.

In addition, aside from instances where overtly political factors influenced policy concerning aid to the region, internal dynamics within organisations also played a role in isolating the cross-border option. For example, recommendations by international NGO personnel who had travelled to TPLF areas in some cases directly contradicted policies established by Ethiopia country offices of the same organisation. In this regard, the history or amount of resources committed to the country programme, or the force of personality of the country director, became as much the basis for organisational policy as other considerations. In other instances, agency offices in Addis Ababa were in open conflict with offices based either in international headquarters or in Khartoum. During 1984/5, for example, the Ethiopia Representative of the International Committee of the Red Cross (ICRC) strongly opposed the ICRC's involvement in the cross-border programme, implemented through its office in Sudan. Shortly after the arrival of a new and less forceful Representative in Khartoum in 1987, a recommendation was made by the ICRC to scale back the cross-border operation significantly.

Equally significant was the degree to which the Ethiopian government was successful in manipulating the provision of international relief assistance for both military and political purposes. The provision of relief assistance in the midst of internal warfare has received much critical attention in recent years, as the international community attempts to address more complex disasters involving both armed violence and collapses in food production. However, analyses of the impact of food aid in conflict situations rarely provide an explicit study of the forms of combat being utilised by all parties to the conflict. Nor do they identify the strategic or tactical opportunities presented by international aid operations to opposing parties. In Tigray, the failure to "study warfare" as a means of understanding the nature of the famine led to an almost unbelievable naivety on the part of the international community concerning the government's use of food aid in the region. In this case, the principle of respect for state sovereignty was extended beyond reasonable boundaries to include the exclusion of information about conditions in rebel-held areas, as well as the avoidance of contact with both relief managers and political authorities from these zones. The consequence was a gross distortion in the public view of how relief operations were proceeding on the ground in conflict areas, as well as the de facto exclusion of some two to three million people from access to the world's food aid until it was too late.

References

Africa Watch (1990) *"Mengistu Has Decided to Burn Us Like Wood": Bombing of Civilians and Civilian Targets by the Air Force*, London.

———— (1991) *Evil Days: Thirty Years of War and Famine in Ethiopia*, London.

Assefaw, T. (1993) "Participatory Relief Management: The Experience of the Relief Society of Tigray", paper presented to Intertect Conference on Refugee Repatriation during Conflict, Addis Ababa, January.

Christian Science Monitor (1985) "Politics Blocks Vital Aid to Ethiopia", Boston, 2 May.

Clay, J. and Holcombe, B. (1985) *Politics and the Ethiopia Famine 1984–85*, Cambridge, Mass., Cultural Survival Inc.

de Waal, A. (1990a) *Famine Survival Strategies in Wollo, Tigray, and Eritrea: A Review of the Literature*, Oxford, Oxfam.

———— (1990b) "War, Markets and Famines in Tigray, Ethiopia During the 1980s", paper presented to Oxford University Department of Anthropology Seminar Series.

Hendrie, B. (1985) *Report on a Visit to Tigray*, Boston, Mass., Grassroots International.

———— (1988) "Disaster Management in Tigray: Report on a Monitoring Visit for the Emergency Relief Desk", Khartoum, Emergency Relief Desk.

———— (1990) *The Impact of Warfare in Tigray Province*, Addis Ababa, Inter-Africa Group.

———— (1991) "The Tigrayan Refugee Repatriation 1985–1987", *Journal of Refugee Studies* 4 (2).

Jansson, K., Harriss, M. and Penrose A. (1987) *The Ethiopia Famine*, London, Zed Books.

Kettle, J. (1985) "Tigray: People in a Multi-Disaster", Oxford, Oxfam.

REST (1985) *Relief Society of Tigray Annual Report 1985*, Khartoum.

———— (1988) *Relief Society of Tigray Annual Report 1988*, Khartoum.

———— (1991) *Report on Health Services in Tigray*, Relief Society of Tigray European Office, London.

Silkin, T. and Hughes S. (1992) "Food Security and Food Aid: A Study from the Horn of Africa", London, CAFOD/Christian Aid.

Smith, G. (1983) *Counting Quintals*. Utrecht, Stichting Oecumenische Hulp Publications.

———— (1985) "New Refugee Arrivals to Eastern Sudan", Khartoum, Interfam Information Project.

———— (1987) "Ethiopia and the Politics of Famine", *Middle East Report*, Washington D.C., March–April.

Wright, K. (1983) *Famine in Tigray: An Eye-Witness Account*, London, REST UK Support Committee.

8

Dangerous Precedents?
Famine Relief in Somalia 1991–93
Alex de Waal

Introduction

Somalia during 1991–93 was perhaps the most spectacular demonstration of the failure of the international relief system in recent years. The major donors, especially the United Nations specialised agencies, failed Somalia both in what they were unable to do and in what they actually did. The task of providing relief in a famine of exceptional severity was left to local organisations, a handful of international NGOs and, above all, the partnership between the Somali Red Crescent Society and the International Committee of the Red Cross. A counterpart to the persistent neglect and incompetence in Geneva and New York is a story of courage, tenacity and imagination by an array of other relief agencies, Somali and foreign, formal and informal. It is necessary to learn from the Somali experience not only to find out where the big actors blundered, but where the small and less visible actors succeeded.

Unfortunately for Somalia, just when those lessons should have been absorbed, when the famine began to wane at the end of 1992, hysterical calls for bolder and massive action struck a sympathetic chord with President George Bush and the secretary-general of the UN, Boutros-Ghali, who launched Operation Restore Hope with the stated intention of saving millions of Somalis from imminent death by starvation. It did not happen according to the script: between June and October 1993, the fighting between United States forces and the militia of General Mohammed Farah Aidid was a bloody debacle that threatened to discredit not just the idea of "humanitarian intervention", but the principle that the USA should play an active role in UN peacekeeping.

The focus of this article is not the international politics of humanitarian intervention, but the nature and dynamic of relief programmes in Somalia, both before and after the military intervention. As in all African famines, relief programmes were but one factor among many that enabled people to survive. Relief did assist hungry and sick people, and saved lives. But it did less than its advocates claimed. Most importantly, the military intervention launched in December 1992 played virtually no role in conquering the famine.

The slow rhythms of academia, along with security concerns, have ensured that the Somali famine has been very poorly documented, even by the low standards of documentation of other contemporary African famines (Seaman, 1993). An added difficulty is the reluctance of villagers to divulge information, fearing reprisals from armed factions or powerful landowners should their allegations become known. One village elder in the Lower Juba remarked, "If we tell you the names, and the names of the plantations, the moment you walk out of that door there will be trouble." In the next village, our research was cut short by the sudden arrival of a "liberator", a man who had looted the local plantation and who threatened to kill anyone he caught giving information. Nonetheless, only a few days' field research are needed to discover some of the complexities of the famine, and the similarities with other famines elsewhere in Africa. A quotation from a village elder in the Lower Shebelle valley (who, typically, wanted both his own name and the identity of his village to remain confidential), encapsulates the common experience of many Somali farmers. The elder was asked what had brought the famine to an end. He replied:

> The assistance has only contributed. The improvement started with the prevailing semi-peace in the area [in early 1992]. Once there was peace, people started some production and began to become self-supporting. This happened in the first season of 1992. So, things began to improve then [in September], after the harvest of the first season, coupled with the first ICRC kitchen.

The story of the Somali famine contains little that will surprise students of famine elsewhere in Africa. Local coping strategies were the most important component in people's survival. Mass migration was both the consequence of the most severe disruption, and in turn the cause of the greatest suffering. Epidemic disease was the cause of most deaths. And, for most Somalis, international assistance was a marginal contribution to survival.

Social Geography of the Famine

The main victims of the Somali famine fall into two categories: traditional minorities and people displaced from their homes by virtue of belonging to the "wrong" clan. The main traditional minorities are the Sab clans, Rahanweyn and Digil, and the non-Somali minorities. The Rahanweyn and Digil are traditionally regarded as "second class" Somalis by the members of the four main pastoral clan families. They speak a different dialect, have variant customs and forms of social organisation, and have consistently been politically marginalised (Lewis, 1982). They are also farmers, inhabiting the Bay region and parts of the Middle Juba and Lower Shebelle regions. Ironically, under the development plans mooted in the 1970s and 1980s, farmers should have been the greatest beneficiaries; in practice, they became the targets for land expropriation and exploitation (African Rights, 1993a).

The non-Somali groups, such as the Cushitic Shebelle (in Hiraan region) and Gabaweyn (in Gedo), and the various groups in Middle and Lower Juba and Lower Shebelle commonly known as Bantu, are even more politically and socially marginal. They live almost exclusively along the main rivers, and therefore have been particular victims of the practice of creating irrigated development projects at the cost of dispossessing the local farmers.

The main "dominant" clans are customarily divided into four clan families: Dir, Isaaq, Darod and Hawiye. Although small groups of Dir and some Isaaq individuals are found in southern Somalia, it is the latter two clan families that concern us here. The Darod dominated Somalia under the former dictator Mohammed Siad Barre. They consist of several clans: Marehan (Siad Barre's own clan), Ogaden, Majerteen, Dulbahante and Warsangeli (the latter three sometimes collectively known as Harte), among others. The Hawiye include the Abgaal, Habr Gidir, Hawadle, Murursade and others.

Most of the rural members of these clans are pastoralists. They suffered much less from the famine than the farmers.

Chronology of the Famine

Like most famines, the Somali famine can be dated from a variety of starting points. Forcible land alienation (of both farmland and pastures) and drought had brought a number of marginalised communities in southern Somalia to the brink of destitution as early as 1988. This combined with a breakdown of basic social services, including veterinary supplies and the maintenance of bore holes. The intensification of rural insurrection in 1989–90 prevented any recovery from the cycle of impoverishment.

This deprivation was sharply accentuated in the early months of 1991, following the overthrow of the government of President Mohammed Siad Barre in January. Throughout the farming areas of southern Somalia, there was fierce fighting. Baidoa, the capital of Bay region, was partly destroyed by a battle in February. Darod communities, including many refugees from the Ethiopian Ogaden, fought with the Hawiye United Somali Congress (USC) forces in various places along the Shebelle river. The Lower Shebelle was comprehensively pillaged by both Darod and Hawiye forces during the military campaigns of March–April, during which Siad Barre's former lieutenants tried to stage a comeback. This was followed by severe fighting and massive displacement in the Lower Juba, first when the USC arrived, and then when the Darod militias took revenge against Bantu villagers who had sided with the USC, naively believing their promises of "liberation". At the same time, hundreds of thousands of people were displaced as much of Somalia was divided into fiefdoms ruled by a single dominant clan or clan family. Members of other clans were forced to flee. There was a massive exodus of Darod from Mogadishu following the fall of Siad Barre, and throughout the Hawiye-dominated areas many Darod fled towards Kismayo or the north-east, looking for sanctuary. There was a smaller flow of displaced Hawiye in the opposite direction.

The military campaigns of the late 1980s and early 1990s were accompanied by massive looting. For the most part, the militias were unpaid and looted in order to eat, or to provide profit for their generals and paymasters. General insecurity, manifested by banditry and extortion, became a prevalent phenomenon throughout southern Somalia.

Two fierce localised conflicts erupted towards the end of 1991. The first was the battle of Mogadishu between the two factions of the USC, led respectively by General Mohammed Farah Aidid and Interim President Ali Mahdi. This lasted until March 1992 and claimed an estimated 11,000 lives (Africa Watch and Physicians for Human Rights, 1992). It also closed Mogadishu port, stifling aid and trade, and drove hundreds of thousands of displaced people into the interior. Famine conditions developed in parts of the city, especially the large camps for the displaced on its outskirts. The second was a less intense war in and around Kismayo between December 1991 and February 1992, between wings of the (Darod) Somali Patriotic Movement, led respectively by Colonel Ahmad Omer Jess and General Mohammed Hersi "Morgan". This closed Kismayo port and devastated the rich agricultural area of Lower Juba. Famine immediately ensued, especially among the displaced Bantu.

Meanwhile, Marehan forces loyal to Siad Barre occupied Bay region, subjecting its Rahanweyn inhabitants to comprehensive and savage looting. Large parts of the area were utterly stripped of livestock and food. The Marehan militia was driven out in April by a campaign launched by the USC under General Aidid, who, allied with Colonel Jess under the banner of the Somali National Alliance (SNA), went on to capture Kismayo. Over 100,000 refugees fled to Kenya in the wake of this campaign and the looting that followed. Between May and October 1992, the nadir of the famine was reached in Bay region and the adjoining areas. Epidemics of water-borne diseases (especially a virulent strain of dysentery) and measles spread rapidly through the population (Center for Disease Control, 1992). Outright starvation was also common right in the centre of the famine-stricken area (Collins, 1993). The number who died is unknown, but a figure of over 200,000 can be ventured with some confidence.

During the worst months of hunger and excess deaths, there was little organised fighting, but endemic banditry and extortion. Militiamen loyal to the USC and the Rahanweyn Somali Democratic Movement operated ruthless extortion rackets, requiring relief agencies, traders and villages to pay large sums for "protection". Coordinated military action commenced again with an offensive launched from Kenya by the forces of General Morgan, who captured the town of Bardhere on the Juba River, and began to move southwards. Morgan achieved his greatest strategic prize in March 1993 when, under the eyes of American and Belgian troops, he succeeded in recapturing Kismayo from the SNA.

Local Relief Initiatives

For most of the famine, relief efforts consisted of local initiatives. During 1990, 1991 and the greater part of 1992, most international relief programmes did not reach into the interior, and were confined to the major towns and villages close to the roads.

There were some remarkable acts of individual and communal generosity and initiative. The weeks following the overthrow of Siad Barre saw a rapid proliferation of civic organisations, enjoying the first freedom from authoritarian government for more than two decades. These organisations included professional and medical associations, community schools, newspapers and, most significantly, voluntary aid organisations. The cases of three of these operations illustrate the role they played and the constraints under which they operated.

Peace Aid Somalia was set up in Kismayo in August 1991 by a group of business people and intellectuals. At first, it raised funds by the members selling some of their personal possessions such as jewellery; later it raised money from the community, focusing on traders; and still later, was supported by ICRC and, to a lesser degree, UNICEF. Peace Aid Somalia provided support to six camps for the displaced in and around Kismayo. However, its activities ceased after the SNA captured the town in May 1992. Many of its leading members were forced to flee to Kenya; others went into hiding. The founder, Zahra Sheikh Mohammed, was injured when SNA militia attacked her house.

Another initiative was the creation of the first kitchen in Mogadishu, by Dhahabo Isse. Dhahabo had worked with development agencies before the war, and in April 1991 she resolved to provide some assistance to the displaced and hungry people in the city. Security was the main constraint: transporting dry rations around the city was an invitation to looting. Instead, Dhahabo resolved to create a kitchen to serve cooked food, on the basis that this would not be attractive to looters. This proved to be the case, though there were repeated security problems surrounding the stores of food, and threats to Dhahabo personally. Rapidly, the kitchen was adopted by the ICRC, and became the model for the ICRC's own relief programme throughout the country, and Dhahabo herself joined the ICRC as a staff member.

The final example is an anonymous farmer in the lower Shebelle, whose story was described by a university lecturer who stayed in the village during the famine:

> This man is a wealthy farmer. He has got a big farm and during this difficult period he opened his own kitchen. Approximately, there were sixty children that he was feeding. He didn't open any centre, but he asked some restaurants to cook for these children, so, to have three meals per day. The quality of the food he was preparing was better than the Red Cross, when they came. After several months he found himself in difficulty because the group was getting larger and larger and he couldn't cope. So he wanted to close the kitchen. We came to him with the idea that we could ask the ICRC to support him. But he refused. He said no, he doesn't want to run a place for other people. His intention is not that his name is known to others, or to take advantage of what is being given, and if he can't do it, he can't, and that's it. He wasn't interested in any way in getting support from outside. I can't tell you his name because he didn't want it to be told.

The ICRC–SRCS programme

The most important of all the local organisations was the Somali Red Crescent Society (SRCS). As the only existing Somali NGO with a nation-wide presence and an integral link to an international agency, the SRCS came to play a central role in the famine-relief efforts of 1991–92. It attracted to its ranks many unemployed professionals and experienced relief workers. More than a dozen SRCS workers were killed in 1991–92, and many others were injured or forced to flee for their lives. Despite running enormous risks, the SRCS consistently and unflinchingly expanded its operations in response to perceived need.

The existence of a committed body of Somali staff was essential to the SRCS programme. Equally essential was the backing of the ICRC, which mounted its largest relief programme since World War II, spending over one third of its entire worldwide budget for 1992 on its Somalia pro-gramme. It delivered 180,000 tonnes of relief – more than the rest of the international agencies combined – as well as mounting seed distributions, veterinary programmes and medical assistance. By any standards, it was an astonishing effort. For this reason alone, the ICRC–SRCS programme must be considered a success.

The ICRC programme was based upon four implicit principles. The first was that the scale and urgency of the need took precedence over all else. This was adopted at the end of 1991, when it became clear that not merely the poorest and most marginal people, but the majority of the population of southern Somalia, faced famine. When any obstacle presented itself, the ICRC and SRCS would find a way around it. Thus, when Mogadishu and Kismayo ports were both closed at the end of 1991, the ICRC launched its "coastal programme", using every available small port, including many beaches, for unloading supplies. When the monsoon changed and its boats could not land, the ICRC used helicopters. It also used a cross-border operation from Kenya. Until the end of 1992, the ICRC was continually increasing the scale of its programme, often in response to the failures of the other main food-aid agencies.

The main reason for the magnitude of the 1992 programme was a recognition that famine threatened almost the whole population of southern Somalia. A supplementary rationale was the belief that the scarcity of food was closely linked to the insecurity. None of the militiamen were paid; they had to steal in order to eat. Famine thus bred banditry, and banditry in turn caused famine. It was noticeable in early 1992 that the level of general insecurity rose and fell along with the price of food. Hence, supplying large amounts of food should itself improve security.

A vital consequence of this principle was that the ICRC took risks, both physical and institutional. One ICRC delegate was killed in Mogadishu in December 1991, and fourteen local staff were killed and more wounded. A major institutional risk was taken early in 1991 when the organisation began employing local armed guards. This began because it was not possible to rent houses or vehicles without also renting guards to protect them, because no owner would agree. It rapidly became policy for a certain number of guards to accompany each convoy or vehicle, and protect each house. This was the first time ever that the ICRC had employed armed guards.

Significantly, this innovation arose directly from the second principle: delegation of authority to the staff members on the ground. The ICRC gave enormous powers of discretion to its delegates. They were allowed to make assessments of need, negotiate with local partners and contractors, and above all, make any security decisions that they saw fit. Thus the decision to hire guards was made and implemented on the ground in Mogadishu by a delegate, based upon an assessment that without private security, operations would be impossible. The debate on the issue in Geneva occurred later. The flexibility that this created was vital to the success of the ICRC–SRCS operation. Equally important, by giving such responsibilities to the delegates, it imbued the operation with a sense of purpose and commitment.

A third element in the ICRC–SRCS programme was active neutrality. The ICRC–SRCS gave assistance wherever it was needed and possible to reach. It gave assistance on both sides of the war in Mogadishu, and similarly in Kismayo. The organisations were active in visiting prisoners of war, monitoring their conditions and often securing their release. They negotiated to protect hospitals in the war zones. These activities were not always successful – for example the ICRC hospital at Keysaney in north Mogadishu was attacked and closed by General Aidid's forces on 14 February 1992, but this involvement continually emphasised the ICRC–SRCS's unique role and its impartiality. It is important to note that the ICRC–SRCS involvement in sensitive issues such as prisoners of war and medical neutrality required diplomatic skills (and training) among the staff. These skills proved just as necessary for the relief programme; a point lost on agencies that tried to treat providing relief as a strictly logistical exercise.

The final key to the success of the ICRC–SRCS programme was the intimate linkage between the international agency and the local partners. The most important partner was the SRCS, but the ICRC also supported local committees, and voluntary groups such as Dhahabo Isse's kitchen committee (it adopted the kitchen model for use throughout the country) and Peace Aid Somalia in Kismayo. The ability to work with these organisations, with a minimum of bureaucratic procedure and a maximum degree of flexibility, was the fundamental reason for the success of the programme.

The ICRC–SRCS programme succeeded in feeding about 1.5 million people, through more than nine hundred kitchens. It also succeeded in "flooding the country with food" so that by September 1992, coincident with the first post-famine harvest, the price of staple food began to fall towards normal levels. But there are several important questions to be asked. How much of the food reached the hungry? According to ICRC records, the great majority was delivered to the intended destination; looting rates were at most 20 per cent. This is, however, somewhat optimistic. Militias, bandits and contractors used a variety of means to divert or extort food. These included registering nonexistent villages and kitchens, obtaining signatures (often by coercion) for food deliveries to villages when some or all of the food had in fact been diverted, and forming false committees to represent real villages, which then sold the food. Village committee members and SRCS staff have a less sanguine estimate for levels of loss; most believe that more than half was looted, pilfered, diverted or extorted (African Rights, 1993a). The diverted food still reached the market, however. It was an unplanned and uncontrolled monetisation programme, and it brought food to markets that would otherwise have been empty.

Did hiring gunmen create protection rackets and reward the warlords? The whole policy of employing armed guards was never thought out in advance, nor thoroughly evaluated afterwards. Certainly, employment with relief agencies became extremely lucrative, not only for individual gunmen but for the contractors and militia leaders who ultimately controlled them. This problem increased over time, particularly when more agencies entered Somalia in mid-1992, driving up the daily rates for guards. Moreover, the ability of the contractors/commanders to provide a secure employment or income for gunmen increased their ability to maintain their militias as organised units. In particular, it enabled them to maintain their fleets of "technical" cars.

It is impossible to quantify the economic and organisational benefits brought to the factional leaders by the relief programmes. However, the benefits were certainly substantial. Moreover, it is difficult to see how this could have been avoided. Did "flooding the country with food" reduce insecurity? This question is also unanswerable. There are many different kinds of insecurity: freelance banditry, commercial looting, organised military campaigns, and extortion rackets. There was certainly much less organised fighting by September 1992 than at the beginning of the year, but extortion was probably greater. In addition, while stealing food to eat may have declined, stealing relief food to sell in order to buy other commodities remained an important means whereby bandits were able to earn an income. There is no doubt, however, that access to food (free and marketed) improved dramatically in the first nine months of 1992, irrespective of the security situation.

The United Nations Programme

The failure of the United Nations relief programmes during 1991–92 was immense. The actions of the UN specialised agencies reflected indifference, incompetence and arrogance. Their presence became almost as dangerous as their absence. This chapter can do no more than summarise this extraordinary story.

The United Nations programme was the antithesis of the ICRC–SRCS programme. The account must also include the role of CARE-International, the most prominent subcontractor of the UN. Relief operations in Somaliland, formerly north-west Somalia, will not be examined here.

During 1991 the UN was largely absent, though it made many vocal promises. The first promises for assistance were made in May. The WFP undertook to provide 40,000 tonnes of food (free and monetised) through Mogadishu before the end of the year, to be distributed by CARE. In the event, just over one tenth of that was actually distributed. CARE reopened its Mogadishu office in September, a few weeks before the first shipment of 12,000 tonnes arrived. A small quantity of sorghum was reconsigned to the ICRC and immediately moved from the port to warehouses in town and then distributed in the Shebelle valley. However, rather than following the ICRC–SRCS mode of operations, CARE delayed while a comprehensive distribution plan was drawn up. In normal circumstances, this would have been the professional response. In the event, it was a disastrous decision. CARE only began distributions in early October, in north Mogadishu. The first, large convoy of vehicles was attacked by looters, so CARE changed its strategy to small convoys. But by the time war broke out in the city on 17 November, almost 8,000 tonnes remained in storage in the port. For the next two months, CARE prevaricated: it had enough food to feed the city for a month, while the city was beginning to starve. CARE did not know what to do: the obvious response to its predicament was that it should not have kept so much food in the port in the first place. Finally, the port militia opened the warehouse doors to all comers and the food was released into the city. It was a highly democratic form of looting, which brought down food prices and appreciably eased tension in the city. In the circumstances it was the best possible outcome.

CARE was put in an impossible situation in late 1991. What is disturbing about this episode is not that CARE made mistakes, but that it, and the UN, failed to learn from them. Almost exactly the same mistakes were committed when Mogadishu port reopened in April 1992, mistakes which were instrumental in creating the crisis that led to the military intervention.

UNICEF did less. Despite receiving emergency funds from USAID at the beginning of the year, UNICEF had no presence in Mogadishu until the last week of December. Consultants and staff members visited. It delivered essential drugs to the city in July, but then kept them in a warehouse for four months for lack of a programme, while the Somali-run hospitals were completely without supplies. Eventually the UNICEF warehouse was looted at the outbreak of the November war. Fortunately, some Somali doctors learned of the looting and went in a group to collect some of the medicines themselves: the supplies helped sustain the make-shift hospital in north Mogadishu during the first month of the war, when it received no external assistance at all. For most of 1991, UNICEF's sole operational programme was in Kismayo, where it supported Somali NGOs caring for street children and the displaced.

The other UN agencies had no presence at all. UNDP sent a consultant in July to investigate reopening the UN offices. His positive recommendations were ignored. WFP, FAO, WHO and UNHCR had no presence. Despite the public launch of the Special Emergency Programme for the Horn of Africa, which included a $64 million budget line for emergency and rehabilitation programmes in Somalia, UN expenditure was confined to the salaries, hotel bills, expenses and allowances of its expatriate staff, evacuated to Nairobi. At least one agency even neglected to pay its Somali employees.

In March 1992, the UN began to talk about an emergency plan of action. A "Ninety Day" plan was one of Under-Secretary-General Jan Eliasson's priorities when he took up the new post of head of Humanitarian Affairs in March. The plan was formally announced in April. The first ship arrived in May; the ninety days expired with almost no progress. In July, CARE was awarded a USAID contract to monetise over 70,000 tonnes of grain as an emergency measure. Monetisation is a difficult process, requiring monitoring of prices in markets, scrutiny of local merchants' performance, and decisions about what to do with the counterpart funds. However, in an emergency, the considerations of running a standard programme should have taken second place to delivering the food to Somali marketplaces. The monetisation programme only became operational in January 1993.

In contrast to the ICRC–SRCS, the UN took minimal physical and institutional risks. Staff rules governing insurance in war zones were cited as a reason for the UN's absence in 1991. On returning to Somalia, after severe international criticism, evacuation was often uppermost in the minds of the UN staff. Many staff were allowed only a two-week stint in Somalia before being rotated out.

The UN failed to delegate authority to staff on the ground. This made its operations extremely slow, cumbersome, and ignorant of realities on the ground. As a result, the UN was almost completely incapable of responding to the situation as it developed. A prime example of this is the failure to utilise Mogadishu port properly. The port reopened in March 1992 after the Ramadhan ceasefire between General Aidid and Ali Mahdi. ICRC immediately used the opportunity, without abandoning their coastal programme through the smaller ports. ICRC's strategy for Mogadishu port was to negotiate separately with each of the two factions for the arrival and unloading of each ship, and then to move the food immediately from the port to distribution points. For the ICRC, the port never closed: one ship docked there each month. The UN instead tried to institutionalise the negotiating structure at the port, by creating a single committee including representatives of both factions. This was a recipe for trouble, which duly occurred. After a few months, the negotiations descended into deadlock, with the different sides exchanging threats and ultimatums. By November the impasse led to WFP first declaring the port closed, and then sending a ship to dock without negotiation save an ultimatum. Meanwhile, thousands of tonnes of food piled up in the port that could not be removed. The lessons of one year before had not been learned.

Other examples of UN inflexibility and ineptitude could be cited. To name but one, UN policy on hiring armed guards was never coordinated among UN agencies or with NGOs, contributing to the spiralling cost of security, dangerous labour disputes, and the near breakdown of negotiated agreements such as the demilitarisation of the area within the airport perimeter. UN evaluations and plans remained secretive, resolved in New York and Geneva before even being shown to staff in the field, let alone talked over with ICRC or NGO staff.

The UN specialised agencies saw their job as a logistical one, rather than one of creative diplomacy. CARE took a similar approach. This was manifest in their attitude to Mogadishu port, and again in a convoy sent from Mogadishu to Baidoa on 11–12 November 1992. The convoy was sent shortly after Philip Johnston, President of CARE-US, was seconded to the UN as coordinator of the new "hundred day" emergency plan of action. Johnston had already called for military intervention to protect the relief effort, saying that "The international community, backed by UN troops … [should] move in and run Somalia" (Johnston, 1992). He was showing considerable impatience with the demands of negotiating and paying his way through roadblocks, and a new, harder line on dealing with militias became apparent at once. In what amounted to a direct challenge to the militias, a CARE convoy was despatched to Baidoa on the night of 11/12 November, with instructions that all the food should be delivered to the townspeople and none to the militias. In Baidoa, residents and agency staff retreated to their houses, sandbagged their doors and put their guards on alert, awaiting the convoy. When it arrived, Somali staff from CARE negotiated with the first set of militiamen, but were instructed not to negotiate with the second. In the gun-battle that ensued, five people were killed and only one truck of food made it through to Baidoa. In the words of one of the Somali staff members, "CARE was a bit strict, which may have cost the convoy." Finally, the UN failed to consult with or learn from local organisations, or even its own Somali staff. Experienced Somali staff became extremely frustrated with their marginalisation within the organisations. Despite its attempts to portray itself as an independent NGO, CARE is bracketed in the same category as the UN by Somali relief workers, including its own staff.

UNICEF re-entered Somalia in December 1991, and WFP in March 1992, but their operations only began to gather momentum in August, after President George Bush announced an emergency airlift, Operation Provide Relief. Bush's decision was dictated by domestic considerations: publicity given to the famine by Senator Kassebaum and the imminent Republican Party Congress. This immediately put Somalia at the top of the agenda for the UN agencies, and James Grant, Jan Eliasson and various "goodwill ambassadors" such as Audrey Hepburn visited in quick succession. This created the climate in which the UN held its emergency conference in Geneva in October and promulgated a plan of action. More importantly, the UN agencies actually put some effort into trying to implement their plan.

The NGO Record

The NGOs in Somalia displayed a variety of practices ranging from extreme consultation and flexibility to near-complete insensitivity to all but the demands of the domestic media. During 1991 and early 1992 there was a very small group of international NGOs in the country: Médecins Sans Frontières, Save the Children Fund (UK), Comitate Internazionale per lo Sviluppo dei Popoli (CISP), SOS-Kinderdorf, and International Medical Corps (all in Mogadishu), World Concern (Kismayo) and ACORD (Lower Shebelle).

The Save the Children Fund record warrants close examination as it worked in the field of public health, a field that was otherwise grossly neglected. Alone among the agencies, SCF recognised the need to maintain a governmental health infrastructure, and to coordinate health information and planning among the operational agencies. It worked closely with the Ministry of Health in south Mogadishu and set up and organised the NGO Consortium, which included both international and Somali NGOs. So eager was SCF to bring UNICEF into Somalia in 1991 that it paid for a UNICEF consultant, recruited him and posted him to Mogadishu to work alongside SCF on the counterpart national health structure (he was withdrawn on UNICEF instructions for security reasons).

Unfortunately, the absence of any functional government with powers to regulate the agencies meant that it was simple for any agency to bypass the coordination mechanisms and quality control set up by SCF and the ministry. Thus, when the Center for Disease Control and UNICEF began a health and nutrition monitoring programme at the end of 1992, the surveys were seriously deficient in their methods, and were criticised accordingly by Somali health professionals, but the "Ministry of Health" had no sanctions that it could impose.

SCF was successful in that the agency's own assistance programme continued uninterrupted until the end of 1993 with virtually no losses due to looting or diversion throughout the various conflicts in Mogadishu, and similarly in Belet Weyn and Bardhere. It also demonstrated the possibility of working with local structures with a view to the long term. It was less successful in persuading other agencies to follow the same course. During the 1970s and 1980s, Somali health professionals built up a fund of experience about dealing with drought, refugees and the health and nutritional problems of camp populations. Very little of this was utilised during the 1991–92 emergency.

Also alone among the international agencies, SCF had a senior staff member, with expatriate status, who was a Somali. This is no coincidence. The presence of Dr Hussein Mursal was critical to the success of the SCF programme. Dr Mursal was far more skilled at dealing with the political and security situation than even the most experienced expatriates. However, while most agencies excluded their Somali staff from discussions of politics or security, considering them "too sensitive", SCF incorporated Dr Mursal, and benefited accordingly. Second, by keeping a long-term perspective and therefore holding out some hopes for the future for Somali professionals, Dr Mursal was able to engender an unusually high degree of commitment to the agency's programme: it was *their* programme.

The other agencies provided surgical teams, ran feeding centres and small relief food distributions, and, in the case of ACORD, maintained an agricultural development programme (by means of solely using Somali staff).

The NGO presence expanded rapidly from May onwards, as the extent of the famine in Bay region became evident. Lutheran World Federation started an emergency airlift to Baidoa in May, and a growing number of NGOs, ranging from Oxfam and Concern to The Samaritan's Purse began operations in the region.

Countdown to Intervention

The circumstances leading up to the military intervention in December 1992 remain murky. Several things are clear: the motivation for the intervention was based upon a very superficial and often false understanding of realities in Somalia; some of this misinformation was deliberately orchestrated, and some of the incidents used to justify the intervention were much less clear cut than the advocates of intervention claimed at the time.

In the report presented to the UN Security Council on 25 November, based upon a report from Mogadishu by the Special Envoy Ismat Kitani, Secretary-General Boutros Ghali made various claims that were immediately refuted (Omaar and de Waal, 1992). Prominent among these was the claim that between 70 and 80 per cent of the food was being looted. This was certainly overly pessimistic, although the counterclaim by the ICRC and NGOs that they were losing at most 20 per cent was probably overoptimistic. A second false claim was that Mogadishu port was closed. Certainly it was closed to the UN – but that was largely on account of the deeply flawed negotiating procedures used by the UN. The ICRC never regarded it as closed.

Boutros Ghali also claimed that there was no-one with whom the UN could negotiate. This was rapidly shown also to be incorrect when the USA began negotiations with a host of factional leaders immediately after the intervention. Moreover, the diplomatic initiatives undertaken by the former UN Special Envoy, Ambassador Mohammed Sahnoun, had shown that progress was possible. When in post between April and October, Sahnoun had succeeded in gaining the confidence of Somali politicians, elders and ordinary citizens from all sides, and had set in motion an extremely promising process of political reconciliation. Tragically, Sahnoun was forced to resign at the end of October, for publicly criticising the UN's failings.

Perhaps the most important erroneous claim was, however, that two million Somalis faced imminent death by starvation. In fact, all evidence indicated that the peak of excess deaths was well past; in Mogadishu, life-threatening hunger had largely been banished since July, and death rates had been falling rapidly in Baidoa since September. The famine had entered a stage at which the overwhelming killers were outbreaks of epidemic disease.

These falsehoods became widely accepted as the truth, largely on account of the mass media. The role of the media in relation to relief agencies and disasters has belatedly become the subject of analytical study (Benthall, 1993); in Somalia it could warrant an account by itself.

In 1991 and the first half of 1992, Somalia was covered by a very small band of committed journalists. It rarely figured in the news outside the specialist press and programmes such as BBC Focus on Africa. This changed rapidly in August 1992, when Somalia suddenly became a news story following the visit to the Kenya–Somalia border by Senator Kassebaum. The media descended, led by prominent television correspondents who were largely ignorant of Somalia, but acutely aware of the demands of portraying a famine for the domestic audiences in Europe and North America. The Somalia story became simplified down to a handful of basic elements: helpless starving victims, cruel gunmen and warlords, and brave and compassionate foreign aid workers. This came about partly through the phenomenon of disaster tourism (de Waal, 1987) and partly through the feeling of correspondents that they should do what they could to help, which they saw as raising more public support for international NGOs (Alagiah, 1992).

This same oversimplification contributed directly to the military intervention; just as the solution to the Somali famine was portrayed as foreign food, the solution to the political problems was portrayed as sending in the US marines. Furthermore, there was deliberate orchestration of the presentation of Somalia to justify an intervention. A number of powerful players were pushing for military intervention from the summer of 1992. Prominent among these were senior officials of CARE. Philip Johnston's public statement of views has been cited. He was extraordinarily influential in the US government, prompting one journalist to write: "Lately, whenever the President of CARE is in Washington, Gen. Colin Powell, Chairman of the Joint Chiefs of Staff, gets together with him to discuss operations in Somalia" (Scroggins, 1993). In October, Malcolm Fraser, president of CARE-International, advocated sending a force of 15,000 international troops (Fraser, 1992), before travelling to New York to lobby the UN secretary-general on this issue. William Novelli, vice-president of CARE-US, aptly described the campaign as "the NGO drumbeat we built up for security" (Odling-Smee, 1993). The UN secretary-general was beating the drum, albeit discreetly. This was certainly part of the hidden agenda behind Sahnoun's forced resignation. Sahnoun's replacement, Ismat Kitani, was sent with the brief to prepare for a military intervention, and behaved with a brusqueness and lack of sensitivity that was the complete opposite of his predecessor.

The actual scale and mode of operation of the intervention was almost certainly decided upon only during the Thanksgiving weekend at the end of November, after Bush's election defeat and before Christmas. At this moment, Somalia caught the public imagination and prominent columnists in the *New York Times* and the *Washington Post* said: "Let's do it" and "Let it be Somalia!" (Gelb, 1992; Cohen, 1992; Raspberry, 1992). The day after the UN Security Council had voted in principle to send troops to Somalia, the InterAction group of US relief agencies held a press conference in which they said that they would be forced to withdraw unless security was improved. CARE was the most prominent agency involved. This was a key event in swinging American public opinion behind the intervention: it seemed as though Somalia's saviours were about to abandon the country to its fate. There is strong evidence that this public pressure stampeded Bush into a much larger operation than he had initially envisaged (Block, 1992), which in turn played upon Bush's personal desire to leave office on a high moral note.

What turned Operation Restore Hope from a mere dream into a reality was that there were powerful institutional interests ready to support any such initiative for "humanitarian intervention" (many of them seeing it as a precedent for Bosnia or Haiti), and little immediate prospect of serious military resistance on the ground. At the time, to the US government, it appeared a risk-free operation.

Finally, it is apparent that some of the incidents were not straight-forward, and may have been partly orchestrated. Two of the main incidents that were used to justify the intervention – the attack on the CARE convoy to Baidoa and the closure of Mogadishu port – reflected systemic weaknesses in the relief programmes. The general escalation in tension in Mogadishu during November was similarly an outcome of provocative actions by Ismat Kitani, which by design or happenstance forced a confrontation between the UN and General Aidid. The new envoy precipitously ordered the deployment of UN troops at the airport the day after his arrival, and refused to take any measures to build confidence between the UN and the factional leaders. The only Somali politician who built any rapport with the new envoy was Mohammed Abshir Musse, a consistent advocate of international intervention. Kitani met Ali Mahdi and Aidid only twice each during his six-month tenure. The developing atmosphere of mutual trust that existed under Sahnoun in September and October was rapidly undermined.

Record of the Intervention

The military intervention set a succession of international precedents. The US-led Unified Task Force (UNITAF) from December to May was the first modern case of the military occupation of a country for avowedly humanitarian reasons alone. The UN Operation in Somalia (UNOSOM

II) from May onwards was the first use of UN forces under Chapter VII of the UN Charter, which allows for the use of force to make peace. (Only the German contingent in Belet Weyn was sent under the more normal Chapter VI peacekeeping rules.) Somalia thus became an experiment, an international test tube in which the instruments of the new world order could be tried out.

The mandate of the forces has therefore been controversial: there was debate about whether the forces should disarm the factions, what the rules of engagement were, and whether troops should be sent to the north-west region, the self-declared Somaliland Republic. Perhaps most fundamentally, there was the question of whether the Security Council resolution of 6 June that empowered UNOSOM to use "all necessary measures" to apprehend General Aidid also allowed it to violate the Geneva Conventions, for example by attacking hospitals. These important issues are not the concern of this chapter. Instead, the question will be asked: what impact did the intervention have on fighting the famine?

Moving food

With characteristically simplistic thinking, the US government and media identified the conquest of famine with the logistics of international food-aid shipments. Hence the intervention force was sent to protect foreign aid workers, rather than Somali civilians. For NGOs that see their role as working in partnership with local people, rather than under the protection of an occupying force, this has proved a disturbing precedent.

In the very early days of the intervention, the movement of food aid was obstructed by a wave of insecurity that spread through the famine regions, especially Baidoa, and by the monopolisation of the port and airport by military traffic. While US troops were disembarking in Mogadishu, the ICRC was still unloading its ships on beaches to the south of the city using small boats. It had to continue doing so for several months. Thereafter, the movement of food aid certainly improved. The difference was, however, incremental rather than a complete transformation. The UN's "Hundred Day" plan of action, due to be completed on 19 January 1993, had to be extended for an additional forty days to enable WFP to meet its target of 87,000 metric tonnes.

Perhaps more important than escorting food aid was the effect of the intervention in breaking extortion rackets. Many of the contracts signed between relief agencies and hauliers and their militia forces could now be broken without fear of violent retaliation. The relief agencies no longer directly fuelled the militias in the way they had done previously. This success was not complete. Violent disputes over contracts continued, armed robbery of houses, offices and vehicles remained a problem, and agencies still employed armed guards for their vehicles and houses.

Overcoming hunger

The record of moving food tells us little about how much of that food actually reached the target population. Certainly this increased. The food supply to Baidoa and nearby villages was much higher, and access to Bardhere was much easier. However, much food was looted after delivery to villages. Moreover, distribution of food within the community remained in the hands of the leaders of the community. As most of the diversion before the intervention had been nonviolent, consisting of corruption by community leaders (genuine and otherwise), the intervention as such had no effect on this. Food was still diverted to the market, and waybills were still forged or not counterchecked. During 1992, the main food-aid agencies had not monitored their programmes adequately for reasons of security; they did not take advantage of the presence of international troops to improve their monitoring.

The absence of both targeting and monitoring means that it is difficult to come to any conclusions about the impact of the relief in overcoming malnutrition. The scant evidence available suggests that the results were disappointing. A survey in February found that more than half of the undernourished children in Mogadishu were not attending any of the feeding centres in the city (Save the Children Fund and Ministry of Health, 1993). A survey in Hoddur came up with similar findings (Brown, 1993).

Public health

The neglect of public health in 1992 has already been mentioned. This continued after the intervention, despite overwhelming evidence that the major killers were already, and would continue to be, epidemic diseases. Measles was probably the single most important cause of death in November, and outbreaks of malaria were predicted for December and January in accordance with the normal seasonal pattern. These outbreaks duly occurred, especially in the Juba valley. There is evidence of a sharp rise in death rates associated with malaria in the refugee camps along the Kenyan border and possibly in Bardhere (Center for Public Health Surveillance, 1993).

There were no programmes to combat malaria, save a small pilot intervention by WHO in Afgoy. The intervention failed to prevent or mitigate this predicted epidemic. The measles programmes were functional, but of very uneven impact. Only a small proportion of the target children were vaccinated, and later surveys indicated that even children who had received vaccines were contracting and dying of the disease, probably indicating a breakdown in the cold chain (African Rights, 1993b).

The third main killer was diarrhoeal diseases, specifically dysentery. The need for sanitation and improved supplies of water had been recognised for many months, but again efforts in this direction were minimal in comparison with the need. The main water programmes implemented during the intervention provided the international troops themselves with supplies.

Economic rehabilitation

The main source of food in Somalia at the time of the intervention was the harvest from the short rains. Farmers in the Shebelle valley had already harvested some significant surpluses the previous September, and food prices had fallen to normal levels in Mogadishu by October (African Rights, 1993a). Following good rains, an excellent harvest was expected in areas where planting had been possible. Many parts of Bay region and the Juba valley expected only meagre crops because of the small planted areas; many people were still refugees in Kenya or Ethiopia or displaced within the country. Nonetheless, the harvest marked an important step towards economic recovery.

The intervention occurred just at the moment when the donors should have been reducing their food aid to Somalia, and turning towards local purchase programmes and agricultural rehabilitation. Instead, the increased and indiscriminate supply of relief food had the predictable effect of driving the price of cereals down to very low levels and providing a serious disincentive to production. As the production areas (particularly the lower Shebelle) were also areas that formerly provided seasonal employment to tens of thousands of casual labourers from Bay region, this also helped to undermine the labour market that was just beginning to show signs of recovery. Thus was a new season of food aid dependency created in many areas.

Saving lives

The basic rationale for Operation Restore Hope was that it would save lives – two million, according to its most enthusiastic advocates. There is no reliable evidence to indicate either how many lives were lost during the 1991–92 famine, or how many were lost in early 1993. However, the available evidence suggests perhaps 200,000 excess deaths in 1992, peaking in June–September and rapidly falling away. During December–February, surveys (of regrettably poor quality) indicated that death rates were falling much more slowly. Deaths in Baidoa (measured by the bodies taken away by the ICRC truck) fell from an average of 204 per day in September to 70 in October, 50 in November and 62 in December (Collins, 1993). Mortality rates in Bardhere, Bakool and elsewhere showed a similar pattern, refusing to fall in the first months after the intervention (African Rights, 1993b). In Mogadishu, the crisis had ended in the third quarter of 1992.

Whether the decline in mortality would have been different in any way without the intervention cannot be known. Influencing the rate of decline of mortality in the final stages of a famine is notoriously difficult. The pattern of famine deaths indicates that malnutrition had ceased to be the driving force behind excess deaths in September at the latest, and that epidemic disease was largely or entirely the cause of deaths by the time of the intervention. Given the failure to deal with the epidemics, it is improbable that the intervention itself had a significant impact on this component of mortality. The evidence that the intervention had any impact on mortality in general is therefore extremely slender.

Conclusion

The failings of the international relief system have been evident for some time. In Ethiopia, southern Sudan, Liberia, Mozambique and elsewhere, the UN succeeded in concealing this fact to all but a handful of people closely involved in their operations. Since Somalia, this view is no longer respectable. Somalia has proved the *coup de grâce*. In Somalia, the failings of the UN and its partners became so self-evident that they could no longer be denied, and the other donors no longer saw it as in their interest to maintain an implausible facade that all was well. Somalia may therefore mark a watershed in the international community's response to "humanitarian emergencies".

The programmes in Somalia in 1991–92 demonstrated the worst institutional traits of the UN and bilateral agencies, and their principal subcontractors. Information, coordination, consultation and courage were all conspicuous by their absence. None of this changed in 1993, save for a brief period after the launch of Operation Restore Hope when, such was the media hype, the relief operation could momentarily be presented as a success. Unfortunately, a number of NGOs, including CARE-International, showed a similar combination of lack of effectiveness on the ground and enthusiastic participation in the "drumbeat" for military intervention.

Meanwhile, the true success during the emergency, the remarkable ICRC–SRCS programme, has been largely overlooked, partly because the ICRC is so self-effacing and partly because of the propensity for international agencies and the international media to ignore the efforts of local relief organisations. There are extremely important lessons to be learned from these successes, and also those of agencies such as SCF (UK). Unfortunately, such is the lack of structural accountability among the major relief organisations, that these lessons seem destined not to be learned.

References

Africa Watch and Physicians for Human Rights (1992) "No Mercy in Mogadishu: The Human Cost of the Conflict and the Struggle for Relief", London, 26 March.

African Rights (1993a) "Land Tenure, the Creation of Famine and Prospects for Peace in Somalia", Discussion Paper No. 1, London, October.

———— (1993b) "Somalia: Operation Restore Hope, A Preliminary Assessment", London, 1 May.

Alagiah, G. (1992) "A Necessary Intrusion", *Independent on Sunday*, 23 August.

Benthall, J. (1993) *Disasters, Relief and the Media*, London, I.B. Tauris.

Block, R. (1992) "White House 'Steamrollered' into Intervention", *Independent*, 10 December.

Brown, V. (1993) "Hoddur/Somalie: Impact of Health and Nutrition Related Activities", MSF and Epicentre, Paris, February.

Center for Public Health Surveillance (1993) "Results of Morbidity, Mortality, Nutritional and Vaccine Assessment Cluster Survey in Bardera, Somalia", Mogadishu, January.

Center for Disease Control (1992) "Population-based Mortality Assessment – Baidoa and Afgoi, Somalia, 1992", *Morbidity and Mortality Weekly Report*, 41 (49): 913–17.

Cohen, R. (1992) "It's Not Another Vietnam", *Washington Post*, 1 December.

Collins, S. (1993) "General Survey of North West Baidoa District", Baidoa, Concern, February.

de Waal, A. (1987) "The Perception of Poverty and Famines", *International Journal of Moral and Social Studies*, 2: 251–62.

Fraser, M. (1992) letter in *Guardian*, 31 October.

Gelb, L. (1992) "Shoot to Feed in Somalia", *Washington Post*, 19 November.

Johnston, P. (1992) letter in *Guardian*, 15 September.

Lewis, I. (1982) *A Pastoral Democracy: A Study of Pastoralism and Politics among the Northern Somali of the Horn of Africa*, London, International African Institute, 1982.

Odling-Smee, J. (1993) "Aid Agency Denies 'Gross Irresponsibility' Charge", *Third Sector*, 4 November.

Omaar, R. and de Waal, A. (1992) "Diplomacy Preferred to Armed Force", *Guardian*, 7 December.

Raspberry, W. (1992) "Let It Be Somalia", *Washington Post*, 2 December.

Save the Children Fund and Ministry of Health, Mogadishu (1993) "Nutrition, Mortality and EPI Coverage", Mogadishu, February.

Scroggins, D. (1993) "A New Role for CARE", *Atlanta Journal and Constitution*, 21 March.

Seaman, J. (1993) "Famine Mortality in Africa", *Institute of Development Studies Bulletin*, 24 (4): 27–32.

9

The Impact of War on Food Security in Eritrea: Prospects for Recovery

Lionel Cliffe

Assessing the Impact of War

A number of countries are making the transition from war to peace: Eritrea, Ethiopia and, hopefully, Mozambique are but some. The achievement of relative peace prompts questions about the prospects for socio-economic and environmental recovery and for longer-term development. This chapter offers some preliminary thoughts concerning post-conflict recovery of food systems. It does so primarily on the basis of a case study of Eritrea, although some parallels and differences with other countries in the Horn and southern Africa are explored in the conclusions.

Three broad concerns provide the starting point for this discussion. First, programmes of recovery need to be based on an accurate identification of the nature and source of the specific crisis inherited in the post-conflict period. This task is complicated in Eritrea and in other war- and hunger-ridden countries of Africa because other major "causal" factors that promote hunger – drought, environmental degradation, economic collapse – all interact with the effects of conflict. Thus, what has to be tackled by way of recovery is the total resulting situation, not just the isolable symptoms of war. The first step, therefore, is a detailed specification of the impacts of these different agents on food security and their consequences. Such an analysis provides a geographically and socially differentiated picture of the *how*, *who* and *where* of hunger.

Second, it will be important to specify what is meant by "recovery". Should the objective be a return to the often precarious status quo prevailing in the pre-conflict period? Such a return may not be feasible, even were it desirable: the multicausal processes causing loss of food entitlement might have become irreversible. Nevertheless, it is helpful to determine whether and to what extent war-related determinants of hunger are reversible with peace, either relatively automatically or with concrete programmes, and those which are more problematic.

Third, the task of seeking "solutions" to wars of hunger has to go beyond the recovery of food security and promotion of social and economic development, for their sustainability will be contingent on future political stability and the development of national and regional capacity to resolve conflicts which generate hunger, and have their roots in the depletion of or competition for food or other resources.

The devastation of war in Eritrea

There are several valuable accounts that have sought systematically to calculate the impact of conflict on infrastructure, productive capacity and human health in Africa (Hanlon, 1984 on Mozambique; UN, 1983 on Angola; UNICEF, 1987 on southern Africa). As yet, there has not been any official attempt to itemise all these costs in relation to the thirty-year-long conflict in Eritrea. Any such account would have to include the deaths and destruction as a result of many different acts of devastation: the years of bombardment of the northern town Nakfa and of many smaller towns, market centres and villages, especially in the north; bombings of the towns of Barentu, Agordat and the port of Massawa after they were taken by Eritrean liberation forces. But overall the war was not marked by the concentrated destruction of the urban landscape seen in Angola for instance. The last stage of the conflict, which involved the capture of Asmara, the capital, and other large towns like Keren, was done without much physical destruction of buildings and loss of civilian lives – although the death toll was considerable among soldiers in the Ethiopian army and the Eritrean People's Liberation Front (EPLF). Rural areas were more directly affected. The numbers of Eritrean civilians killed by direct violence may never be known exactly but must be counted in many tens of thousands; and the casualties suffered by the Ethiopian army, many of them peasant conscripts, were probably even more numerous.

Some measure of the direct toll can be obtained from some systematically collected evidence as a by-product of surveys conducted in 1987 and 1991 to assess relief-food requirements (Leeds Food Needs Surveys (LFNS) 1987; 1991; see also Cliffe, 1989). They allow some estimation of such other effects as the number of conscripts (and loss of youthful male labour), the loss of livestock, and arable land lost to minefields. These are summarised in Table 9.1. The data reveal the much greater indirect effects of war and years of martial law on the production systems, livelihood entitlements and trade.

To evaluate the impact of these natural and man-made threats to food security, it is necessary to situate producers in a context shaped by two factors: the pre-conflict systems of livelihood; and the particular character and spread of the war.

Table 9.1 Estimated direct military impact on rural Eritrean civilian population, reported up to 1987 and 1991

	1986–87	*1988–91*
People killed	1,500	7,000
People imprisoned	3,500	10,500
People conscripted (since 1984)	13,000	40,000
Houses destroyed	2,500	50,000
Land destroyed/mined (hectares)	23,000	47,000
Animals lost		
camels	1,600	13,500
cattle	5,500	80,000
sheep/goats	34,000	290,000
pack animals	3,000	41,000

Sources: Leeds Food Needs Survey, 1987; 1991

The interaction of war, drought and socio-economic change

Two broad agricultural systems characterised Eritrean production in the years before the war. In the highland plateau in the south of the country, sedentary agriculture is practised. In the west and coastal lowlands, pastoralism and agro-pastoralism predominate, while a quarter of the population lives in urban settlements.

The recent disruptions within Eritrea need to be set against a distinctive array of "external" forces that have operated over the past century to reshape the economy, patterns of food production, and livelihoods. The coastal area had been involved in trade and other contact with the Indian Ocean, the Mediterranean and Arabia for centuries; the highlands have a long history of interaction – of conflict as much as linkage – with the highland kingdoms of Abyssinia. An intensification of links with the world market occurred under Italian colonialism from the 1880s, which placed indigenous production systems in a context of commercial relations. This was also accompanied by the effects of settler colonialism, including alienation of land, the generation of an agricultural and urban wage labour force, and the subordination of indigenous agriculture in terms of access to markets and technical improvements (Negash, 1987). The promotion of some settler agriculture, and of growth of infrastructure, urban economic activities and capitalist social relations in the 1930s was put in reverse by the economic decline under British administration from 1941, after the defeat of the Italians.

The incorporation of Eritrea into a federation with Ethiopia during the 1950s, and the subsequent imposition of more direct Ethiopian overrule since 1960, accelerated this decline. Eritrea was subject to domination by an Ethiopian social formation that was in many respects more under-developed than its own, and by a polity which, unlike Eritrea, had never experienced anything but absolutism. This overrule changed its social character, if not its authoritarian style, with the Ethiopian revolution in 1975, but rural Eritrea has shared little of the agrarian policy changes pursued in Ethiopia proper, except for the general lack of provision of public investment in peasant agriculture. The 1975 Ethiopian land-reform proclamation had only limited application in Eritrea, as some reform had already occurred under British colonial or Eritrean nationalist auspices in many areas, and there were relatively even fewer "peasant associations" formed by the Ethiopian authorities than in Ethiopia proper. There were far fewer people subject to forced resettlement than from the adjacent province of Tigray.

As Eritrean resistance grew, successive Ethiopian regimes were drawn into the logic of alien rule, despite formal protestations about "one Ethiopia" and shared history and culture. The Ethiopian state sought to contain a people's war in the 1960s, and in the 1970s it increasingly engaged not just in a war against liberation fighters but in widespread repression directed at the mass of the population. At the same time, the Eritrean People's Liberation Front developed its policies and programmes of building grassroots participatory structures, of land reform and of provision of social services in the agricultural highlands, which they controlled, albeit clandestinely, and in the three northern provinces that remained liberated from 1979 onwards.

The consequences for the different systems of agricultural and livestock production and of food security and people's survival have to be set against the actual patterns of conflict in the thirty years of protracted war of national liberation. The particular character of the war from 1980 has been one which combined both guerrilla infiltration and hit-and-run tactics in the highlands and all areas of direct Ethiopian presence, with a conventional war of major proportions in which the two armies faced each other's trenches. The Eritrean nationalists successfully but bitterly defended this 300-kilometre front line and thereby directly controlled almost all of the three northern provinces of Barka, Sahel and Senhit, which were also more predominantly agro-pastoral and pastoral. Most of these three latter provinces were, as a result, exposed to sporadic aerial or artillery bombardment, which curtailed daytime life in specific ways. But the secure front line allowed some EPLF-run administration, which guaranteed food supplies and promoted some development.

The rest of the country, containing much of the agricultural areas, was the site of guerrilla war and was exposed to Ethiopian counterinsurgency measures and attempts to maintain their control. These actions had a quite different impact on the people's way of life, depending on the intensity of conflict and repression, and on how far they were contested areas. There had been a flood of refugees in the late 1970s as the Ethiopian army reasserted its control of formerly liberated territory, and a steady stream continued through the 1980s, fuelled by bombardments of liberated areas, by increased confrontation and repression elsewhere, and by the imposition of conscription on young Eritrean males.

From 1987 a major shift occurred in the pattern of conflict. The EPLF moved from the defensive and pushed their front line some hundred kilometres to the south and east, close to Keren – the strategic getaway town to the highlands and Asmara capital. In 1990 an encircling move gave them control of the main port Massawa, and eventually access to the southern part of the highlands. The "liberated" areas and thus the need for cross-border relief food were dramatically expanded, and for the last two years of the war the Ethiopian army was itself pinned down in an area of the highlands from Keren to some 50–100 kilometres south of Asmara.

War, drought and hunger

Apart from direct suffering and destruction, conflict and repression had consequences for agricultural and livestock production, food availability and the functioning of the overall economy. These began before the major drought of 1983, but this lethal combination of factors increased the population's vulnerability to starvation, and threatened its capacity to recover when more favourable climatic conditions prevailed. Tracing some of the specific effects of war on food and livelihood security in each of the two main agro-ecological zones, as we shall now do, also pinpoints some of the debilitating elements that will have to be overcome in these systems and in the economy. Table 9.1 indicates a picture of greater direct destruction of life and livelihoods in the period 1987–91, reflecting the greater contestation in the highlands in that period. The figures underscore the extent to which the civilian population was itself a major target in a country at war. The numbers of animals stolen or number of people injured may be inexact, but they do give some idea of the scale of the war and the psychological effect on the people as a whole of what they perceived as an overall threat to their livelihood and way of life.

One direct impact of the fighting was on the availability of labour, which constrained land use and the survival prospects for some households. Large numbers of young men were conscripted into the Ethiopian army. Almost all were from the three highland agricultural provinces – perhaps 4 to 5 per cent of the adult male labour force in 1987, rising to a massive 15 per cent by the end of the war in 1991. These figures do not include the recruits to the EPLF forces, totalling perhaps 100,000 by 1991. These losses were vastly increased by the flood of refugees and internally displaced. Labour available for agricultural activities also suffered indirectly: if homes were destroyed, labour could be displaced from crucial seasonal tasks for emergency rebuilding.

The direct loss of labour has to be seen against a context of labour migration to destinations in the Gulf oil-producing countries and Libya, and to Europe and the United States, which has grown over the last generation. This, and the underlying exodus of young men, prompted a major redistribution in the gender division of labour, placing a much greater burden on women. This labour shortage was reported as one reason why surprising amounts of land were in fact not cultivated in a small but significant number of villages, especially among the poorest peasant families. Even when labour shortage did not lead to noncultivation, it clearly was a constraint facing many vulnerable households, particularly the significant proportion that were "female-headed". Developing strategies to overcome the labour shortage underlying food insecurity will present formidable difficulties in the recovery period.

Conflict also curtailed further the availability of land. Villagers reported that trenches were dug across fields; areas near highways were left idle for fear they would invite harassment from passing convoys; fields were abandoned, as people sought refuge in neighbouring hills; dwellings were burned and few people ventured back to farm. In one village 90 per cent of land was left idle as people simply "did not dare work it". Many villages, especially in the highlands, reported some form of restriction on land used because of the military presence: the curfew reduced time for ploughing; people were not allowed onto distant lands; fields were taken for camps or training grounds. Reports from 1991 suggest that as much as 400,000 hectares of land were lost to production: while much of this was used for grazing, a sizeable amount of arable land was also taken out of production. Most of these direct threats and restrictions were, of course, lifted with peace in 1991.

Land mines were a major problem in some villages, and one with long-term consequences: almost 10 per cent of the villages in 1987 reported that some land had been mined. The actual effect on production in the affected villages may be marked even if the area mined is a small proportion for the country as a whole. One district, Zagar, lost thousands of hectares on that small part of the eastern escarpment which receives two annual rains. Land that has been mined can only be put back into production after the war if painstakingly cleared. The UN estimates that it may cost $1,000 to clear a mine that could have been produced for $1. Over twenty people lost their lives as they attempted to clear land during 1991. In most cases mined land is still left idle.

The chronic depletion of productive resources in agricultural areas

The problem of land mines illustrates a more general issue affecting prospects for recovery of agriculture. The evidence does not support the commonly held view that there is some terminal land shortage, particularly in the highlands, nor that there has been some major and lasting deterioration of the farming environment due to overcultivation. Indeed, what is remarkable is that arable land was not cultivated on a significant scale: some 40 per cent of villages in 1987 and 70 per cent in 1991 reported significant areas left idle. But overall, the evidence points to a more general long-run decline in the resource base during the long years of war and hunger, with increasing proportions of households drifting down from the "middle" peasant to the "poor" category.

The Leeds surveys conducted in 1987 and 1991 confirmed the findings of other studies conducted in Ethiopia (McCann, 1987; Holt and Lawrence, 1993), that loss of oxen has been consistently the most significant factor undermining crop production, increasing people's vulnerability and inhibiting long-term recovery after famine. The 1987 survey indicated how even the middle peasant households, on average, were left with fewer than the pair of oxen needed as a minimum to do their own ploughing; whereas the poor peasants, the majority, had already fewer than they needed, only 0.7 each on average, even before the calamities of 1983. The problem continued to worsen, and the 1991 survey reported that shortage of oxen was considered to be second only to that year's poor rainfall as an explanation for low crop production for "middle" and "poor" households. It was also cited as the main reason why some households cultivated no land. Those without oxen were by far the largest single group of households considered "vulnerable". Of some 76,000 households in the 1991 survey, 24,000 were left with no oxen.

Even at the best of times, those without oxen become beholden in some way to those who do own oxen. There are a number of arrangements open to poorer peasants whereby they can get the use of other people's oxen, each of which may increase vulnerability over the longer term. For example, poorer peasants practise a form of "share-cropping" where they promise a share, usually a third, of the harvest in exchange for the use of a team, and a quarter or less if they only borrow one ox. In effect their position is not unlike those forms of land tenure where they used to pay land rent. Some 12 per cent of all villages reported that such methods were used by nonowners of oxen in 1991. In-kind payment reduces their chances of building up a grain stock or a marketable surplus in good years, but involves paying less in bad years.

What is known about this and other various hiring and borrowing arrangements does not support the cosy and unsubstantiated conclusion of a recent FAO report (1994) that "traditional sharing arrangements and the exchange of labour for ox-time appear to deal with this problem satisfactorily." Rather, there is evidence of an overall national shortage of oxen to plough the cultivable land, plus a process affecting the large majority of highland farmers of irreversible impoverishment and continued dependence.

For most households the dearth of oxen and their maldistribution mean that some sort of unequal exchange of their labour, cash or crop share has to take place. The same is true of pack animals. Lack of a donkey means that household members, usually girls and women, have to do more fetching and carrying of water. Not having a camel for the long haul means a similar labour or cash exchange, or paying considerably more for food to be transported from distant markets in these times of shortage. For the rich peasant with pack animals, however, such arrangements represent an additional source of income and accumulation. These inequalities in access to means of production other than land, and the consequent antagonistic relations of production, tend to be intensified by the effects of war and drought.

Some instances of collective action with more egalitarian implications are to be found, however. Even before the end of the war, the Eritrean Relief Association (ERA) relief and recovery programme sought to replenish oxen; and in some cases, where there was a viable village assembly, a small common pool of draught animals was made available to spread the benefits of the few oxen provided. Whether collective provision of these crucial means of production is sustainable in the long run is debatable, although some provision for access to draught power would be necessary to complement any land reform as long as the present farming system continues. Recovery plans provide for extra oxen, through credit, but such provisions do not automatically guarantee their availability to the poorest households unless social mechanisms equal to the task have survived or can be built up.

All too often the rapporteurs from highland villages emphasised in the 1991 survey this shortage of oxen, but almost as frequently coupled it with pleas for mechanised equipment. The same requests were also being passed on by Eritrean government officials to aid donors as part of the emergency transitional support required. But while tractors might help to fill the immediate gap and bring more land into cultivation sooner, there must be grave doubt about the long-term costs to the national accounts of the fuel imports and the effects on the indigenous farming system, which would become less "sustainable", more dependent on imported energy and on supplies from government, cooperatives or "tractor capitalists".

Strategies for Recovery

The deterioration of the pastoral economy and prospects for recovery

Land-mines, harassment, aerial bombardment and general impediments to movement had serious effects on grazing and livestock husbandry, as well as on crops. The numbers of livestock killed or confiscated by the

Ethiopian army were small in proportion to the total livestock population, although to the people affected they represented a significant proportion of those required to rebuild their herds after the severe drought of 1983–85. One village reported that "home grazing is mined" and that, therefore, herding of all animals all year round had to be done further afield – with more demands on time and loss of milk to children in the home. One village in Barka reported that, "Ethiopian pilots seem to have special interest in camels." The curfew imposed on many areas under partial or total Ethiopian control also affected herding: "We can't go looking for lost animals after dark ... so herds can only go limited distances." Such incidents, reinforced by restrictions on movements, cut people off from the normal grazing areas, which were often quite distant from their homes, and posed a more general threat to that pattern of regular movement to new pastures so critical to pastoral and trade activities. In 1991, one third of all villages reported that during the war they had faced some restriction on grazing, and 70 per cent of them indicated that they had not been able to travel easily to market, or that if they did goods were confiscated, or they had to provide a bribe or "levy". But by then only a small proportion, mostly in the highlands, felt that such restrictions still had serious consequences for livestock production in that year. Another and more widespread effect of these bans, uncertainties and fear meant that herders became hesitant to send beasts to the rich pastures in the southwest along the Gash and Setit rivers, used seasonally by so many people. Hence one report from a village in Senhit in 1991: "Even those who went to Gash returned to say we lost our livestock."

The direct loss of animals, and difficulties placed in the way of herding and trading animals for grain, during the war merely amplified the widespread and devastating losses to pastoral activities in the hunger years of the 1980s, when the severe famine years of 1983–85 were followed by rainfall that was below normal in every year except 1986. The overall effect of drought and war was to reduce livestock numbers by 1985 to a quarter of what they had been before the major drought. A partial recovery in 1986–87 only brought the national herd up to a figure still less than half the 1980 figure. The numbers reported in the two surveys point to further massive losses by 1991 of more than half of 1987 numbers. These rather crude data point to a postwar situation which is the culmination of a long-drawn-out, debilitating decline in the animal resources on which many Eritreans depend for food and exchange entitlements. These overall declines in entitlements have been accentuated by a long-term decline in the terms of trade of animals for grain. One consequence of these declines has been a reduction in the proportion of rural households who can be classified as pure "pastoralists" as opposed to agro-pastoralists: from 10 per cent to 6 per cent between 1987 and 1991. The evidence points to a paradoxical situation whereby "rich" pastoralists can survive perhaps better than any other rural people, but many more less-well-off former pastoralists may have had their return to that way of life irreversibly cut off.

The catastrophic decline in numbers cannot of course be immediately reversed with the peace-time resumption of "normal" grazing patterns, even with good rainfall. Natural increase in herds depends on the gender and age composition of existing herds; whether breeding stock have survived; as well as the gestation period of the beasts concerned. Goats and sheep tend to lead the way in recovery if conditions are favourable, being able to generate growth in herds more or less immediately; cattle and camels regenerate more slowly. It is not the condition and amount of grazing land or veterinary services which alone determine whether regeneration of herds occurs at the rate that is scientifically feasible. Crucial too are the calculations of those who live off the herds, which represent an income and a source of entitlement only as far as they are disposed of through trade, exchange or direct consumption. The more urgent their need for current income and the fewer other sources of income/food available to them, the bigger the proportion of the herd that will have to be disposed of immediately. Fortunately, this contradiction between fostering the growth of stock and maximising current income from livestock is not completely incompatible. As only a small proportion of male cattle, sheep and goats are worth keeping as breeding stock, some 90 per cent of the young males can be disposed of once they reach maturity without slowing down the long-term regeneration of herds. But if the circumstances of the most impoverished force them to dispose of animals before they mature, or to sell more than 90 per cent of the young males, recovery is slowed, and may be indefinitely postponed. Decline may thereby continue even though the objective conditions of war and drought that caused the loss of herds are reversed: people may have entered an irreversible decline in the pastoral means of livelihood.

Further evidence of the impact that the steep declines in the size of the Eritrean livestock herds have had on the feasibility of household "coping strategies" has been the growing dependence on food aid. In 1987, "animal sales" were the most important method by which all households expected to make up the harvest shortfall. The 1991 survey found that "animal sales" took second place to "relief aid" even amongst rich households, who are now, as we have seen, in a small minority. For poor households, animal sales hardly figure: they were expected to be a "very important" means of making up the harvest shortfall in only 30 villages of the 400 surveyed (8 per cent). It is conceivable that our respondents held these expectations because they thought food aid would be so abundant in 1991–92 that animal sales would be unnecessary; in view of the inadequate levels of food aid received in recent years, it is more likely that "coping" by selling animals was realised to be impossible when there were so few animals to sell.

Recovery for the majority of that third of the rural population dependent wholly or partly on livestock is thus problematic. They will have begun to reap some "peace dividend" from the restoration of some grazing land, from the greater freedom of movement to distant pasture, especially those for certain seasons or used as drought reserves, and to markets. Soon after the end of the war, we saw thousands of animals being traded in the market in the northern town of Keren, from which most of the herders of the northern provinces had been cut off for twelve years or more. One rapporteur conveyed these general feelings from a highland village in Akele Guzai: "Before, the enemy had destroyed pasture; people had so many problems in travelling from place to place; they were killed and assaulted; the market prices for things we bought were high. Now we can move and prices are much lower." But these improvements alone cannot guarantee against further decline without efforts to restore the livestock asset base of the most vulnerable. Some programme is needed to supply additional animals to the poor, perhaps by purchasing from any surpluses in markets in eastern Sudan or Tigray, if they are to have any basic food or livelihood security. Fortunately, another form of subsidy to herd regeneration exists apart from the obviously limited possibility of shipping in animals from outside the country. Provision of income support, especially in the form of continued food aid, would have the inestimably valuable effect of reducing the pressure on the most vulnerable herders to mortgage their future by selling off too many of their livestock assets. However, the first FAO Mission (1993) to independent Eritrea provides no other proposals that would assist resource recovery for the majority of poor among the agro-pastoralists and pastoralists.

Refugees and displaced

One enormous, tragic effect of the long war was the displacement of over half a million Eritreans across the border into Sudan, in addition to the many thousands of people who fled their homes but remained within the country. Half of the refugees made some kind of life in camps set up by the Sudanese authorities, sometimes alongside Tigrayans or other Ethiopians, receiving some relief rations and some allocation of land for self-sufficient livelihood support through the UN High Commissioner for Refugees (UNHCR), the Sudanese government and NGOs. The remainder were self-settled, living in towns throughout Sudan, making a living through trade or wage labour. The Eritrean Relief Association in its 1985 annual report estimated there were 140,000 other "displaced" people within liberated areas, most of them whole communities from villages that had been bombarded or overrun by Ethiopian forces, or just uncomfortably close to the frontline. They were more often from the pastoral/agro-pastoral areas, and only the more fortunate were able to save and take with them some of their livestock.

By mid-1993 the trickle of refugees who had returned to Eritrea spontaneously had amounted to an estimated 80,000, but the main organised repatriation from Sudan was held up. In part this was to allow the new Eritrean government to make plans for their return and reabsorption after the referendum and independence in 1993, and to conclude long negotiations with the UN as to what outside financial and other support would be available. Even then the eventually agreed government–UN programme (PROFERI) envisaged that the official return would be in three phases beginning in February 1994 and continuing until 1997. The long delay might well allow for an orderly process of resettlement, but it does betoken an administrative insensitivity that gives primacy to the formal specification of project timetables and bureaucratic convenience. The government's Commission for Eritrean Refugee Assistance (CERA) used the delay to carry out a careful survey of the refugees, their status, origins and preferred place to resettle in Eritrea. Apparently many opted for districts other than their home areas, perhaps reflecting their and the government's perception of the availability of land and other opportunities.

A quarter of the refugees have been in Sudan for a decade or more; a simple "return" to a home area and reabsorption into an existing household with its own means of livelihood is not possible. At an aggregate level, the return of a higher proportion to highland agricultural areas might well be possible given the apparent labour problem and existence of unutilised land. However, access to land would still be very much a problem for any who do return, as the existence of some unutilised plots does not mean that the land is "available" to newcomers, unless and until there is some kind of land reform which would allow land to be reallocated. In the event, the joint Eritrean government–UN programme for resettlement envisaged virtually no refugees returning to the highlands. Whether a result of the refugees' own preferences or not, the programme envisages up to 88 per cent moving to the northern and western provinces, which are predominately agro-pastoral; 43.5 per cent of this group are expected to settle in Gash-Setit where land, although at a lower altitude, is sufficiently well-watered for permanent crop husbandry, and is regarded as relatively abundant – and, moreover, legally "available". This pattern will, de facto, mean some settling of people from the highlands (who probably form a substantial minority of the refugees) into the western lowlands. Already inhabitants of Gash-Setit are contesting the notion that land there belongs to the state. The possible resentments about land distribution in that area are being fuelled by the clamour for "concessions" for sizeable holdings for commercial farming to entrepreneurs, many of them well-educated and well-off returnees from the more distant diaspora.

The government programme envisages the provision to refugee households of a year's food supply; the necessary seeds, tools, livestock; plus help in building houses and the provision of social infrastructure. Given the sizeable numbers of people involved, equal to a 20 per cent increase in the existing rural population, the cost of even a minimum provision runs to over $400 million. Almost 30 per cent of this sum is to be found by the government, perhaps with the help of a World Bank loan. Even deferred repayment of this loan will place an enormous strain on the Eritrean economy, which is one of the world's weakest in terms of its per-capita GNP and foreign-exchange-earning capacity.

Even with such expenditures, the particular problems of the 39 per cent of refugee households which CERA estimates are headed by women may not be adequately met – although provision has been made for them to have the use of tractors for ploughing in the first year. Such a minimum programme will, however, be faced with political complications: households who have grown used to an allocation of reasonably fertile land in eastern Sudan sufficient for a small surplus, in addition to UNHCR provision of school and health facilities, will have high expectations.

An additional source of discontent may emerge as refugees are re-patriated in different areas of the country. One dimension of this problem will derive from the fact that many of the refugees will be settling in areas characterised by different language, culture and possibly religious beliefs – and perhaps different farming systems and livelihood strategies. How will highlanders cope with the demands of using spate irrigation on the hot and unhealthy coastal flood plain? What will be the language and content of interaction between returnees and locals?

Another aspect of this absorption in areas with different backgrounds relates specifically to the allocation of land. The programme refers to resettled refugees being given one hectare of land in the highlands, two in the lowlands – little enough for subsistence. But crucial questions re-main. On what terms? What rights will they have? What security will they enjoy? In this respect the resettlement of refugees prioritises the whole complex issue of national policy on land tenure as requiring immediate attention. A further complication is the provision of animal draught power. The government plan for repatriation understandably cannot afford to provide a pair of oxen for each returning household; that would be more than most peasants have, as we have seen. But to make the easy assumption that oxen will automatically be "shared" through traditional mechanisms understates the problem of constituting a community among these reset-tled people. This problem, and perhaps many others, are likely to be underlined by the plan which envisages that most of the refugees will form separate, new settlements rather than being an element grafted onto existing communities. The plan to provide oxen also implies the transpo-sition of the highland farming system onto areas where the tradition is that camels, donkeys and even cows are just as likely to be used for ploughing. The implicit assumptions guiding current plans are further revealed by the formula of providing land to people designated "agriculturalist", and herds to the "pastoralists". The formula implies that after many years of exile refugees are immutably, and presumably by ethnic definition, set in one of two categories – a distinction made even less useful by the fact that most refugees will be resettled in areas where the "agro-pastoralist" mix presents the best survival prospect.

Demobilisation of combatants

This interrelatedness of problems applies to the many ex-combatants. The very considerable army of the former Ethiopian regime which was stationed in Eritrea was captured and returned to Ethiopia proper, fled or was slaughtered in the terrible final battles of May 1991. The Eritrean People's Liberation Army and the other cadres of the EPLF, all calling themselves "fighters", were left as the only armed force in the country, and were not demobilised. The weapons have thus stayed for the most part in the hands of this highly disciplined army. Nevertheless, there is little immediate threat of armed banditry, gratuitous violence or a descent into warlordism.

The EPLF announced in May 1991 that all fighters would remain as a volunteer force, be provided only food, shelter and pocket money (50 Eth. Birr: aproximately £8 per month), and be expected to assist in rebuilding, including taking senior posts in government. At the same time, all former Eritrean civil servants were kept in post on salaries, thus avoiding that source of discontent, although the full integration of these two elements into an effective public service may take further time.

During the war, the numbers of the EPLF was a closely guarded secret. But in an interview in September 1991, EPLF secretary-general, Issayas Afeworki, suggested that they might number 100,000. The absorption of this large number of cadres and soldiers into gainful work represents an enormous task with implications for other problems of repatriation and recovery. A significant but small number will be essential to the new administration. It is also intended that a much larger minority will be absorbed into a new professional national army. The constraint will be to find sufficient financial resources in this impoverished country to pay even those extra numbers, to give ex-fighters a full salary along with the salaries of existing officials. But what of the other tens of thousands? Some have (often half-completed) qualifications, and/or acquired literacy or some educational upgrading in the trench and bush classes that were developed during the war years. Formal employment creation will occur as the war economy is replaced – the textile and other closed factories and the plantations, might be reopened – but will not be on a scale sufficient to absorb more than a small proportion. For the rest to be gainfully occupied will require the fostering of individual or small-scale cooperative self-employment in crafts, farming and herding, and services, as well as the necessary training, support services and credit.

Meanwhile, a decision of the EPLF Central Committee in mid-May 1993 asked fighters to be content with another two years of limbo on pocket money and subsistence, with no concrete promise of a programme of demobilisation. The reaction was swift. Four days before the independence celebrations, several hundred fighters paraded with arms through the main city centre of Asmara, closed its main arteries and the airport, just as foreign visitors to the celebrations were beginning to arrive. They demanded to see Issayas Afeworki and voiced their protests about their economic prospects, but also about the unusually nonconsultative way the Central Committee was reaching such decisions. This demonstration was carried out in a typically disciplined manner, but underscored the centrality of this additional task of recovery, the need to avoid future conflicts or a self-demobilised drift of armed fighters into civil society and likely banditry. The government is seeking support from international funds by donors who have realised the importance of such demobilisation in postwar countries of Africa.

Land reform for recovery: the politics of sustainability

We have seen how the needs of refugees and ex-combatants require some predetermination of land tenure policies, and also how land reform was part of mobilisation strategies of the EPLF. Land reform would thus seem likely to be on the postwar development agenda – but of what kind, and at what stage of recovery? The pre-conflict systems of land holding were diverse and complex. The highlands have been characterised by one system, *diesa*, under which land was supposedly associated with a clan, *enda*, which allocated plots to newlyweds or periodically reallocated to take into account changing needs, but the household would have guaranteed access subject to these clan rights. It seems that this pattern emerged during colonial rule from a "traditional" system of family holdings and inheritance (*tsilmi*), which still remains in some areas; but increasing population and the loss of areas to Italian settlers meant there was little spare *diesa* land to allocate, and led to an indefinite postponement of reallocations. Hence the permanent occupation by established households and confirmation of landlessness among those with less secure de facto rights. In these changed circumstances, younger generations could acquire access to land, if at all, through inheriting small plots subdivided by the family, thus leading to fragmentation.

Such evolving variations on "traditional" tenure have been further modified in some areas by either the Ethiopian government's policy of peasant associations redividing land in the 1970s and 1980s (implemented only to a very limited extent in Eritrea), or land reform promoted by ELF or by EPLF during the war. Under this latter formula, the needs of the landless were addressed in a "democratic" process under an elected village committee, overcoming the risks of favouritism being shown by elders of the *enda*. What exists on the ground in any one locality in the highlands tends to be a mixture of "tradition", tempered or supplanted by the legacy of land reforms introduced by either or both the Derg or the EPLF.

The new Eritrean government has, in turn, to decide quickly whether simply to leave the complex realities well alone, consolidate some land reform based on EPLF's past experience or a variant of it, or introduce some consolidation of holdings under individual titling or some other form of secure access. It cannot issue land rights to refugees which are at variance with those that apply to their neighbours. Different calculations will have to be made with respect to land in nonhighland areas, most of it classified as *domeniale* since the Italian period, and also to grazing lands in the highlands themselves where at present animals have access to common land. *Domeniale* was a legal formula designating land as state-owned; de facto "ownership" could be claimed by those who cleared it. This system offers an apparently simple administrative mechanism to mount a resettlement programme. However, people in Gash-Setit, now faced with a 50 per cent increase in the province's population under the resettlement programme, are already voicing their unease, also claiming that the Italians' decreeing their areas *domeniale* overlooked their pre-existing systems in which whole areas, including land not cultivated at any one moment or used for grazing, belonged to the community.

Complexities and political pitfalls could emerge with refugees in the other pastoral and agro-pastoral provinces. There is a tendency to demarcate certain areas to receive refugees, and to adopt a technocratic view which equates "recovery" with the use of what is seen as virgin territory for settled agriculture. This tendency for bureaucratic heavy-handedness toward the agro-pastoralists' way of life, their considerable crop-growing activities, combined with livestock, and their need for restocking of their herds, would not only aggravate any tension with the state, and between agriculturalists and agro-pastoralists, but would sharpen fault lines that could set ethnic and religious groups at odds.

It is this latter possibility of tension between highland, Tigrinya-speaking Christians and other nationalities, mainly Muslim, which is the remaining, at present insignificant, potential for future conflict inside Eritrea. The past bases for the long war were to do with the nature of, and overrule by, the Ethiopian state – which for the foreseeable future is no longer a threat. The only possible leverage offered to neighbouring governments to exacerbate internal conflicts – which has bedeviled so much of recent history in the Horn of Africa – is the possibility of a fundamentalist regime in Sudan exploiting the religious fault line. It is therefore crucial that policies pursued in the name of "recovery" or "development" do not foster any such polarisation. In practice that means that the needs and voices of the agro-pastoralist, northern and western people must not be ignored in favour of urban-based or highland-centred development or elite returnee interests.

Towards Sustainable Recovery

In sum, Eritrea two years after the end of war has a peaceful and stable political situation, which is undoubtedly one of the prerequisites for sustainable recovery, one not guaranteed in many other post-conflict situations. Some normal economic intercourse between town and country, liberated and contested areas, has been re-established as a result of the automatic peace dividend. Plans for recovery and development are being formulated. But the social and economic problems being faced are of enormous proportions. The underlying economic structure is extremely limited, even by African standards. The limitations of the agricultural sector were put into context after a good rainfall year in 1992, in which the harvest managed to meet perhaps 60 per cent of food grain needs, prompting hopes of further progress to self-sufficiency. The poor rains of 1993 put the harvest back down to 30 per cent of food needs. The opening-up of internal and regional trade does allow for some of the shortfall to be made up through commercial channels, but food aid must continue for some years to come. Indeed it is an imperative for recovery, in order to guarantee household food security for the resource-depleted majority of farmers and herders, and to "subsidise" the recovery of livestock holdings.

Few died of starvation in Eritrea, despite the horrors of war and drought, largely because of food aid and an efficient distribution system developed by the EPLF's relief arm. However, evidence from the Leeds Food Assessment Studies suggests that available rations have been consistently below minimum requirements, and, as a result of war and economic stress, people have been forced to sell off every available asset. They have run out of "coping strategies". It is for this reason that there is a need for continuation of food and other relief aid, while at the same time reorienting what had been "emergency" assistance so that it dovetails with development initiatives.

This transition from relief to development is a difficult one, currently being attempted by several countries in Africa. Wars throughout the continent have led not only to massive destruction, especially of those productive resources needed to maintain livelihoods, but also to long-term processes of impoverishment from which self-sustained recovery of both the national economy and the majority of households may no longer be possible. Such circumstances require more than food aid in the first stages of recovery. They demand programmes of replenishment of productive assets for rural poor, beyond that which is likely to be generated by peaceful stimulation of the market or private investment alone. In Eritrea, this recovery of rural productive potential requires in particular the assisted acquisition of seed and tools, but above all *oxen*, in the agricultural zones – a requisite which would also be crucial to some areas of Ethiopia and parts of southern Mozambique. The drier areas of Eritrea, as in Sudan, Somalia and parts of Ethiopia, demand the assisted provision of livestock, through purchase schemes and credit, to those whose herds are too small to provide both regenerative growth and income. The specific resources required in other countries may be different, but the emphasis on restoring productive assets of peasants and returnees is everywhere essential if the persistence of a legion of permanent "refugees" or impoverished, and the continuing threat to peace that they bring, are to be avoided. Even in countries like Mozambique and Angola, which do not share the potential land pressure of the Eritrean or Ethiopian highlands, many people face a fate equivalent to landlessness, by virtue of being without other agricultural resources or livestock.

Eritrea's need for continued food aid and for agrarian recovery programmes to generate food security is the greater because of other predicaments that it shares with other conflict areas. First, it has no significant export products from the agricultural sector, with the exception of a post-recovery potential for livestock and fisheries sales across the Red Sea, nor from industry. Its production of crops for local industry was decimated by the war; its previously existing industrial base has been undermined, but hopefully not permanently, by wartime destruction, shortage of spares and raw materials, and by being overtaken in the meanwhile by competition. Like Somalia and Mozambique, its foreign-exchange-earning potential is primarily from remittances from exiles, refugees and labour migrants.

Second, the threadbare state of the formal sector of the economy and its chronic shortage of foreign exchange, which further inhibits productive investment from internal or outside sources, means that there is even less prospect of formal employment creation than in most African countries. The tensions of trying to find livelihoods for the high proportion of the population who are returnees or ex-combatants are thus likely to be great, but even more marked unless the recovery of agriculture provides livelihoods for more people and not merely expanded output.

A third factor conditioning post-conflict food aid and recovery involves recognition of the fact that, even with the restoration of agricultural productive capacity, the country as a whole and perhaps a majority of rural households will not be self-sufficient in grain production. Any development/recovery programme has thus to give just as much priority to nonfarm sources of supplementing income: initially, and perhaps for many years to come, some public works or food-for-work programmes, plus casual wage-earning and informal activities. The same conclusion is stressed in a recent survey in the neighbouring Ethiopian highlands (Holt and Lawrence, 1993).

Eritrea may be relatively better off than other war-ridden countries in that the political conditions for a sustainable peace – a stable regime not subject to destabilising internal or external conflicts – would appear to be in place. However, that situation is still precarious in the long run without sound strategies for recovery of national output and of livelihood prospects for all. Like other such countries, Eritrea's current resource base is so limited that it will require outside assistance, but of a sort that does not ignore these imperatives.

References

Cliffe, L. (1989) "The Effects of War on Two Different Agricultural Systems in Eritrea", *Development and Change*, 20 (4)

Food and Agriculture Organisation (FAO) (1994) *Eritrea Review*, Report of a Mission, UN Food and Agricultural Organisation, Rome.

Hanlon, J. (1984) *Mozambique: The Revolution under Fire*, London, Zed Press.

Holt, J. and Lawrence, M. (1993) *Making Ends Meet: A Survey of the Food Economy of the Ethiopian North-east Highlands*, Save the Children, London.

Leeds Food Needs Survey (1987) *Eritrea: Food and Agricultural Production Assessment Study*, Final Report, Centre for Development Studies, University of Leeds.

———— (1991) *Eritrea 1991: A Needs Assessment Study*, Final Revised Report, Centre for Development Studies, University of Leeds for Emergency Relief Desk.

McCann, J. (1987) *From Poverty to Famine in Northeast Ethiopia: A Rural History*, Philadelphia, University of Pennsylvania Press.

Negash, T. (1987) *Italian Colonialism in Eritrea, 1882–1941: Policies, Praxis and Impact*, Uppsala, Uppsala University Press.

PROFERI (1993) *Programme for Refugee Reintegration and Rehabilitation of Resettlement Areas in Eritrea*, Joint Government of Eritrea and United Nations Appeal, Vol. I, June.

UN (1983) *White Paper on Acts of Aggression by the Racist South African Regime against the People's Republic of Angola*, Angolan government, reprinted by UN Security Council, 7 December.

UNICEF (1987) *Children on the Frontline: The Impact of Aprtheid, Destabilization, and Warfare in Southern and South Africa*, New York.

PART III

Towards New Approaches:
Implications for Policy and Practice

Gender, War and Food
Judy el Bushra and Eugenia Piza-Lopez

Introduction

War places extreme stress on social relations, including gender relations.[1] The subordinate status of women may be exacerbated during warfare, leading to extreme physical, material and emotional hardship. Yet in the longer term, the stresses war places on social relations may provoke a re-evaluation of women's role and status, and open up opportunities for new and more constructive gender relations. Are these longer-term changes fundamental, or merely a functional adaptation to the new situation? And to what extent can the changes that take place during wars be used as a springboard for social transformation?

"Gender" refers to those characteristics of men and women which are socially, rather than biologically, determined, and to the relationships between men and women in social settings. Since gender is socially constructed, its manifestations differ from one society to another, and may change over time. In all situations women tend to occupy roles and positions which are subordinate, in some fundamental way, to those of men. This imbalance between men and women, however, must be seen in relation to other imbalances existing in human society, such as those based on ethnicity or economic class. The challenge of a gender approach to development lies in the transformation of unequal gender relations to provide a basis for justice and equity, not only between men and women, but between all members of society (Brett, 1991).

Social relations are distorted, profoundly altered, and sometimes re-defined by war. Conflict threatens the physical and social integrity of communities and calls into question their ability to survive. It involves widespread physical violence, both against the person and against the basic resources on which people depend for their survival. There are important reasons for exploring the gender dimensions of conflict. Since World War II changes in the nature of conflict have brought civilians, particularly women, to the forefront of most contemporary wars (Summerfield, 1990).

A further reason for stressing the importance of this topic is the need to refine our understanding of the social processes that lead to, determine the outcome of, and have the potential to heal conflict. How men and women acquire, develop, express and adapt their gender identities may be an important element in this. Armed conflict can highlight the "fault lines" of society, pointing up expressions of injustice and indicating needs for transformation. Understanding the evolution of armed conflicts will be incomplete unless gender differences are addressed, both at individual and societal levels and in terms of the international and global political dimensions.

This chapter looks primarily at the impact of armed conflict on households in their productive and reproductive roles. The first section focuses on changing gender relations within the household during wartime, looking particularly at women's economic role and at some of the constraints faced by women in carrying out that role. The second section comments on issues that may arise in post-conflict situations and what they tell us about long-term changes in gender roles and relations. The final section presents some lessons that policy-makers may wish to draw for the planning and implementation of assistance programmes in conflict situations.

Women as Household Providers during Wartime

The immediate consequence of war in most communities is likely to be the absence or incapacity of large numbers of men. Women are then obliged to take over many of men's functions in household economic and support systems, taking on more and heavier work, a new and more varied range of tasks, and greater responsibility (and with it, greater psychological stress).

Conflict damages a family's means of earning money and feeding itself. Farming may no longer be viable if there is insufficient labour available, seed stocks have been eaten, or produce looted. Marketing outlets and sources of essential supplies may have been destroyed. Those who are obliged to seek refuge away from home lose access to their land and often their animals, and as refugees they may have few opportunities to earn a living.

Women heads of households, however, have a double burden. They face multiple disadvantages, the most obvious being the lack of male adult labour and income-earning power. Beyond this is the problem of access to resources. At the best of times, women on their own without a male interlocutor experience difficulties in making claims to land, in arguing with officials, or in persuading merchants of their creditworthiness. Community structures providing economic support may be restricted to men, or women may have only passive roles within them. Thus, although women may have increased economic responsibilities, this is not necessarily matched by increased power in decision-making and resource-allocation.

A report from a town in southern Somalia in 1991, describing the chronically reduced production levels as a result of looting, insecurity and lack of fuel for transport, highlighted the importance of women's economic role in this crisis:

> Formerly, the women were confined to such activities as water delivery, occasional farming, limited business involvement, looking after the children, food handling. Now, with this circumstance, they have to assume full household management, including securing income for survival, maintaining livestock, etc. The Sablaale market, therefore, is overwhelmed by women, selling bits of sugar, salt, tea leaves, maize, beans, eggs and meat. (ACORD, 1991)

Survival strategies

Family providers must meet their basic needs and those of their dependants in whatever way they can. This may mean adopting survival mechanisms which they are ill-equipped or untrained for, as well as those which in normal times would be considered socially unacceptable (el Bushra and Piza-Lopez, 1994).

The first set of survival strategies aim to enable households to adjust to stress by adapting existing roles within the constraints of the existing environment. Women will "make do" by cooking cheaper foods, reducing the number of meals eaten per day, reducing the size of food portions. For many women this includes eating last and going without. Families may decide to divest themselves of assets by selling jewellery or land, and slaughtering animals. Such decisions require judicious balancing of short- and long-term options based on an intimate knowledge of the local environment. Economising is likely to precede selling off assets; when it comes to selling assets, those of lasting long-term utility are preserved for as long as possible. Such strategies do not challenge, and may indeed reinforce, the decision-making power of men within the household.

Women who have not previously worked for payment may set up as food sellers or tailors in towns, work for wages on farms, in domestic service or in low-paid jobs with the military, turning skills normally practised within the home to commercial advantage. Farmers may switch to planting short-cycle crops, those which can be stored in the ground until needed, those which are rich in carbohydrates, or those which can be grown close to the house for security. Farmers may have extensive knowledge of crops suitable for such circumstances and may keep aside seed for such eventualities.

One of the long-term consequences of conflict may be the loss of crop varieties specially adapted to local conditions. This is particularly significant in cultures where women are habitually responsible for farming certain specific crops: often these "women's crops" are the more "old-fashioned" varieties, as opposed to imported varieties produced as cash-crops by men (ACORD, n.d.). Strategies like these, based on exploiting resources more exhaustively than usual, can be effective only as long as the resources continue. "Making do" is therefore a good strategy only if it enables gaps to be bridged until normality returns.

In situations of chronic stress, people may feel they have no choice but to take up activities that are socially unacceptable, or unacceptable in normal conditions. In some cultures that discourage women from working outside the home, petty commerce may be seen as acceptable for women if they have no other choice. Selling narcotics and alcohol may be acceptable in some societies but not others. Still other roles may be so badly regarded that women who perform them risk being rejected by their family and community. Prostitution and associated roles such as working in bars fall within this group, as does black-marketeering. Associating with enemy soldiers is perhaps the most ill-regarded activity of all, from which women may never be able to regain their families' estimation and support.

The factors that push women into taking on socially unacceptable roles are complex. They include economic pressures such as the lack of other viable options for making a living; but economics alone does not explain why women take such drastic steps, which undermine their own feelings of self-respect and threaten supportive relationships. Some liberation movements, those of Eritrea and Tigray for example, have sought to address this by promoting women's feelings of self-worth through political education, through a better understanding of their situation of double subordination, as well as by diversifying their economic skills through training.

Women's health and well-being and their impact on household survival

The majority of contemporary wars are not fought on formal battlefields, but in the homes and fields of ordinary civilians. Whether people are directly attacked or not, the threat of personal violence constrains them from pursuing their normal business. Working in their fields, searching for food, water or fuel, selling produce by the roadside or attending community occasions, they risk being attacked, raped, blown up by land mines or caught in crossfire.

When women become sole providers, their safety becomes critical to the survival of their families. A recent report from Malange, Angola, quoted an aid worker as saying that up to fifty mothers a week were being killed in crossfire or by land-mine accidents: "The mothers have gone out to the country to get food and have been either killed or blown up by mines... You presume they've been taken prisoner, they're dead or have had a leg blown off by explosions" (Shiner, 1994).

Conflict reduces levels of resource availability in society as a whole, and destroys health, welfare and education services. Women are particularly vulnerable to this reduction in resources and support. Their vulnerability is both physical (especially in the case of pregnant and nursing mothers) and social, in that women are at a disadvantage in accessing command of the resources of the community.

Reports from Somaliland (northern Somalia) describe how the destruction of health infrastructure during the war, which ended in 1990, continues to affect women's health. In the absence of effective medical services and personnel, complications of pregnancy and childbirth remain untreated. Disability is another serious problem following a war in which thousands of anti-personnel mines were scattered throughout the countryside by President Siad Barre's retreating army. Most of those who lose limbs from land-mine injuries are women and children, since they often need to stray off the beaten track (where mines are more likely to be sown), to work on their crops or round up goats and sheep kept near the homestead. With no prostheses available, disabled women have found it difficult to carry out routine household tasks: rejection by the husband often ensues (African Rights, 1994).

Beyond this, women are particularly vulnerable to sexual violence and rape. Media attention has recently focused on Bosnia, where soldiers have reportedly been urged to rape and kill women as part of the "war effort". Estimates of the numbers of women raped in Bosnia range from 20,000 to 50,000 or higher (Vulliamy, 1993). Yet it appears that rape may be routine in conflict situations, carried out mainly by troops, with or without the encouragement of their commanders. Burma, Philippines and Uganda are but a few of the countries where the number of women and girls raped by soldiers runs into the thousands (el Bushra and Piza-Lopez, 1994).

Marriage and prostitution enforced by the military are variants on the use of rape as a war strategy. Reports from Mozambique describe the virtual enslavement of young boys and girls in Renamo camps, where boys, themselves traumatised by violence, frequently inflict violent sexual encounters upon the girls, who risk being killed or starved if they resist. Long-term repercussions include unwanted pregnancies in girls barely old enough to cope with the demands of motherhood (McGreal, 1993). Women's testimony from northern Uganda also makes extensive reference to women being abducted from their children and husbands and forced into new "marriages" with their captors (ACORD, 1993c). For many women, accepting sexual relations with soldiers or other men in positions of power may be their only means of protection or escape. This strategy is a particularly important one in the case of young women, as for example in Northern Uganda where some mothers have adopted the tactic of marrying their daughters to soldiers at puberty to limit the risk of rape (Cécile Mukaruguba, personal communication).

The consequences of rape are extremely serious for women from the point of view both of their mental and physical health, and of their long-term economic survival. Emotional and physical impairment is increased if unwanted pregnancies or unwelcome marriages have also resulted. The loss of honour following rape may lead to the women concerned being ostracised, rejected by their husbands, or unable to find marriage partners later in life (Musse, 1994). The consequences for the community include, amongst others, accelerated spread of HIV/AIDS, the impact of which, in many countries, tends to be graver amongst women (Mworozi, 1993).

Personal self-esteem is part of the web of factors affecting people's physical and mental survival capacity. Self-esteem may be reflected outwardly in dress and personal hygiene, and may require standards that are difficult to maintain in a war setting. In Rwanda, married couples were found sharing the one garment they possessed: whichever spouse had to leave the house, wore it (ACORD, 1994). Somali refugees in Kenya valued the provision of shrouds by Oxfam as highly as food and shelter, and Oxfam emergency projects in Bosnia have recently been sending items of personal hygiene such as soap, sanitary towels and underwear in relief packages (Oxfam Emergencies Unit staff, personal communication). This is not simply an extension of the range of items covered, but an acceptance that maintaining self-respect is as important a need as those of physical survival.

Women's personal identities may be tied closely to issues of sexuality, marriage and family, and to values of loyalty, motherhood and conformity to culturally defined norms of behaviour. All these come under threat in conflict situations, as a result of rape, the death of, or separation from, husband and children, and lost potential for marriage and child-bearing. For many women, the family is the principal arena of self-identification; inability to provide food and protection strikes at their personal feelings of self-worth.

The issue of psychological stress and trauma in conflict remains underresearched. Reactions to stress involve a sequence in which initial shock is followed by efforts to cope with and manage the situation. This "coping" phase is critical and is highly influenced by a person's circumstances. Additional stress factors, such as the need to struggle to find food, have a negative effect on coping, while factors that offer support such as good social networks can aid recovery.

Studies carried out in refugee communities in Mozambique, Zambia and Central America have pointed to differences between men and women in the way people deal with trauma. These differences tended to reflect differences in gender roles and identities. Women worried most about family issues such as their relationships with their children and husbands, while men worried most about external factors such as access to health facilities. Women tended to show greater feelings of helplessness than men and, in these studies, to have less access to social-support networks and less time to make use of those that existed. The studies also indicated that single women or women who had lost their families or other social support were most at risk. However, marriage itself was an additional stress factor for some women (Oxfam Health Unit, 1993; Summerfield, 1990).

Gender relations in the wider community

Gender relations do not operate only at household level, but are reinforced by other social institutions of both a political and an ideological nature. For example, the relegation of women to domestic, private and "invisible" spheres within the household may be justified by reference to religion or tradition, and is reflected in – and reinforced by – women's relative lack of participation in public affairs and their absence from decision-making fora at national and international levels.

When families are under pressure during times of conflict, women often seek protection or support from the village leadership and committees, largely represented by men. Indeed, men may be instrumental in promoting mechanisms for protecting the vulnerable. In Palestine, for example, research done by a male academic showed that wife-beating is practised at some time in up to 50 per cent of households. The researcher was shocked by the high proportion of men (and some women) who accepted violence against women as normal, and even, in some circumstances, desirable (Bhatia, 1994).

The commonly held "ideal" view of women as being unable to participate in warfare, and hence vulnerable and needing protection, lends ideological support to community mechanisms for their protection. However, such attitudes are not well-suited to the reality of women's lives in wartime, which obliges them to become independent economic actors. Major adjustments are often required in order to enable women to participate in mechanisms for control of economic resources such as land, food-aid distributions, or market space. In Somalia and Somaliland, for example, the existence of elders' committees has been an important factor in keeping communities together during wartime and in guaranteeing survival and protection. However, these male-dominated organisations have often been reluctant to accept women into their ranks as producers and decision-makers. Elders expected benefits accruing to the community, such as food aid, to be channelled to the family through community structures (that is, men), rather than to individual adults (Jacques Gagnon, personal communication).

When fighting takes place within the community (that is, in civil war) the general level of violence tends to increase, including gender-related violence, and threatens interpersonal relations including those between women (Zur, 1993). Attitudes to women's personal behaviour often become more conservative and rigid during wartime. Women's idealised roles as guardians of the honour and identity of a culture may come under special scrutiny, and societies undergoing stress have been observed to erode women's human rights as a reaction to pressure from external forces. Thus, at the height of the Gulf War, Iraq introduced a law legitimising the murder of women suspected of offending family honour; while in Somalia the de facto military authorities instituted the death penalty for women suspected of mixing too freely with foreign soldiers (Maier, 1993).

However, new forms of organisation which promote effective mutual support have also emerged. Informal gatherings may coalesce within refugee settlements, around medical or feeding centres, uniting women who have been through similar experiences. On a more formal level, women's organisations may start up, often at the instigation of determined individuals, in order to offer concrete assistance such as health care or advice on joint income-generating or for specific strategic purposes. Women's groups in Mogadishu, for instance, aim to challenge the hardening of misogynist attitudes in an increasingly tense conflict situation (ibid.).

Much has been made of the fact that wars are waged mainly by men. However, stereotypes are belied by the presence of women in the military in many countries, and by the active support (logistic, cultural, economic) that women give male combatants. While men may be the ones who go to war, they are nevertheless taught ideals of manliness and stories of past battles by their mothers, wives and sisters, and are supported in their military tasks by the activities of women (Cock, 1989). Nevertheless, evidence from many conflict sites describes initiatives taken or led by women, lending moral force to non-violent resolution of problems. This may be done on an individual basis – giving food and shelter to travellers, for example – as well as by the use of more formalised means for expressing opinions. In the past, women in the southern Sudan, for example, joined up their girdles and stretched them between opposing forces when they felt that fighting had gone too far (Berhane-Selassie, 1994). The women of Juba, southern Sudan, in 1988 petitioned the government to help end the fighting, sick of seeing their husbands being killed, their children dying of malnutrition, and women falling to land mines (Lado and Yatta, 1988). The role of women in peace movements worldwide has been extensively documented by the Swedish Life and Peace Institute (Ferris, 1992).

Long-Term Changes to Gender Relations

Changes to the division of labour

The new productive activities which women adopt in wartime challenge previous perceptions about appropriate roles, and women's newly acquired responsibilities are likely to persist after the conflict period is over. In northern Uganda, the division of labour in maize cultivation, once rigidly defined, is unclear now: both women and men can be seen doing most tasks (ACORD, 1992b). Women's work now includes the provision of basic household supplies such as soap and sugar, which twenty years ago was the responsibility of men. Returning menfolk have not necessarily readopted their old roles; rather, women have tended to continue taking responsibility for essential household provisioning. This creates problems of readjustment for men as well as women, potentially leading to family breakdown and social dislocation (ACORD, 1993c).

The adoption of new roles may be welcomed by women as they recognise that their new skills can be empowering. Women who have learnt to express their previously untapped inner resources do not want to return to the dependency of their prewar lives. Women in Somalia, for example, declared that, having learned how much the community depended on them, they would never agree to return to their old roles (ACORD, 1993b). In particular, the new economic skills women may learn as a result of crisis may lead them to greater economic independence and hence self-confidence and respect.

The impact of demographic changes

The absence of men and the increase in proportion of female-headed households is one of several changes in household structure that may result from conflict. In time, this may lead to a demographic imbalance with short- and long-term consequences for patterns of marriage and household labour arrangements. In Cambodia, the demographic imbalance has had several negative consequences for women's personal life. Their "value" in the marriage market reduced, they have few choices of marriage partners: either accepting junior status as a second or third wife, not getting married at all, or continuing in unhappy or violent marriages. Educated and economically independent women may find themselves "on the shelf" if they are seen as being not compliant enough. Yet the stigma of being unmarried and the difficulties of coping alone economically are serious disincentives (Pok, 1994).

War, however, sometimes encourages women to rely less on marriage as a means of support. Having survived war with little help from men means that women may be less willing to "carry" husbands who do not contribute to the household economy and related tasks, and less willing to bow to social pressure against divorce (ACORD, 1993b).

Liberation movements

In exceptional situations, the community, instead of being overwhelmed by a set of conflicting interests over which they have little direct control, is led by a movement that explicitly bases itself on their needs. Such movements that promote popular participation in political processes at the grassroots may or may not adopt a strategy of positive reinforcement of women's position. But where they do, the outcome seems to be significantly different. In Eritrea and parts of Ethiopia, for example, the conflict has earned for women rights to have their voices heard in political fora, to be trained and educated, to fight in the army alongside men, and to be free from oppressive legislation and tradition in their personal affairs (Hammond, 1994; Wilson, 1993). Political understanding of the reasons for one's situation may be an important factor in trauma recovery (Summerfield, 1990; Zur, 1993).

However, the ability of liberation movements to maintain such gains after the revolutionary period is questionable. There appear to be significant problems in replicating these changes outside urban centres and in maintaining them over time. In Eritrea, for example, women with experience of political participation at the highest levels, who might be able to carve out opportunities for other women, are relatively few and have a struggle to maintain their access to funds, training and influence. Moreover, women who adopted new roles during conflict often find that in peacetime they must revert to more conventional "feminine" behaviour if they are to be accepted socially (Oxfam Gender and Development Unit, personal communication)

The potential for social transformation

Communities often face difficulties of reintegration once a conflict is over. Individuals are left with physical and emotional disabilities, communities with broken and distorted households, and nations with political sores to heal. Demobilised soldiers, many equipped with little but stolen arms, need to be rapidly integrated within their families and within the economy if they are not to become footloose and reckless. Recovery from conflict is thus a strategic threshold from which the outcome may be either positive, towards rebuilding, or a degeneration towards renewed conflict.

Changes to gender relations have undoubtedly taken place as a result of conflict. The most significant changes appear to be the loosening of the division of labour, changes in household structure and marriage relationships, the emergence of more and stronger women's organisations, and the challenge to stereotypes of women's and men's roles raised by the involvement of women in liberation movements. These changes provide openings in which more fundamental issues can be addressed if a climate of mutual confidence is maintained.

Changes such as these have been welcomed by women in many cases. Yet they have negative sides too. Often where changes in the division of labour allow women more flexibility, the main result has been to enable them to fulfil their responsibilities more efficiently, rather than promoting greater understanding of their position. In most post-conflict situations women have not acceded to increased control over economic resources even though their practical need for such control has increased. Reduction in support to women (through government services, for example) has been reinforced by international initiatives such as structural adjustment programmes, and the lack of protection for women and lack of respect for their human rights observed on the ground during war situations has not been seriously or effectively challenged by the international community (Ashworth, 1992).

Conflict rarely changes gender relations at a fundamental level, but simply rearranges them in a more or less functional way. Conventional images that men and women have of themselves and each other, which underlie their overt behaviour, may not change at all. Indeed, conflict may simply provide a stage on which existing conceptions of gender are played out and refined, resulting in women's subordination becoming sharper, if seemingly offset by new advantages. Juxtaposing conflict and gender raises questions about men as perpetrators and women as victims of violence. Women may participate actively in wars as soldiers and support personnel, and those who do not may still encourage or incite their menfolk to violence. And men are often unwilling victims of war just as women are – killed and maimed, driven from their homes, dragged off reluctantly to fight and be fought.

Yet armed conflict involves struggles for power in which women and men are caught up in different ways, given their differential access to power. Empowerment implies entrusting people with the means – intellectual and emotional as well as material – to exercise control over the decisions and resources that are important to them. Conflict is on balance more likely to disempower women than to empower them, as it attacks their physical and mental health, places obstacles in the way of their economic self-sufficiency, enhances the social attitudes which maintain their subordination. In short, the impact of conflict on women mirrors the impact of conflict on all the more marginalised members of a community, and indeed on all vulnerable communities. Rape is a critical element of this conjuncture, bringing together gender, conflict and power. It exemplifies the total domination and humiliation of the powerful over the powerless, and hence takes on the nature of a symbolic representation of conflict. The challenge of development in the context of conflict is to create the conditions where balanced interests, openly expressed and accorded respect by all, succeed in outlawing domination whether of women by men or of one group over another.

Development in Conflict: The Challenge to the Aid Community

Armed conflict situations represent critical thresholds in gender relations, in which options for positive change and re-examination of old assumptions present themselves. At such critical junctures, aid, if administered strategically, has the capacity to contribute towards the creation of a more equitable balance. Yet aid agencies, which on the whole fall victim to the same unequal gender relations that prevail elsewhere in the world, have been slow to develop the internal structures and mechanisms that would promote a holistic and developmental approach to emergency work. Much has been written elsewhere about the effectiveness of responses to conflict emergencies (see, for example, ACORD, 1992a, 1993a; Agerbak, 1992). From the point of view of gender work, however, there are several key objectives to keep in mind.

First, agencies should change the basic assumptions on which they plan their responses, away from the formulaic application of service projects (food, water, medicine) and towards a planning framework based on assessment of a broad range of community and individual needs – including those which do not appear to an outsider to be a priority but which may be vital in raising levels of women's self-esteem, such as recognising needs for underwear or sanitary towels, rape counselling or cooking pots.

Second, since these needs will include those of women and others who may be relatively "invisible" – often indoors, probably afraid to go out, and anyway outside conventional power structures – the assessment capacity of agencies must be upgraded to enable such people to be consulted and actively engaged in the planning process. This will involve, as a minimum, recruiting sufficient staff able to consult participatively with men and women at grassroots level.

Third, agencies must develop a clearer focus on investing in people on the ground, whether this means capacity-building for their own staff, recruiting greater numbers of women staff, making greater efforts to support a broad range of local groups, or changing their own management structures to encourage flexibility and sensitivity throughout the organisation.

Finally, the development community will not be able to rise to the challenge of gender and development in conflict situations unless they as organisations address the lack of gender awareness and gender competence within their own hierarchies, particularly at senior management level.

Note

1. This chapter is based on a report entitled *Development and Armed Conflict: The Gender Dimension* by Judy el Bushra and Eugenia Piza-Lopez, to be published jointly by Oxfam and ACORD.

References

ACORD (1991) "Sablaale District Development Programme (SOM 4): Proposal for a One Year Interim Phase Jan/Dec 1992", mimeo, London, ACORD.

———— (1992a) "Operationality in Turbulence", RAPP Document No. 5, mimeo, London, ACORD.

———— (1992b) "Rural Development Promotion Programme in Gulu, Uganda, Annual Report 1992", mimeo, London, ACORD.

———— (1993a) "The Relief/Development Debate; Some Lessons and Suggestions for the Future", Background paper for the ACORD Assembly Workshop, mimeo, October.

———— (1993b) "Sablaale District Development Programme Annual Report 1993", mimeo, London, ACORD.

———— (1993c) Unpublished interview notes of ACORD Gulu staff interview with Panos Institute.

———— (1994) "Development and Armed Conflict: Report of a Workshop Held in Kampala, Uganda in October 1993", mimeo, London, ACORD.

———— (n.d.) "Programme of Assistance to Southern Sudanese Refugees in Northern Uganda", mimeo, London, ACORD.

African Rights (1994) "War, Women and Family Life", project proposal for research and advocacy work, mimeo, London.

Agerbak, L. (1992) "Breaking the Cycle of Violence: Doing Development in Situations of Conflict", *Development in Practice*, 1 (3):151–8.

Ashworth, G. (1992) "Women and Human Rights", background paper for the OECD/DAC Expert Group on Women in Development, mimeo, London, CHANGE.

Berhane-Selassie, T. (1994) "Towards Conceptualizing African Women in Conflict Resolution", draft paper presented to seminar Institute of Social Anthropology, mimeo, Oxford University, 19 February.

Bhatia, S. (1994) "Arab Refuge Lifts Veil on Battered Wives", *Observer*, 20 March.

Brett, A. (1991) "Why Gender is a Development Issue", in T. Wallace and C. March, eds., *Changing Perceptions*, Oxford, Oxfam, pp. 1–7.

Cock, J., (1989) "Manpower and Militarization: Women and the SADF", in J. Cock and L. Nathan, eds., *War and Society: The Militarization of South Africa*, Johannesburg, David Phillip, pp. 51–66.

el Bushra, J. and Piza-Lopez, E. (1994) *Development in Conflict: The Gender Dimension*, Oxford, Oxfam-UK/ACORD.

Farah, A.Y. with I.M. Lewis (1993) *Somalia: The Roots of Reconciliation*, London, Action Aid.

Ferris, E. (1992) "Women, War and Peace: An Issue Paper", mimeo, Life and Peace Institute, Uppsala.

Hammond, J. (1994) "Women and Liberation Struggle in Northern Ethiopia", paper presented to seminar on Women and War, Institute of Social and Cultural Anthropology, University of Oxford, mimeo.

Lado, M and Yatta, R. (1988) "Petition to the Acting Governor of Equatoria Region", mimeo, Women's Development Centre, Equatoria Region, Juba.

Maier, K. (1993) Women Fall Victim to Somalia's Prejudice", *Independent*, 5 January.

McGreal, C. (1993) "Renamo Conceals Child 'Brides' of Boy Soldiers", *Guardian*, 11 June.

Musse, F. (1994) "Rape of Somali Refugees in Kenya", paper presented to seminar on Women and War, Institute of Social and Cultural Anthropology, Oxford University, mimeo.

Mworozi, E.A. (1993) "AIDS and Civil War: A Devil's Alliance", *AIDS Analysis Africa*, November–December.

Oxfam Health Unit (1993) "Effects of Conflict on Women", background paper for workshop on Development in Conflict: The Gender Dimension, Pattaya, Thailand, January, mimeo, Oxford, Oxfam.

Pok, P. (1994) "Gender in Armed Conflict Situations in Cambodia" Paper presented to workshop on Development in Conflict: The Gender Dimension, Pattaya, Thailand, January, mimeo, Oxford, Oxfam.

Shiner, C. (1994) "Children Starve in City of Orphans", *Observer*, 20 February.

Summerfield, D. (1990) "The Psychosocial Effects of Conflict in the Third World", *Development in Practice*, 1 (3): 159–73, mimeo, Oxford, Oxfam.

Vulliamy, E. (1993) "Pope Warns Raped Women on Abortion", *Guardian*, 1 March.

Wilson, A (1993) "Eritrean Women – The Beginning of a New Struggle", *African World Review*, May–October.

Zur, J. (1993) "The Psycho-Social Effects of 'La Violencia' on Widows of El-Quiché, Guatemala", *Focus on Gender*, 1 (2): 27–30.

UN Reform in a Changing World:
Responding to Complex Emergencies
Hugo Slim and Angela Penrose

Introduction

Humanitarian emergencies have never been simple, but since 1991 it has become increasingly common for the international community to describe a variety of humanitarian crises as "complex emergencies". The term is applied to what are regarded as a new breed of post-Cold War humanitarian crises, which are distinguished by multiple and simultaneous factors such as civil conflict, famine, displacement and a breakdown of national government. These ingredients have always been features of humanitarian crises, and, while such situations may have been increasingly common in recent years, they are by no means unprecedented. The complicating factor in recent years, therefore, is not so much the tragic ingredients of the emergencies themselves, but the widening range of international options for responding to them. These options have become available to the international community primarily through the post-Cold War United Nations and the new political space open to powerful Member States to explore in the "new world order".

Today's emergencies are just as complex as they ever were for the people who are affected by them and who endure them. To them, the addition of the word "complex" is gratuitous, and verges on tautology. It is the United Nations, and the leaders of its member states, for whom today's emergencies are really much more complicated, largely because they can now choose to get more directly involved on the ground, militarily. It is not just the options of more direct involvement which complicate today's emergencies, but also the nature of that involvement: once the international community intervenes through the United Nations, its actions all too often become part of the problem. This has been seen most clearly in Somalia where, as Farer (1993a) has observed, inappropriate management of the military intervention made "the UN a player rather than an honest broker in the country's unruly political life and ... [thus] set the stage for confrontation".

This chapter sets out the main reasons for frustration with the international community's response to humanitarian emergencies through the UN and its operational agencies. In the last three years, the UN has conducted a series of experiments in responding to complex emergencies in Iraq, Bosnia and Somalia. Each of these has demonstrated that, while the international context of UN action has changed dramatically, major structural obstacles remain within the organisation which potentially limit its capacity for conflict prevention, mitigation and resolution. The results show that there are no simple solutions. There remains a need for fundamental reform to tackle issues of mandate, coordination, resources and accountability.

New Scope for Humanitarian Response

The international community's new humanitarian dilemmas have come about since the disintegration of the former Soviet Union, and the subsequent rapid transformation in the international political order. With the end of the superpower standoff, the international community has become more free to act in humanitarian emergencies, and expectations of the UN have risen accordingly. In its 1993 Human Development Report, the United Nations Development Programme (UNDP) describes the changing situation as follows:

> Worldwide, there have been more than 100 major conflicts in the past four decades, taking the lives of some 20 million people. The United Nations was often powerless to deal with these conflicts – paralysed by vetoes by major powers on both sides of the East–West divide. Since May 1990, however, no such vetoes have been cast, and there has been growing demand for UN support with such conflicts. (UNDP, 1993: 10)

Since 1988 the UN has launched more peacekeeping operations than in the whole of the previous forty-three years of its history. At the beginning of 1992 there were 10,000 peacekeeping troops; at the beginning of 1993 there were 60,000 and by the year's end, some 100,000 UN troops were deployed in twelve operations worldwide (Lewis, 1993).

In January 1992, the UN Security Council met for the first time at head-of-state level, symbolising the new importance Member States attached to the role of the UN. The incoming secretary-general, Dr Boutros-Ghali, was requested to produce a report on ways in which the UN could more effectively carry out its peacekeeping and peacemaking roles. *An Agenda for Peace* was subsequently published in July 1992, and considered the capacity of the UN to increase its preventive diplomacy, peacemaking, and peacekeeping roles, alongside additional proposals for "post-conflict peace-building" and the all-important issue of adequate financing for peacekeeping operations.

During this period, a more immediate process of trial and error was moving ahead in humanitarian emergencies in Iraqi Kurdistan, the former Yugoslavia, and in the African countries of Somalia and Angola. The international community's initial policy vacuum on humanitarian crises was mirrored operationally by an institutional vacuum, particularly in the area of overall coordination and consistency of response. In Africa, this institutional confusion has exacerbated existing humanitarian crises, particularly in Somalia and Angola.

There can be no doubt that the UN has made serious attempts during the period to establish mechanisms that will ensure that complex emergencies receive an appropriate response. Working to its Agenda for Peace, it is more actively pursuing the resolution of conflict and humanitarian crises. But in its efforts, the UN is encountering numerous difficulties, some of which are the result of the limitations of its own charter and structure. Others are due to the priorities of its more powerful member states, and a general reluctance of the international community to develop and invest in the UN's long-term humanitarian emergency capacity.

Obstacles to UN Engagement in Complex Emergencies

The UN's new-found freedom to act and intervene in humanitarian emergencies has also revealed the inherent limitations of the UN Charter in the post-Cold War world, most notably in the way it is restricted in its ability to engage with the various parties concerned in humanitarian emergencies. The UN was created by, and is accountable to, nation-states and is not authorised to intervene in matters which are essentially within the jurisdiction of the state. The UN is therefore defined in its Charter as an organisation of states, and is established to relate politically and operationally to the institutions of state as its prescribed partners. This tension between the UN as a supranational body harmonising the actions of nation-states, yet restricted in its actions by what the governments of those states would allow, has been continuously present in the role of the UN.

In situations of disputed sovereignty like Somalia, Angola, Mozambique, Sudan and Liberia, where major emergencies may exist in areas beyond the control of the nominal state authorities, the UN has repeatedly found itself bound and gagged by its interstate mandate in the many sided realities of intra-state conflicts. As Scott (1993) has observed, the fact that the UN centres on the notion of national sovereignty, represented by its Member States, means that in recent years "humanitarian needs are often greatest at the point at which the international community has the least clear mandate to respond". The inability to adapt and respond to intrastate dynamics of conflict in many of today's emergencies has rendered the UN an unwieldy and often paralysed player in complex emergencies.

The examples of Somalia and Somaliland are illustrative in this respect. Since the international community's refusal to recognise the declaration of the new Republic of Somaliland in 1991, the United Nations agencies have encountered serious difficulties in working with national and regional health and educational structures. Official UN policy during much of the 1991–92 period was to enforce unity and reconciliation with the south. In this context, the UN continued to view Somaliland as part of Somalia and to manage their programmes there from Mogadishu as part of UNOSOM I and II. The refusal to treat Somaliland as a separate entity with administrative structures of its own, and with a less severe level of crisis, resulted in two policies that led to the inevitable withholding of resources from the area at a crucial time of potential rehabilitation and recovery. The first was the decision to bypass government structures in Somaliland and only to provide resources to NGOs in the area. This meant that key ministries were seriously under-resourced, lacking multilateral and bilateral funding.

Second, because Somalia was considered to be in a state of emergency, the situation in Somaliland, although much more stable, was considered to fall under the same blanket emergency definition. Consequently, it was only subject to categories of emergency funding with no prospects of longer-term development aid more appropriate to its needs at the time. In the health sector, for example, the extremely short and ad hoc planning cycles that resulted were not conducive to the long-term reconstruction and development required. A recent report describes how the "classification of international assistance as emergency aid affected the overall planning process for assistance ... in 1992 the UN produced a 90 day plan followed by a 100 day plan ... and NGO plans dependent on donor funds were also developed around a short-term planning cycle. The emergency classification intensified the perception of a need for urgent interventions rather than for rehabilitation and development programmes" (Forsythe, 1993).

In Somalia during 1991 and 1992, opportunities for rehabilitation and reconstruction were also missed by the UN's difficulties in engaging with the latter days of the Barre government and its successors. The failure of the UN to provide support to the vestigial professional institutions in the country prompted the following criticism:

> In its slowness to engage at that early period, the UN missed the opportunity of conserving and strengthening government structures and supporting the many committed and competent Somalis who demonstrated their willingness to keep systems operating. As the situation deteriorated, the humanitarian imperative became predominant, but from the end of the civil war there was also the imperative to halt the damage being done to the development process. It was vital to re-establish and resuscitate the local economy. It would have been easier to attempt this in early 1991 than very late in 1992. Undoubtedly, representatives of the UN agencies found it very difficult to deal with Siad Barre's regime

towards the end of its period of rule and the distaste felt for the lack of co-operation, the corruption and nepotism experienced by many of those attempting to administer assistance programmes was shared and understood by NGO representatives. The decision not to engage with those who had ousted Siad Barre is not so easy to understand, however. UNDP, despite having $50 million remaining in its budget, said that there were no government structures to work with and its budget could only be used for development purposes. It also appeared to be the policy of UNICEF and other agencies not to work through government structures. (Penrose and Timpson, 1993)

This kind of engagement crisis, which has afflicted the UN in Somalia and Somaliland, is partly the result of the organisation's state-centred mandate. But with so many of today's humanitarian emergencies involving disputed sovereignty and government breakdown, it is essential for UN operations to find mechanisms to support professional and civil institutions, even in the absence of formal political government structures.

Security considerations have proved to be another factor which have prevented UN humanitarian engagement with an emergency, and stopped UN relief operations for long periods. Somalia is perhaps the most extreme example, where UN staff were evacuated for a total of some eleven months during 1991. In the same period, organisations such as ICRC and Save the Children Fund were able to maintain expatriate and Somali staff throughout. Save the Children, for example, only evacuated their staff for a total of seven days in 1991, and like other NGOs was otherwise expanding its programme throughout the year.

The UN is not simply a humanitarian organisation. It is also a political organisation – a negotiator, a peacekeeper, a peacemaker and even an occupying force. There is, therefore, the need to clarify and disentangle the multiple, and potentially conflicting, objectives of the UN involvement in complex emergencies. In particular, this means drawing up clear ground rules for the modus operandi between humanitarian relief and military interventions. Recent experience of the so-called "military–humanitarian interface" needs careful examination, and a more rigorous code of conduct which seeks to define when and how the two functions need to be combined (as in food convoy protection or air supply), and when and how they need to remain separate (as in peacemaking).

Reform: Responding to the New Political Landscape

Attempts at institutional reform

An Agenda for Peace focuses primarily on the issues of peacekeeping and peacemaking. However, the UN's emergency capacity faces major operational challenges in other areas too. The equally important issues of the coordination, resourcing, budgeting and provision of emergency relief all hinge upon UN agencies' ability to work effectively with each other in crises. Such synergy is traditionally worked out on a case-by-case basis, through a combination of mechanisms including the nomination of Special Representatives, lead agencies and inter-agency groups to oversee the UN response in any given emergency. These ad hoc structures have proved to be of varying quality. Even where they work well at country level, there remains a big hole at the centre of the UN system, where coherent humanitarian policy, clear operational strategies and mechanisms to ensure accountability, are lacking.

The absence of systemic policy is not particular to its humanitarian operations, but is symptomatic of a wider institutional problem. The UN was not constituted as a supranational authority, and since its establishment the problem of policy coordination and coherence has persisted. The system is "polycentric", comprising a large number of different agencies, each with different and overlapping mandates. Yet these agencies are neither effectively integrated nor coordinated by "a central brain" (Taylor, 1993). Under existing arrangements, "the specialized agencies have constitutional independence from each other, and from the centre, and there is no central institution which has legal authority over them" (ibid.). In this context, the failure of the Economic and Social Council (ECOSOC) to manage the various components of the system as originally envisaged has been particularly marked, leaving no other UN institution with a specific watching or coordinating brief over the international community's response to humanitarian emergencies. In such emergencies, the multiple agencies which constitute the UN remain, as usual, largely independent.

In recent years, a twin-track approach has developed in response to this problem. First, as humanitarian crises have grown in their international political significance, the Security Council has emerged to take the lead in humanitarian policy-making and in setting the parameters for intervention. Second, the UN created the Department of Humanitarian Affairs (DHA) in December 1991, in an attempt to develop a new coordinating mechanism for its agencies' humanitarian operations. The DHA is discussed further below.

The Security Council: into the driving seat

The emergent role of the Security Council has been most striking in its various resolutions setting new precedents for humanitarian intervention. The first of these was Security Council Resolution 688 in 1991, which "insisted" that "Iraq allow immediate access to international humanitarian organizations to all those in need of assistance in all parts of Iraq", and initially provided the appropriate military muscle to back up such insistence (United Nations, 1991, para. 3). In Africa, the most notable example of

Security Council intervention to date has been its Resolution 794 on 3 December 1992, which authorised military intervention in Somalia by a Member State (the USA) under Chapter VII of the UN Charter "to use all necessary means to establish as soon as possible a secure environment for humanitarian relief operations in Somalia" (United Nations, 1992, para. 10). More than ever before, it can now be argued that at policy level the UN's response is determined largely by the Security Council itself. However, there are serious questions about the Council's selectivity and consistency, and its ability to distinguish between the humanitarian and the political dimensions of an emergency.

There have been growing fears among humanitarian agencies, both inside and outside the UN system, that "humanitarianism" is being increasingly equated with military aspects of international operations in complex emergencies. Whilst improved coordination between the departments of Political Affairs, Peacekeeping Operations and Humanitarian Affairs is necessary and desirable, closer integration has implications for the impartial and neutral provision of humanitarian assistance in conflict situations, as the military and the humanitarian agendas in such settings become increasingly inseparable. Current proposals aim to provide a framework for cooperation in both the planning and the implementation of humanitarian and peacekeeping operations, to ensure that humanitarian factors are taken fully into account in the planning of peacekeeping missions.

The Department of Humanitarian Affairs: leadership at last?

As mentioned earlier, the establishment of the Department of Humanitarian Affairs (DHA), following General Assembly Resolution 46/182 entitled "Strengthening the Coordination of Humanitarian Emergency Assistance of the United Nations", reflected the desire of the international community for the effective operational coordination of the UN agencies' humanitarian response. It was the result of considerable debate, consultation and reflection, and as such initially represented a potentially significant advance in the development of a global strategy for humanitarian relief.

The impetus for the creation of the DHA came from Western governments, international NGOs and others concerned by the inability of the international community to establish mechanisms to ensure the operational effectiveness of the UN response to humanitarian crises. DHA was given the responsibility of defining and asserting its role in terms of those functions: information gathering; early warning and preparedness; prompt and effective response; resource mobilisation; the management of the relief-development transition; training and capacity building; and accountability. The guiding principles of the resolution sought to establish a framework which recognises the linkages between the underlying crisis in development faced by many less developed countries and complex disasters, and which requires the provision of adequate resources to address the root causes of such humanitarian crises. In many respects these guiding principles represent a considerable advance in UN thinking on these issues. The importance of prevention, early warning and preparedness are emphasised, and the need to acknowledge a "continuum" from relief to rehabilitation and development is recognised as a key principle of UN humanitarian policy, around which UN agencies should cooperate and plan.

The wording of the resolution was the result of laborious negotiation between those who thought that UN assistance can only be initiated by the request and consent of the affected country, and those who felt that in certain situations of civil conflict such a request is unlikely to be forthcoming. The resolution tilts the balance towards humanitarian intervention, but carefully avoids any talk of the "right" to do so. As a final compromise, reference is made to the consent of the affected *country* and not the sovereign state. This terminology provides flexibility in exceptional circumstances, and allows the UN to provide humanitarian assistance in the absence of a government request. In this way, it is in line with the thinking of the secretary-general in *An Agenda for Peace*, which notes that "the time of absolute and exclusive sovereignty, however, has passed" (Boutros-Ghali, 1992). To address the issue of internally displaced people, the resolution calls upon those states whose populations are in need of humanitarian assistance to facilitate the work of those organisations providing relief aid.

At an operational level, the resolution gives the DHA a number of specific tasks which are intended to be the core functions of its co-ordinating activities. These include the preparation of consolidated appeals on behalf of the UN system during emergencies, and the management of a new Central Emergency Revolving Fund (CERF) of $50 million, which is to be drawn on by UN agencies in emergencies as immediate loans, but guaranteed against other donor pledges. The DHA is also responsible for chairing an inter-agency standing committee (IASC) to link UN and NGO operations. Crucially, the Resolution makes clear that the DHA is also responsible for "country-level coordination" of the UN system.

Personnel

The problem of inappropriate personnel and the lack of an emergency cadre of humanitarian professionals is also cited repeatedly, particularly by NGOs, as a crucial factor affecting the DHA's ability to carry out its coordination role, and a major brake on its performance and credibility in emergencies. In a 1993 briefing, Oxfam noted that "the quality of staff in the specialised agencies and DHA is uneven. Although very many of the UN staff with whom Oxfam has worked are very effective, the overall standard needs to be improved" (Oxfam, 1993). Similarly, the director-general of Save the Children Fund, Nicholas Hinton (1993) has identified a key area of improving the UN's "practical performance" in emergencies as "ensuring that important posts are filled with people of proper competence as leaders and managers".

Resolution 46/182 lays emphasis on the DHA's role in "country-level coordination". All too often, however, both the quality and quantity of DHA staff operating at field level has been inadequate. As Save the Children Fund has argued:

> Strengthening DHA's activities at field level remains a major priority and is best achieved by the deployment of high quality personnel with appropriate skills and sufficient management support.... Only with such staff and expertise, will DHA effectively achieve a comparative advantage in a coordination function within the system and maximise its contribution. (Save the Children Fund, 1993)

In addition to issues of staff quality and quantity, many of the UN agencies experience a tension – common to many NGOs as well – between relief and development professionals. In the case of the DHA, Paul Taylor (1993) has described "a visible clash between the traditional culture of diplomacy in the UN, and the new culture of relief provision, which requires rapid response, impatience with routine, and imaginative innovation". He further notes that for the DHA this clash of cultures is symbolically represented in the split sites of DHA's headquarters between the "traditional pin-striped suit" of New York, and the Geneva branch which is "straining to take on new clothes".

Since its creation the DHA has made disappointing progress: it has fallen short of expectations, and missed the opportunity to reform significantly the UN approach to complex emergencies. This has been most apparent in Somalia, where traditional approaches to humanitarianism have been visibly marginalised within the UN system in the wake of more military-oriented options. So far, DHA has failed to take, set and lead the humanitarian agenda with all its political, development and security components.

This failure has resulted from the institutional inadequacies described earlier, as well as the reluctance of the main agencies involved in humanitarian activity to explore enthusiastically a different model of coordination. With varying degrees of sincerity and commitment the various heads of agencies – UNHCR, UNICEF, WPF, UNDP, FAO – have all welcomed DHA in speeches to the Economic and Social Council and elsewhere. UNDP has issued comprehensive guidelines for cooperation between it and DHA. Yet an effective model of coordination as suggested by resolution 46/182 has yet to be constructed and implemented in a concerted fashion in a number of emergencies.

Resources and the commitment of Member States

A lack of donor support, compounded by inappropriate and still overly reactive budgetary procedures, has left DHA underresourced and therefore underrepresented in emergencies. In 1993, donors were asked to contribute $6 billion to humanitarian assistance, but committed about half that amount (Eliasson, 1993). Jan Eliasson, the first head of DHA, has spoken of "being constantly preoccupied with the question of resources", and has emphasised that "the level of humanitarian assistance in any situation ultimately relies on the donor community's willingness to contribute" (ibid.). The reluctance of Member States to invest in prevention-led systems in particular has meant that DHA has been unable to secure a foothold in emergent crisis situations where they might have been able to develop a coordinating role from the start. The essentially short-term approach to humanitarian emergencies remains a major impediment to the UN's ability to resource and develop a more integrated and coordinated humanitarian strategy.

Plugging the gaps?

Despite these constraints, the DHA itself has also been slow to make the most of its existing resources and mandate. From the start in 1992, DHA could have taken firmer and swifter measures to determine its role and identity by building on the full range of functions covered by resolution 46/182. The DHA's under-secretary-general's emphasis on "humanitarian diplomacy" was not enough. The specific tasks identified in the resolution are still undeveloped within the system, and DHA has yet to prove that it can coordinate these functions across a broad range of emergencies.

In particular, DHA has not attempted to take the lead in embedding early warning and prevention as the core of UN humanitarian strategy, both in political, technical and financial terms. The resolution authorised DHA to take this lead, but it has not done so intellectually or conceptually in its strategy or ECOSOC papers, nor operationally in the field. Like many of the concepts that proliferate in the literature on humanitarian response (including the related concepts of the relief–development continuum, and the strengthening of indigenous structures and local capacity) early warning and prevention are frequently discussed, but rarely operationalised. The importance attached to these issues in the resolution was neither accidental nor superficial, but the result of extensive study of vulnerability, and the accumulated experience of complex emergencies over two decades. The failure of the DHA to prioritise these aspects of its mandate suggests that past emphasis on conflict mitigation rather than prevention is likely to persist.

The one positive aspect of the enormous cost of peacekeeping operations is that they may provide the stimulus for a more serious look at what prevention really means. The lessons are legion, yet the press, the public, the politicians and donors, and it appears the UN itself, would rather spend huge sums on peacekeeping operations (higher by a factor of ten in Somalia than the humanitarian operations) than adequately resource early warning, prevention and rehabilitation measures. The cost and extent of possible peacekeeping operations and the experience of Somalia have prompted a further international reappraisal of UN strategy and operations.

In speeches to the opening session of the UN General Assembly in September 1993, US President Clinton and the British Foreign Secretary, Douglas Hurd – both representing governments which had urged the enhancement of UN peacekeeping capacity – backed away and demanded restraints on such activities in the future. They both insisted on strict tests before peacekeeping operations could be authorised. Both speakers underplayed the decisive role of the US in promoting peacekeeping and enforcement operations in the early 1990s, and the difficulties of adhering to tests and criteria for Security Council interventions in a climate where such interventions had become highly politicised and selective.

Issues of selectivity and consistency

Central to current policy discussions of humanitarian intervention or enforcement actions is the question of the equatability and consistency of response. Present thinking in this area is characterised by two views: those who are seeking greater adherence to the UN Charter and who wish to standardise the international legal framework for UN intervention; and those who take a case-by-case approach, arguing that practice will eventually create effective precedent. At the heart of these two views, there is on the one side a rejection of the principle of selectivity and on the other a preference for it. In *An Agenda for Peace*, the UN secretary-general made the case for uniformity and consistency by stating that "the principles of the Charter must be applied consistently, not selectively, for if the perception should be the latter, trust will wane and with it the moral authority which is the greatest and most unique quality of that instrument" (Boutros-Ghali, 1992).

At present the principles and practices regarding UN action are not applied consistently in every situation. Humanitarian crises are absorbing more and more time of the Security Council and the secretary-general, but each one is treated in an ad hoc manner, reminiscent of the way in which security threats were responded to in the past. With the end of the Cold War, the dominant powers on the Security Council, notably the USA, continue to take dramatic decisions almost unilaterally. Major decisions relating to peacekeeping and peacemaking are being taken without adequate consultation with UN humanitarian officials and without attention to possible negative impacts on civilian populations. There is a fundamental but complex opportunism at work here. Devoid of an overall international humanitarian policy, powerful nations are labelling selective interventions "humanitarian" in accordance with their own political priorities. This selection is therefore not so much based on the rights of the affected populations and principles of equity, as on meeting non-humanitarian national and international objectives, and the feasibility of intervention.

The humanitarian emergency in Angola is one obvious casualty of this selective approach. In the last forty-two years, Angola has suffered almost continuous war, from the struggle for independence from Portugal began in the 1950s to the present civil war still ongoing in early 1994. During that entire period, it has known only five hundred days of peace. However, UNAVEM II, which was set up after the Bicesse peace accord in 1991, has received considerably less support from Member States than other similar UN operations. The UN programme for demobilisation has been described as "just one example of how Angola's peace process has been undertaken on the cheap". It is reported that the UN had allocated less than $70 million to its peacekeeping and monitoring role in Angola, compared to $2 billion in Cambodia and $340 million on UNTAG in Namibia. On her arrival in Angola to oversee UNAVEM's operations, the UN secretary-general's Special Representative, Margaret Anstee, warned that she had been asked "to fly a 747 with only enough fuel for a DC3" (Economist Intelligence Unit, cited in Scott, 1994). Clearly the reasons for the foundering of the peace process, the resumption of the civil war and ensuing suffering were complex, but the lack of commitment by the UN's key Member States – most notably the ambivalence of the USA and France – seriously undermined the UN in the run-up to the elections and were a significant contributory factor to the renewed violence.

Accountability

A persistent feature of humanitarian assistance in recent decades has been the lack of a transparent system of evaluation and accountability of the international community's response to emergencies. Both the UN and NGOs are guilty on this count. The need for accountability is increasingly recognised in two main areas: assessment of operational performance, and human-rights monitoring. The former relates to the effective delivery of aid by relief institutions; the latter concerns the rights of the victims in emergencies, in terms of their entitlement to relief, and any abuses they may have endured at the hands of the relief system.

The recent emergency in Somalia has led once again to calls for the establishment of a permanent and independent body to monitor and report on the international community's conduct in emergency operations. In

May 1993, the human-rights organisation African Rights called for such accountability in the case of Somalia: "It is imperative that there should be a Commission of Inquiry into the events leading up to the launch of Operation Restore Hope ... The Commission should also investigate the success of UNITAF in achieving various security, humanitarian and political objectives." In the case of human-rights abuses, African Rights recommended that "UNOSOM II should set up an independent tribunal which can review any cases of complaint that Somalis have against soldiers belonging to the UNOSOM forces." Professor Tom Farer, the former legal consultant to the United Nations Operation in Somalia, has also called for a human-rights ombudsman to monitor human rights during the pursuance of UN emergency operations in Somalia, and in other similar humanitarian emergencies (Farer, 1993b).

The case for accountability of this kind is by no means confined to the Somalia emergency. The need for a standing commission, independent of humanitarian and military agencies themselves, to monitor international performance and to represent the rights of the victims, during and after all humanitarian assistance programmes, is now surely beyond doubt. Even if the extreme form of the "*devoir d'ingérence*" (the imperative of intervention) and the "*droit d'ingérence*" (the right of intervention) are unlikely to be accepted universally by the international community, there is a growing consensus that humanitarian assistance must be seen in terms of the rights of victims to relief, and the obligations on the international community to meet these rights as effectively as possible. Several decades of the current system of humanitarian assistance, with its individual agency mandates and the selective priorities and interests of its major donors, have shown it incapable of effective self-regulation, and it remains one of the few areas of human rights without an independent reporting mechanism.

Beyond its contribution to any particular emergency, the standing or permanent nature of such a commission to monitor the international response to humanitarian disasters would also encourage the development of institutional memory, and act as a depository for the lessons learned in humanitarian assistance. Many such lessons are all too often dissipated between agencies by their own in-house and often confidential evaluation process. By acting as both an arbiter and a centre of expertise in humanitarian assistance, a commission could also make a long-term contribution to the understanding and improvement of good and just practice in the field of humanitarian assistance.

Conclusion

The early 1990s have marked a sea-change in the scale and nature of humanitarian relief. The new freedom of the international community to act and intervene in humanitarian emergencies via the Security Council and through UN military operations is unprecedented. The operational options that this freedom has spawned have contributed to the increasing complexity of humanitarian disasters. In the face of such complexity, the main institutional arrangements for the UN's humanitarian response are still weak and confused. While UN humanitarian policy may now have found a "brain" in the form of the Security Council, the DHA has by no means asserted itself as the system's coordinating body. Instead, the DHA and resolution 46/182 are in danger of being totally ineffectual, in stark contrast to the military who look set to become the more natural partners for the Security Council and its "humanitarian" strategy.

At a more fundamental level, there are obvious signs that the current UN Charter is creaking under pressure both from raised international expectations of UN operations and the intra-state dynamics of the emergencies it is attempting to meet. Its ability to engage with all the appropriate parties in such emergencies remains in doubt, and its lack of overall policy on humanitarian emergencies leaves the UN vulnerable to potential abuse by those favouring a selective rather than a consistent response. Eliasson (1993) has identified the UN's "ability to deliver" as the acid test of the UN's humanitarian role. Major efforts still need to be made to improve the UN's coordination and its performance at the field level in emergencies if it is to develop this ability in the future. In political terms, the international community must also redefine the UN's terms of engagement with local structures, and be consistent in its response to humanitarian crises, if the UN's delivery of relief is to be flexible and fair. Finally, the creation of an independent commission to monitor humanitarian assistance and protect the rights of the victims of conflict-related disasters is essential if progress in this area is to be made and the commitment to humanitarian relief is to become anything more than a reactive and opportunistic part of the foreign policy of powerful member states.

References

African Rights (1993) "Operation Restore Hope: A Preliminary Assessment", London, May.

Boutros-Ghali, B. (1992) *An Agenda for Peace*, New York, United Nations.

Eliasson, J. (1993) "The Humanitarian Challenges for the UN: Lessons to be Learned from Bosnia and Somalia", address to Foreign Policy Association, New York, 15 December.

Farer, T. (1993a) "United States Military Participation in United Nations Operations in Somalia: Roots of the Conflict with General Mohamed Farah Aideed and a Basis for Accommodation and Renewed Progress", submission to the Committee on Armed Services of the House of Representatives, 14 October.

——— (1993b) "The Lessons of Somalia: The UN and the Future of Humanitarian Assistance", address to Somalia Symposium, London, Action Aid, December.

Forsythe, V. (1993) "Save the Children Fund Health Intervention in Somaliland: A Critical Analysis", London, Save the Children Fund.

Hinton, N. (1993) "Family Emergency at the Heart of the UN", *Financial Times*, 5 February.

Lewis, P. (1993) *New York Times*, 12 December.

Oxfam (1993), "Improving the UN's Response to Conflict-affected Emergencies", Oxfam briefing, Oxford, November.

Penrose, A. and Timpson, A. (1993) "The United Nations and Humanitarian Assistance: A Case Study on Somalia", presented to the Development Studies Association Seminar on the United Nations and Humanitarian Relief, Oxford, January.

Save the Children Fund (1993) "Briefing Note on the Role of the UN Department of Humanitarian Affairs", London, July.

Scott, C. (1993) "Humanitarian Intervention Revisited: A Review of Current Commentaries on the Legality and Practice of Humanitarian Intervention in the Light of Recent International Experiences", unpublished MSc dissertation, London School of Economics and Political Sciences.

―――― (1994) "Options for the Reform of the International System for Humanitarian Assistance: Liberia Case Study", London, Centre for the Study of Global Governance and Save the Children Fund, February.

Taylor, P. (1993) "Options for Reform of the International System for Humanitarian Assistance", Centre for the Study of Global Governance and Save the Children Fund, London.

United Nations (1991) Security Council Resolution 688 of April 5.

―――― (1992) Security Council Resolution 794, 3 December.

United Nations Development Programme (1993), *Human Development Report*, New York and Oxford, Oxford University Press.

Engaging with Violence:
A Reassessment of Relief in Wartime
David Keen and Ken Wilson

Introduction

Relief organisations have tended to conceptualise famines in terms of food shortages and needs, and accordingly to construct relief operations as logistical exercises. However, effective relief in conflict-related famines depends on understanding the relationship between aid and the dynamics of conflict. Without this understanding, relief operations may actually exacerbate famine. The crudest version of current practices involves assessing national grain production and population and deducing a figure for overall grain needs. A slightly less crude version involves subtracting exports from total grain production. Another involves assessing the numbers "in need" in particular locations, and dispatching a corresponding amount of relief goods, most often grain. While assessing needs during a famine is clearly important, this chapter suggests that those involved in relief also need to think about the relationship between relief and the local political economy. It is argued that more attention should be given to the impact of relief operations on the ability of different groups (both winners and losers) to pursue their own economic and military strategies. Of course, this means considering the strategies both of those suffering from famine and of other local actors. Groups in the latter category may include those affected indirectly by an influx of famine migrants, those in a position to relieve famine, those benefiting from famine and displacement, and those helping to create famine; clearly, these categories may overlap to some extent. Relating relief programmes to the strategies of winners and losers in conflict-related famines is essential, not least because the "delivery of commodities" approach is often impossible to implement during modern conflicts, due to political and logistical obstacles. With recent crises in Bosnia, Somalia and Angola highlighting the inadequacy of the current system of humanitarian response, a re-evaluation of current practices is long overdue.

What is urgently required is a better understanding of the complex web of political and economic goals which together determine patterns of famine and relief during civil wars. These will include strategies for political and military control and for profit. They will also include strategies for survival and attempts either to maintain livelihoods or to develop new ones. Organisations involved in international relief need to think about how they are responding to the dynamics of conflict, about which strategies they should be facilitating, and which they should be discouraging. This chapter therefore describes the articulation between the dynamics of conflict and the organisation of international relief, and uses this analysis to identify alternative strategies for humanitarian aid which are more likely to support losers than winners.

Depopulation: Functions and Response

Some functions of depopulation

Securing the depopulation of particular areas is likely to serve important functions for government and/or rebel groups. The classic counter-insurgency strategy involves attempting to deprive a rebel movement of recruits, material support and civilian "cover" by ejecting the civilian population (or large parts of it) from areas of rebel strength. Typically, these areas are rural areas, with the government attempting to maintain a series of garrison towns. Counterinsurgency tactics may also involve trying to scare people away from the rebel movement by attacking groups that are even vaguely associated with the rebels. This tactic is also likely to lead to depopulation in particular areas.

In addition to such military considerations, depopulation may hold out the prospect of important economic benefits, including access to natural resources like land, minerals and oil, economic exploitation of people once they are displaced (notably as cheap labour), and appropriation by the army and local elites of relief that was intended for the displaced. The importance of economic considerations in propelling depopulation is underlined by the fact that raiding, for example in Sudan, has sometimes been directed against groups minimally associated with rebel movements, allowing a transfer of assets from such groups but at the same time helping to turn these groups against the government. Thus, an unintended but perhaps also predictable side effect of economically inspired violence may be to strengthen the rebel movement in certain respects.

Mass migration is often regarded and presented as a by-product of famine; in fact, mass migration has frequently been an intended consequence of artificially created famine. This was the case during the famine in northern Ethiopia in 1983–85, which led to mass migration from Tigray to Sudan (see, for example, Human Rights Watch, 1991). It was also the case during the southern Sudanese famine that peaked in 1988, a famine that led to mass migration to Ethiopia and northern Sudan. In countries such as Ethiopia and Sudan the state has sought to deprive rebel movements of the populations on which their survival depended. A range of techniques was used: relief was obstructed and aid agencies barred from many famine-affected areas; market supplies were restricted (for example, through impeding transport or actual attacks on markets); normal routes for economic migration and remittances were blocked; gathering of wild foods was impeded; livestock were stolen or killed and crops destroyed, with government-supported militias helping to devastate rural areas. In these countries, drought served both to supplement and to disguise the techniques being used to create famine. In Mozambique, the forced removal (known as "recuperation") of rural people to government-held relief camps became widespread by 1989–90.

For their part, rebel movements may attempt to drive out populations from government-held garrison towns or from artificially created "villages" where people have been concentrated. In effect, the rebels are often attempting to reverse a process of forced urbanisation that has been sponsored by the government. Rebel movements may also contribute to the depopulation of rural areas which they cannot fully control or which are sympathetic to the government, exploiting the local populations for economic, military or even sexual purposes. Even in rebel-controlled zones, a rebel movement's overexactions, often carried out by weakly disciplined troops, can lead to the unwanted flight of peasants to government-held towns. This pattern was particularly marked in Mozambique, where Renamo alienated large numbers of people through its violence (including widespread sexual abuse) and heavy taxation.

In general, rural devastation and depopulation harms rebel movements since they rely on exactions – voluntary or involuntary – from the rural population. In Mozambique, rural devastation (with drought precipitating serious famine in 1992) helped to bring Renamo to the negotiating table and led to the 16 July agreement on humanitarian corridors. This proved to be a landmark in the peace process, even if the relief provided under it was limited. Whilst in part a victory for the government's counterinsurgency tactics, this rural devastation in Renamo areas also owed a great deal to the economic and military unsustainability of a looting and taxing war economy run by an authoritarian and extremely violent rebel movement.

The need for relief had earlier softened the stance of the rebel movement in Sudan. In 1989, the rebel Sudan People's Liberation Army (SPLA), desperate for relief for its areas from which there had been large-scale population movements, softened its opposition to relief supplies for government garrisons in southern Sudan. Together with a shift in what had been a clear pro-government bias on the part of international donors, this helped make possible – if only temporarily – a relief operation under Operation Lifeline that reached government- and rebel-held areas.

Depopulation, famine and the geography of relief

Humanitarian relief, while often presented as politically neutral, is rarely so in practice. As with development aid, it may be profoundly shaped by political inequalities, often reinforcing them. Given the functions of rural depopulation, particularly for governments, it may require firm action from international donors if such depopulation – with all the associated damage to rural livelihoods and risks to health – is to be prevented. Yet although international agencies were able to meet some of the needs of people displaced from southern Sudan in 1986–88 and northern Ethiopia in 1983–85, these interventions came at a point when the famine process was already far advanced and when people had already been forced to abandon their livelihoods. The degree to which rebel-held areas are helped may be more closely related to geopolitical contingencies than to actual need. In Sudan, the pattern of international operations tended to facilitate government attempts to depopulate parts of Bahr el Ghazal and Upper Nile. These areas were deprived of significant assistance until 1989, while substantial relief was provided to those who trekked east to Ethiopia, and limited relief was provided in 1988 to areas of northern Sudan that adjoined the war zone in the south. Similarly, bar a few muted protests, the international agencies facilitated a massive depopulation of the key war zones of Zambezia/Nampula and central Mozambique in 1990–91 by providing relief in the camps that were created.

Of course, relief agencies may find it difficult or impossible, from an ethical point of view, to decide *not* to provide relief to people displaced into government zones as part of a counterinsurgency tactic. It should be emphasised, however, that foreign governments and multilateral organisations – often conceiving of famine as no more than a "disaster" and frequently adhering stubbornly to the idea that a host government is essentially well-meaning – have typically been slow to react to famine in rebel-held areas. A concern with not infringing the "sovereignty" of host governments has been a major impediment, as has the (related) lack of any UN organisation with a specific responsibility for helping internally displaced victims of conflict or for working with non-sovereign governments. UNICEF has some tradition of flexibility, attempting to meet children's needs wherever they are, although this organisation too has been constrained by host government sensitivities. In the case of Mozambique, the reluctance to assist rebel-held areas has been overlaid by widespread international revulsion at the tactics of the rebel Renamo movement and evidence of its South African backing, leading to an almost total lack of relief to rebel areas.

The pattern of international relief in Mozambique at any given time appears to have had a profound effect on the course of the civil war. In 1986–87, when even government-held areas lacked large-scale international assistance, Renamo was able to extend its areas of control substantially. At this time, Renamo benefited not only from the lack of relief in government areas but also from the weak logistical support government garrisons were receiving. However, after 1987 and more especially after 1990, international aid played a key role in expanding government military control in northern Mozambique. International relief made it possible for large populations to live in government-held areas; it encouraged depopulation of rebel zones; it helped establish government legitimacy by facilitating the provision of government services; it provided indirect logistical assistance to the army; and it gave a kick-start to the floundering economy. Some people, for example Hanlon (1991), have suggested that international aid had the effect of weakening the state at the national level by taking over many of its functions. Whatever the merits of this argument, it seems clear that international aid also allowed an *extension* of state power at the local level (Wilson and Nunes, 1993).

It could be argued that this bias in assistance towards the government-held areas actually served to reduce the quantity of suffering in Mozambique, not only by maintaining at least a framework of government and services but also by shortening the war. This line of argument, while probably accurate, is a profoundly uncomfortable one. Many will feel it is inappropriate for relief organisations to "play God" and withhold relief from suffering people; after all, the same arguments about relief helping the rebels and lengthening the war have been made by the Sudanese government in relation to the SPLA. On the other hand, providing relief to Renamo areas might have carried the danger of institutionalising conflict. Most wars are resolved when one or both sides can no longer sustain military logistics or the economic and human costs of the war.

Depopulation, famine and the timing of relief

Unfortunately, donors' relief interventions are typically geared towards relieving the *final stage* of famine (starvation) through nutritional and health interventions, rather than tackling the political and economic processes (including human-rights abuses) that lead to this final stage and the out-migration accompanying it. Conflict-related famines frequently involve a loss of livestock, grain and other assets as a result of raiding, drought, forced sale, or some combination of these. These phenomena are often sponsored or manipulated by powerful groups to gain maximum profit and to provoke maximum distress. Donors need to use this type of analysis to redesign their responses and to redefine their mandates.

In southern Sudan, Oxfam did attempt to counter the process of asset loss at an early stage: it bypassed normal market mechanisms, controlled by powerful political interests, when it bought and distributed livestock to the poorest. However, bilateral and multilateral donors tended to take the view that relief interventions should not interfere with market mechanisms, and that helping those who still had assets could promote "dependency". When Oxfam lobbied the European Commission for a substantial relief response in the spring of 1987, Oxfam's Country Representative noted:

> When tackled on the question of nutritional indicators not being helpful in relation to pastoralists, [the EC official] replied that to make good a claimed food deficit when people still have livestock could cause dependency.... In his view, pastoralism was, in any case, non-viable and in decline all over the region.... It is important to note that USAID, UNICEF and EEC have all recently expressed similar views concerning pastoralism in the South, that it is on the way out and in twenty years would have disappeared anyway. (Oxfam-UK 1987)

Supporting coping strategies

Even when people have been uprooted from their home areas, their own economic strategies are likely to be the key to their survival. Many studies have shown that this was the case for Mozambican refugees and those internally displaced within Mozambique (Wilson, 1992). The greatest mortality in Mozambique was in places where the pursuit of livelihoods was curtailed or impossible; death rates were rarely simply a function of lack of food aid. Similarly, for famine migrants moving from southern to northern Sudan in 1987–88, it was not just the inadequacies of relief that led to very high mortality rates; also significant were adverse prices and restrictions on survival strategies pursued outside market mechanisms. Adverse prices included artificially high grain prices, low prices for livestock the migrants were selling, and low, even non-existent, wages in the context of resurgent slavery. As in most conflicts, restrictions on non-market strategies included constraints on freedom of movement and on gathering wild foods, constraints arising from the danger of attack by government-supported militias as well as from specific prohibitions by government officials. In many conflicts, landmines are also used to restrict civilian movements and activities, so as to reduce livelihood options. Despite the centrality of deliberate attempts to destroy or constrain people's survival strategies in conflict-related famines, aid organisations rarely seek to tackle this issue.

Relief and the Dynamics of Violence

Relief as an incentive for violence

The importance or relating relief interventions to specific patterns of conflict is underlined by the fact that, in some circumstances, relief may *increase* levels of violence.

The prospect of appropriating future relief supplies may be one motive for raiding. It may also encourage a range of other measures designed to restrict people's movements and group them in areas where they will attract international relief. In Mozambique, the prospect that concentrations of civilians would attract international aid served as a motive for raids and roundups by government forces and militias associated with the government. In Sudan too, the prospect of appropriating relief was one of the foreseeable benefits of famine for the loose coalition of army officers, merchants and militiamen who helped create the famine by organising, funding and carrying out raids on Bahr el Ghazal and Upper Nile.

Appropriating relief is unlikely to be confined to stealing it. It may involve the manipulation of exchange rates for imported relief supplies and logistical backup. It may also involve demanding "protection rents" or lucrative transport contracts to take relief through areas where "insecurity" can to some extent be controlled. This phenomenon was important during the famine in Somalia. In the later years of the Mozambique conflict, some aid agencies found they could get private convoys almost anywhere by giving generous contracts to local businessmen. The costs of such strategies were still much lower than airlifts.

Sometimes attacks may simply be motivated by a desire to obtain relief already distributed. During conflict in Mozambique, the arrival of relief supplies in a given area tended to intensify the fighting. For example, Renamo would often assault Frelimo-held towns shortly after aid had been delivered there. Reconstruction efforts and investment in particular areas of Mozambique also sometimes attracted raiding. In addition, locations playing a key role in relief logistics were commonly a focus for conflict. In circumstances where relief is scarce, the delivery of relief to one group or area may be particularly likely to incite violence. Correspondingly, in Somalia, the Red Cross stressed the value of *widespread* distributions.

Because relief resources are often large in relation to the budgets of governments and rebel movements, the struggle for control over these resources may be a key element in political conflicts *within* government or rebel movements. This can in itself expose aid agencies to significant delays and dangers. Splits within the rebel movement in southern Sudan have been linked with disputes over access to relief resources, as well as with a number of other issues such as whether the south should be separated from the north. In 1991, when elements of the Nuer attacked Dinka people around Bor and Kongor, one contributory cause seems to have been Nuer resentment at apparent discrimination against them in relief efforts (WFP/FAO/UNICEF, 1991). Later, in 1993, a perception that the largely Nuer "Nasir" faction of the SPLA was being favoured in United Nations relief operations appears to have fed into attacks by the mainstream SPLA on Nuer.

Recent civil wars in Africa appear to have been driven to a significant extent by economic devastation and an attempt on the part of various groups to escape destitution by violent means. This dynamic, which has apparently contributed to increasing factionalism and has added to the difficulties of securing peace agreements that are binding at local level, cannot be addressed when the only concern is to "target the most needy".

The potential of relief to diminish violence

If particular patterns of relief can increase levels of violence, the potential of relief for reducing violence also needs to be recognised. In so far as raiding and theft are being perpetrated by groups who are themselves in need of food (or funded by merchants speculating on grain price rises), bringing down grain prices may tackle some of the causes of violence. Even stolen relief grain could play a part in this, as has been noted in relation to Somalia (de Waal and Omaar, 1992).

In Mozambique, diverted international aid may have played a role in reducing raiding by impoverished government soldiers, in improving the morale of civilians, and in enhancing the protection the government was able to provide for them. These effects have to be weighed against corresponding dangers inherent in diversion, in particular the danger of encouraging raiding and roundups.

Specific kinds of relief can bring specific "payoffs" in terms of increased security. A cattle-vaccination programme among the Mundari in Equatoria, Sudan – organised by Oxfam and a local NGO – appears to have contributed to relatively peaceful relations among local chiefs, who realised that they could not hope to gain access to vaccines unless peace prevailed in their respective areas (Almond, n.d.). In 1989, relief to southern Sudan under Operation Lifeline brought important benefits, as did the July 1992 agreement on humanitarian corridors for Mozambique. These probably lay less in the direct effects of relief delivered than in the limited peace which accompanied deliveries, and the associated opportunity to resume something approaching normal economic activities (see, for example, Deng and Minear, 1992).

In many parts of the world, the prospects for a lasting peace depend on weaning various groups away from violent strategies that have, for them, served important economic as well as political purposes. A related task is to use aid to bolster democratic, peaceful elements in any given society, and to enhance their ability to secure the loyalty of those elements (often young men) who may be lured into more violent strategies by the absence of other kinds of opportunities. In Somalia, promising approaches include channelling significant rehabilitative aid through clan elders, and supporting the administration in the nascent northern republic of Somaliland. In Iraq, the democratic administration of the Iraqi Kurds faces a slow decline unless international aid is used to counter the economic blockade imposed by Baghdad (Keen, 1993). Properly directed, aid can play a vital role in reducing violence and human-rights abuses, and in allowing people to carve out some form of political protection for themselves. This means understanding how power is exercised *at the local level*, and not simply engaging in (probably counterproductive) military strikes against villainous and allegedly all-powerful figures "at the top", as for example in Somalia against General Aidid and in Iraq against Saddam Hussein. In so far as aid can reduce levels of violence, the benefits may vastly outweigh any direct benefits involved in distributing particular commodities, such as food.

The presence of foreign relief organisations in areas outside government zones may counter rural devastation and depopulation not only by providing material relief but also by deterring, or at least publicising, human-rights abuses in that area. These human-rights abuses require careful investigation and analysis and are unlikely to be confined to outright fighting or the use of food as a "weapon of war" by one side or the other. In particular, abuses of human rights facilitated by war (permitting the powerful to co-opt labour, demand payments for physical protection, and various other forms of exploitation of groups considered "fair game" in the context of civil war) may be more detrimental than damage arising directly from fighting. Markets are likely to be severely distorted by the threat of force, even where actual violence is not carried out. The potential role of aid agencies and international donor governments in restraining and publicising these abuses is considerable, but, to date, very few have given proper attention to this role.

The relationship between aid donors and human-rights issues has an additional disturbing dimension. A key reason for this continuing neglect of human rights is the risk of disfavour from the host government. For NGOs this may mean their expulsion from the country. In situations of conflict, the interests of security services and international aid agencies frequently converge. Ever since the Malaya and "Mau" emergencies of the 1950s, and drawing on the Anglo-Boer war at the turn of the century, military strategies against guerrillas have involved the creation of concentrated settlements or camps in which civilians can be more easily controlled. The main constraint on this option for governments is the enormous cost of sustaining people in these camps. Meanwhile, international relief aid is dependent on the visibility of aid provision in the media and on logistical access to concentrations of people in the terminal stages of distress. Despite two decades of recognition that camps are a menace to life, livelihood and long-term recovery for the people involved, it has proven almost impossible for large-scale relief programmes run by international agencies to take place outside camp environments, where delivery and distribution can ostensibly be made more easily, to discernible numbers of beneficiaries with measurable results. Particularly in the context of conflict-related famines, aid agencies have often focused on ambitious programmes in relatively easily accessed, controlled environments, where staff, visitors and donors can tell something "significant" is being achieved. This was the pattern discerned in programmes supporting Mozambican refugees in Zambia (Black et al., 1990).

Thus, whilst agencies may disagree with the brutality of roundups of refugees and the displacement of people in war zones, these actions nevertheless provide them with the context for their work, and they may therefore share a macabre and indirect common interest in creating camps. Even for the relief agencies who strongly oppose such actions – and the number is increasing – there remains a dilemma. On the one hand, the urgent humanitarian needs of populations rounded up demand attention: they are likely to be among those in greatest need and may otherwise face the prospect of mass mortality. Moreover, cooperation with the government authorities offers the hope of influencing the government "from the inside". On the other hand, to support such populations is to invite further displacement. It also poses the risks that the agency will lack staff and resources for other important activities where more cost-effective action might be possible; for example, interventions aimed at populations who have not yet reached the stage of destitution. Furthermore, separating refugees or internally displaced people into camps may constrain their ability to pursue economic activities; for example, by restricting relationships with the local community, or by confining people to areas where there is intense pressure on resources. The apparent assumption that refugees and internally displaced people are passive victims waiting for aid is likely to be particularly unhelpful, as is an excessive focus on providing novel socio-economic systems for refugees in settlements and camps (for example, production and trade in handicrafts or foodstuffs). Such schemes have been common for refugees across Africa, but have rarely met with success (see, for example, Black et al., 1990).

Anticipating obstacles to relief

Relief will be affected by, as well as affect, political and economic processes in a given society. Quite apart from the manifold military and economic benefits that may be offered by processes of depopulation, famine brings a range of price movements from which there are likely to be powerful beneficiaries. In Sudan, as in many African countries, army officers played a role in restricting supplies of relief and commercial food to garrison towns where they were profiting from the sale of expensive grain. In part because of vested interests in famine itself, targeting relief to particularly needy groups may be difficult or impossible if no account is taken of the needs and strategies of more politically influential groups, whose cooperation in relief operations is likely to be essential. Political difficulties in targeting should be acknowledged – and planned for – in advance, rather than simply noted in retrospect. And aid agencies' perceived neutrality may depend on distributions of assistance to a wide range (geographically and socially) of beneficiaries. Reaching the rural poor may depend on planning distributions to powerful clans or ethnic groups, to government officials and/or soldiers, or to urban groups more generally (de Waal and Omaar, 1992; Keen, 1991; Keen, 1994).

Aid donors face another dilemma here, however, since such "sweeteners" may increase the numbers of people with a vested interest in continued crisis, as well as providing resources for escalating violence. In so far as resources are directed at groups not suffering from famine, it will be important to direct them at groups who have some interest in promoting peace and perhaps in using relief resources to secure support for a non-belligerent stance.

Conclusion

The broader effects of relief aid – on the strategies of those suffering from, or in some sense contributing to, famine – are unlikely to be easy to assess. However, famines cannot be properly tackled without considering these effects. Even grain distributions may flounder unless the attitude of powerful local groups towards such distributions is understood. Proper attention to the impact of relief programmes – and their relationship to the dynamics of conflict – is too often pushed aside by a narrow focus on counting "numbers in need" and sending them a corresponding quantity of grain.

In the context of internal conflicts, it is important to go beyond analyses which see famine as occurring when victims are "caught in the crossfire". Indeed, the main problem of civilians in contemporary civil wars is that they are themselves the central object of the conflict. Famine, displacement and relief dependence are usually not so much a by-product of war as a specific military and political objective. The case of the former Yugoslavia has further highlighted the shortcomings of purely humanitarian relief interventions in circumstances where population displacement is a primary *goal*, rather than simply an unfortunate consequence, of conflict (see, for example, Jean, 1992).

Whilst in the short term relief may be important as a purely nutritional or health intervention, in a wider sense relief will affect (and be affected by) the political and economic processes contributing to famine. International aid does not and cannot stand outside economic and political processes in some separate "humanitarian" sphere. This is only too well understood by local elites or military factions seeking to manipulate hunger and international aid; it is ignored by international governments and organisations at their peril.

What is urgently required is for aid donors to give greater attention to protecting the human rights and economic strategies of the most vulnerable groups. Of course, this is easier said than done. One key starting point in any attempt to improve the effectiveness of international aid is to obtain a deeper understanding of political and economic processes in societies where aid organisations are intervening. Involving civilian organisations in the design and implementation of relief is another key area. A third is providing institutional and relief support to local authorities or elders with a genuine interest in protecting civilians from violence. A fourth is giving greater attention to the development of infrastructure and markets in areas where refugees and internally displaced people find themselves. A fifth is setting up proper systems for monitoring human-rights abuses, and introducing mechanisms which allow monitoring to be translated into corrective action. This means changing what is counted and measured – moving away from a concentration on measuring nutritional status and towards assessing levels and types of violence. Donor organisations, notably within the UN, need specific mandates for assisting the victims of conflict at a point before they begin to starve.

References

Almond, M. (n.d.) *Pastoral Development and Oxfam in the Sudan*, Oxford, Oxfam.

Black, R., Mabwe, T., Shumba, F. and Wilson, K. (1990) *Ukwimi Refugee Settlement: Livelihood and Settlement Planning. A Preliminary Report of Field Research and Recommendations*, King's College, London/Refugee Studies Programme, Oxford.

Deng, F. M. and Minear, L. (1992) *The Challenges of Famine Relief: Emergency Operations in the Sudan*, Washington, The Brookings Institute.

de Waal, A. (1989) *Famine that Kills: Darfur, Sudan, 1984–1985*, Oxford, Oxford University Press.

de Waal, A. and Omaar, R. (1992) "The Lessons of Famine", *Africa Report*, November/December.

Hanlon, J. (1991) *Mozambique: Who Calls the Shots?*, London, James Currey.

Human Rights Watch (1991) *Evil Days: 30 Years of War and Famine in Ethiopia*, New York, Washington, Los Angeles, London.

Jean, F., ed. (1992) *Populations in Danger*, London, Médecins Sans Frontières/John Libbey.

Keen, D. (1991) "Targeting Emergency Food Aid: the Case of Darfur in 1985", in S. Maxwell, ed., *To Cure All Hunger: Food Policy and Food Security in Sudan*, London, Intermediate Technology Publications.

—— (1993) *The Kurds in Iraq: How Safe is Their Haven Now?*, London, Save the Children Fund.

—— (1994) *The Benefits of Famine: A Political Economy of Famine and Relief in Southwest Sudan, 1983–89*, Princeton University Press.

Oxfam-UK (1987) "Policy Situation Report no. 6", 1 March, Oxford, Oxfam.

Quan, J. (1987) *Mozambique: A Cry for Peace*, Oxford, Oxfam.

WFP/FAO/UNICEF (1991) "Crop, Food and Emergency Needs Assessment Mission, Southern Sudan", October–December.

Wilson, K. (1992) *A State of the Art Review of Research on Internally Displaced, Refugees and Returnees from and in Mozambique*, Swedish International Development Authority/Refugee Studies Programme.

Wilson, K.B. and Nunes, J. (1993) "Repatriation to Mozambique: Refugee Initiative and Agency Planning – The Case of Milange District 1982–1991", in T. Allen and H. Morsink, *When Refugees Go Home*, London, James Currey.

Conclusion
Mark Duffield, Joanna Macrae
and Anthony Zwi

Introduction

Complex emergencies engendered by war present one of the most formidable challenges to the post-Cold War order. As the contributions to this book suggest, responding to this challenge will require far more than increasing the numbers of food parcels sent from North to South, and from West to a fragmenting East. The causes of conflict are deeply rooted in historical and contemporary economic and political relations, and will not be subject to simplistic solutions. Indeed, it has been argued that international "solutions" may be part of the problem. The poverty of existing responses to war and hunger has become increasingly apparent in the events of Rwanda, Kurdistan, Bosnia and Angola, placing new strains on the international community.

This book has sought to analyse the nature of contemporary conflicts and humanitarian crises, and to re-evaluate existing responses to them. This concluding chapter aims to draw the multiple strands of earlier analyses together and to identify more appropriate approaches to conflict. It reviews the changing nature of conflict and changing perceptions of conflict; it then re-examines the international response to conflict-related emergencies, concluding with a discussion of priorities for future policy action.

Complex Emergencies: Changing Contexts and Changing Concepts

In the past, conflict, economic decline and famine were often examined in isolation. Such an approach is no longer tenable. As the rationale of the Cold War has been stripped away, the deep-rooted and interrelated structural factors which continue to promote war have been revealed. The limitations of past paradigms have been exposed and new analyses have developed which explore the linkages between famine and war. In examining the factors promoting national and local conflicts, these new

approaches have highlighted the limitations of existing humanitarian interventions. At a time when the international community is experimenting
with an increasing range of instruments to respond to conflict, developing
further our understanding of the origins of war and vulnerability will be
particularly important. This section draws on earlier chapters to highlight
the features of contemporary conflict which promote hunger.

The genesis of conflict

Until the 1960s, African economies typically enjoyed significant growth
and development, albeit inequitably distributed. Since the 1970s, Africa's
fortunes have been reversed. The pace of its decline has coincided with
a period when the economies of Southeast and East Asia have developed
rapidly, enabling them to compete effectively with those of an ailing West.

In response to the global crisis of the 1970s, African governments, and
their Western advisers, sought to intensify the production of exports,
particularly those destined for Western markets (see Chapters 3 and 5).
Ironically, as they were doing so, Western economies began to disengage
from the continent, increasing the concentration of the global economy
within and between the emerging North American, Western Europe and
East Asian economic blocs. As the economies within these blocs under-
went a historic technological and materials revolution, in Africa trade and
exports were dominated by the same raw materials that it had traditionally
farmed and mined.

This policy failed in several respects. Increasing state investment and
borrowing saw the massive growth of debt as terms of trade for exports
from Africa declined. Perhaps more importantly, intensification of production accelerated environmental decline, asset depletion and the erosion
of the subsistence base, leading to increased impoverishment. In market
economies – for example, in Sudan – intensification took the form of the
expansion of mechanised agriculture. Vast areas of land, once the domain
of pastoralists, were farmed to exhaustion. In planned economies such as
Ethiopia, intensification took the form of substantial population movements in villagisation and relocation programmes. In Angola, the needs of
large-scale commercial farms were promoted at the expense of the land-
based majority. These programmes eroded the asset base of the rural
poor, promoted the spread of poverty, increased the rate of urbanisation,
and exacerbated tension over remaining resources.

These transformations in the economic foundations of Africa, inspired
by increasing commercialisation and changes in the relationship between
producers and the state, have had a profound effect on social relations.
As households and communities attempt to survive in an increasingly
hostile environment, many of the coping strategies they have been forced
to employ have further hastened the pace of economic, environmental

and social decline. The growth in labour migration, for example, has undermined the position of elders, as the youth have sought, and occasionally found, new sources of wealth and influence. Gender relations have also been transformed, and new burdens have been placed on women as family units have split, and conflict and HIV disease have taken their toll (Duffield, 1981; el Bushra and Piza-Lopez, Chapter 10 in this volume). Relations between ethnic groups have changed as a shrinking resource base has reinforced the value of subsistence assets and increased local tension. Violence has emerged as a strategy to secure economic and political power and survival under these unstable conditions.

The structural crisis in Africa's formal economies provides a starting point for the analysis of war and violence. Since the end of the Cold War there has been a shift away from an emphasis on the external causes of conflict in favour of attempting to analyse the internal factors that shape the nature and form of conflict (see Duffield, Chapter 3; Keen, Chapter 6; de Waal, Chapter 8; Keen and Wilson, Chapter 12). Such analyses explain conflict and famine as the outcome of competing strategies between rulers and ruled, the powerful and the weak, the winners and losers in the complex socio-economic situations which have arisen.

The emergence of war economies

A number of common military strategies have emerged in Africa. Governments have pursued tactics which typically depopulate areas as an attempt to corral populations, deny opposition movements any source of potential support, and gain control over large areas of land. Depopulation has been achieved through a variety of means: commercial and transport infrastructures in opposition areas have been destroyed, civilians have been intimidated and terrorised, and land mines have been planted widely. Food aid and other essential supplies have also been denied to such areas, or supplied selectively, in an attempt to attract and sustain populations.

Opposition movements have used more diverse strategies. In the conflicts in Tigray and Eritrea, relations of political reciprocity between movements and people developed during the 1970s and 1980s, (see Hendrie, Chapter 7 in this volume). In such cases, the experience of conflict has promoted accountability and democratic forms of organisation: whether these can be sustained in the post-conflict period, remains to be seen. More typically, however, many of today's movements have adopted a predatory relationship to civilians (see Duffield, Chapter 3; and de Waal, Chapter 8, in this volume). In government-held areas, especially in southern Africa, opposition movements have targeted the educated middle class for elimination, and systematically destroyed the physical infrastructure. Predatory and nonreciprocal relations toward civilians in areas controlled by movements have typically hinged around taxing systems.

These range from direct appropriation under varying degrees of coercion, to the establishment of peasant agricultural areas to support the movement. These patterns of political and economic predation have been perpetrated in Mozambique by Renamo, in Angola by UNITA, and in southern Sudan under the various factions of the SPLA.

These predatory regimes and movements in Africa, and increasingly elsewhere, have contributed to the development of what might be called autonomous war economies. Through control and development of parallel economic activities, internal taxation, asset appropriation and manipulation of relief aid, such economies support political structures which can now function beyond the bounds of conventional state relations. To a large extent the dominant groups within such economies are sanction-proof. Such war economies, now common in many parts of Africa, Eastern Europe and the Caucasus region, have to be seen in relation to the collapse of the formal economy outlined above. In the absence of legal means of survival, extra-legal structures have emerged. In this respect, war economies are a relatively new phenomenon. The political solidarity which characterised the popular movements in the Horn, for example, belongs to a more orderly Cold War era (Jean, 1993; African Rights, 1993). The movements and rogue regimes of today have far more narrow interests.

The costs of war

The fact that such regimes and movements are predatory in nature means that they are intrinsically disaster-producing. The survival strategies of the politically dominant centre upon the displacement and impoverishment of the losers, a key component of today's emergencies.

Past attempts to gauge the formal costs of war in Africa have focused on assessing the impact of conflict on mortality, the physical damage to infrastructure and the loss of GNP. While important, the danger in this approach is that it may assess the effects of war primarily in terms of physical destruction. The corresponding relief and rehabilitation strategies that have developed from this view concentrate on physical inputs; for example, drugs, educational materials and the refurbishment of buildings and roads. It defines the emergency in the only way that donors are prepared to respond. Yet the social and civic costs are of far greater importance. That is, the erosion of the subsistence asset base creates a growing pool of impoverishment, the loss of a skilled and educated middle class to run the economy and education and health services, the loss of capacity at government and policy-making levels, and the emergence of alternative and extra-legal forms of survival. Unless such issues are tackled, present relief strategies that focus on the delivery of commodities and, at best, on physical repair, will simply continue to feed the emergency.

The social costs of war have been immense. Yet these costs must be placed within a wider context of the social costs of structural under-development and maldevelopment inherited in the post-colonial and inde-pendence period, deepened by subsequent national economic policies, and reinforced by global inequalities of aid and trade. The growth of insecurity and the manner in which internal wars are fought, especially the availability and employment of modern weapons, have accentuated these earlier trends.

Banditry and the emergence of predatory movements, for example, have further eroded the position of traditional structures, threatened first by colonial policies and subsequently by the commercialisation of rural life. An extreme form of this inversion of social life and values has been the appearance of child soldiers. Shorn of the sanctions of kinship, rape and the sexual exploitation of women have also become a common ad-junct to violence. Following the breakdown of normal relations between ethnic groups, in several places slavery has reappeared.

The International Response to Complex Emergencies

The response of the international community: putting NGOs on the front line

Since the mid-1980s, international agencies, particularly NGOs, have become major players on an African stage characterised by political instability and economic decline. Bilateral and multilateral agencies have promoted the development of the private, not-for-profit sector to imple-ment their programmes. This increased reliance on NGOs to implement international policy has been particularly heavy in the sphere of inter-national relief. The expansion of NGOs in Africa has been the result of international attempts to respond to the crisis of social development associated with governmental collapse, war and violence, and the sub-sequent breakdown of public welfare structures.

An important development is that NGOs have, of necessity, had to find ways of working in the context of ongoing conflict. Lacking a man-date or means to end violence, faced with the limitations of the UN, and with bilateral donors unwilling to deal directly with national governments and popular or predatory movements, NGOs have been placed on the front line of complex emergencies, as they seek to deliver humanitarian aid in war situations. Feeding the victims of ongoing structural and armed violence represents an essentially new response to Third World conflict, whether in the context of compensatory programmes implemented under structural adjustment programmes or that of a conflict-generated emergency.

Until the mid-1980s, most UN peacekeeping missions had demanded a ceasefire before the international community intervened (Goulding, 1993). Being able to mount humanitarian operations in war situations became a hallmark of NGO "flexibility" during the latter phases of the Cold War and its immediate aftermath.

NGOs have played an important role in mitigating the effects of humanitarian crises accompanying conflict, often enabling the survival of significant numbers of people. However, evidence from the Horn and southern Africa suggests that their interventions, supported by international donors, have had significant and unpredicted side effects: relief operations have often contributed to the conflict dynamic, and supported the growth of war economies (see Chapters 3 and 12; also Scott-Villiers, Scott-Villiers and Dodge, 1993).

While there have been a few cross-border operations such as those into Tigray and Eritrea, NGO safety nets have usually operated in government-controlled areas. From such locations, relief operations have often provided indirect support for counterinsurgency tactics. Where governments and movements have depopulated areas, for example, NGOs have often taken on the role of supplying food aid to the displaced population. While such support may be crucial in the short term, in the longer term it may tacitly reward military strategies which herd civilian populations into closed camps with all their associated health risks. The sharp moral dilemmas raised by such situations are often lost in the high-profile media attention given to food deliveries. These images in turn are often used to sustain support for such interventions among Northern constituencies.

The international aid system may tacitly fuel conflict in a number of other ways. Since the 1970s, the diversion of food aid for military purposes has been widely acknowledged. In the 1980s, more substantial gains were made by governments able effectively to tax relief inputs by imposing fixed exchange rates; large-scale relief operations have therefore constituted a major source of hard currency for regimes at war. This has been clearly apparent in Sudan and Ethiopia. Equally, they may contribute to the further decline of remaining civil institutions if they operate largely through parallel channels, which limit the development of national capacity for coordinated action for relief and development. Hanlon (1991) argues that such a pattern emerged in Mozambique where government institutions were typically bypassed by humanitarian agencies, reducing still further the government's capacity to ensure the equitable distribution of resources. Similarly, in Somalia and Somaliland, the UN's reluctance to work with the vestiges of public institutions undermined attempts to redevelop the shattered civil institutions that are essential to a sustainable peace.

While the international relief system has readily taken on a role in the provision of physical resources, it has been less active in developing strategies concerned for the protection of conflict-affected communities. NGOs and other operational agencies, such as UNHCR, have often been reluctant to speak out openly about human-rights abuses, of which they often have direct evidence. The advocacy role of NGOs is frequently underplayed in favour of operational activities, despite, or perhaps because of, their often close relationship with bilateral and multilateral donor communities. The independence of many NGOs has thus become sacrificed to the wider international need to be seen to respond to humanitarian crises in an apparently "neutral", apolitical way. The reality of conflict situations suggests, however, that relief aid cannot be politically neutral.

The international response: the changing role of the UN

Freed of the constraints of the Cold War, since 1989 a "new" UN has emerged which has proven to be more interventionist than previously. The main feature of the current approach is that it builds on the earlier NGO strategies to attempt to work with ongoing conflict. From the failed Operation Rainbow (1986) in South Sudan, to Operation Lifeline Sudan (1989) and the Special Relief Programme for Angola (1990), through negotiated "corridors of tranquillity", there have been examples of UN attempts to deliver humanitarian aid in the absence of a formal ceasefire. Central to these early attempts at intervention, however, was the growing politicisation of relief aid. Corridors of tranquillity were founded on the belief that humanitarian aid could somehow end conflict by bringing warring parties together. In Sudan and Angola such policies have failed.

A second, more aggressive, phase of intervention and consequently politicisation of humanitarian aid began with the Gulf War. Member states of the UN, particularly the United Kingdom and the United States, themselves became directly involved in relief operations. The safe havens of Kurdistan (1991), together with the protection of the safety net in the former Yugoslavia (1992) and in Somalia (1993), are cases in point. Like the earlier failure of humanitarian diplomacy, militarisation has also floundered. Where the UN has achieved success with such policies, as in El Salvador and Namibia, it has been because the parties concerned have wanted peace. Unfortunately, in the majority of current conflicts this does not appear to be the case.

Since the end of the 1980s, the UN has had to confront the nature and consequences of internal conflict. More specifically, it has had to acknowledge the emergence of political formations which exist beyond the bounds of conventional international and state relations. In facing this challenge, the UN has shown major weaknesses. One of these relates to the legality of some relief interventions. The humanitarian operations that are held to be the keystones of the "new" UN, such as Kurdistan, Bosnia and Somalia, have all been based upon little more than ad hoc Security Council resolutions.

While the need for a case-by-case analysis of the operational environments and objectives is clearly necessary, the lack of a clear set of criteria and legal provisions for intervention risks reinforcing the perception that the process of selection of strategy is directed primarily by international political factors and the interests of the key actors, not by the needs of conflict-affected populations. Such a perception clearly undermines any claims by the UN and its member states that the provision of humanitarian aid is politically neutral, and should therefore be protected from military action by warring parties.

Second, the safety nets provided by the UN are characterised by weak coordination and fragmentary delivery. The establishment of the Department of Humanitarian Affairs cannot be said to have overcome this problem. It is still an open question whether traditional rivalry between UN agencies will wreck the drive for coordination. One of the most serious weaknesses has been the lack of clear objectives within the new-style humanitarian operations. Such operations display an alarming tendency not to examine the underlying causes of conflict, and thus frame clear strategies for their political resolution. This political simplicity is vividly revealed in the case of Angola. Here, the elections held in 1992 were seen as an end in themselves, which would prove a magic solution to the structural problems exposed and exacerbated by years of war and bitterness. The resurgence of UNITA's military onslaught, weeks after the election results indicated that they had lost, points to a frightening and negligent degree of naivety on the part of the international community. Review of current complex emergencies reveals that the international community is willing to treat only the symptoms, and even then, only in selected places.

Consequences of international failure

UN intervention in recent complex emergencies suggests that not only has it been a failure in the majority of cases, but that it has often further polarised the situation, leading to renewed conflict. Somalia and Angola are cases in point. The trend for the "new" UN to attempt to provide humanitarian aid in the context of ongoing conflict has built upon earlier practice established by NGOs. In the same manner as argued above, the UN is in danger of institutionalising conflict. The risks of this occurring are heightened by the fact that the UN, unlike NGOs, is not simply a humanitarian agency; it is also a political organisation. Even more care, therefore, needs to be taken in ensuring equitable distribution of its resources and energies.

As the situation in many countries switches from ordered to unstable war economies and generalised insecurity, the "flexibility" of many humanitarian agencies has also begun to reach its limit. The inability of many agencies to operate effectively in Kurdistan and Angola, together with the noticeable absence of established NGOs in Bosnia, all suggest that the dramatic expansion of NGO activity during the 1970s and 1980s in fact relied upon the security that a government framework conferred. Given these weaknesses within the relatively flexible operational mandates of NGOs, the capacity of the UN system to replicate these models is sorely questioned.

The Challenge of Complex Emergencies: Priorities for Action

The conflict and insecurity that presently shape many parts of the globe have deep-seated, structural causes. The emergence of proactive war economies in response to economic decline is an important aspect of the crisis. These economies, and the predatory and autonomous political movements they support, suggest that attempts simply to mediate between protagonists or impose parliamentary elections are destined for failure. A long-standing solution must encompass reform of the global economy. Unless the formal economies of Africa can be revitalised and given room to grow, and the fruits of economic reform and development distributed more equitably, for many there will remain no perceived alternative aside from extra-legal parallel activity, often including violence.

The international community's response to these structural economic and political crises has been limited and equivocal. The recent conclusion of the Uruguay Round of GATT (General Agreement on Tariffs and Trade) suggests that the terms of trade between Africa and the rest of the world will continue to deteriorate, particularly in the short term. The marginalisation of Africa since the 1970s occurred at a time when the level of protection within the multilateral system was declining. Further reductions, and therefore growing competition, cannot help but further weaken many African countries.

Structural adjustment programmes that focus upon export-led development potentially limit investment in national educational, health and agricultural systems, further weakening the human resource base. In addition to the bewildering array of economic conditionalities on development assistance, a new generation of conditionalities has been placed on the agenda. The growing emphasis in the 1990s on "good governance" as a prerequisite for sustainable development has a confusing ring after a decade of policies which uncritically supported the privatisation of public action, further limiting the development of accountable and legitimate political and civil structures. Yet even as individual and civil human rights at last appear on the development agenda, the international framework to support the right to development remains unfulfilled. There is a clear need to reappraise the impact of international aid and trade policies on the development of appropriate political and economic structures in the Third World, and to assess the corresponding obligations that this places on the international community to support institutions, to resolve rather than promote conflict.

Development of sustainable peace is therefore deeply related to developing new mechanisms of international accountability and to promoting new strategies for disbursing international relief and development assistance. As the contributors to this volume have shown, increasing the accountability of international public action will rely upon:

- Developing a framework for development which explicitly acknowledges the structural conditions that promote violence. Just as environmental impact assessment has become a common feature of development planning, so the potential for conflict to arise from inappropriate and inequitable development projects and strategies needs to be identified, and ways found to support the development public and private institutions required to manage conflict.

- Developing a framework of international law which promotes the rights of victims of violence and underdevelopment, and reverses the current trend to protect the rights of the international community to implement its, often untested, solutions.

- The ad hoc framework for intervention in complex emergencies needs to be clarified, if it is to avoid becoming a selective political tool of a unipolar world order. Developing criteria for military action and humanitarian aid must be based more on the analysis of the local conditions of conflict and on the needs of conflict-affected communities, and less on the political and military objectives of powerful Member States of the UN.

- An independent, international monitoring system should be established to monitor international operations in conflict situations, and to ensure the rights of conflict-affected communities to adequate protection.

- Greater emphasis must be placed on developing tools to monitor and evaluate the impact of relief assistance on the evolution of conflict. Currently, such programmes are evaluated within the confines of crude data regarding the direct impact on mortality and morbidity rates, and pay little attention to the political economy of relief aid in complex emergencies.

- Conflict-affected communities, and especially those most vulnerable within them, must be given a voice in determining the course of international action to prevent, mitigate and resolve structural and political violence. Only by reversing the process of disempowerment engendered by structural violence and conflict can sustainable strategies for development be achieved.

Conclusion

Complex emergencies reflect the failure of national and international communities to respond adequately to the complex web of violence, and predatory economic strategies, developed in response to maldevelopment and inequitable allocation of resources. The moral dilemmas confronting policy-makers and practitioners concerned with alleviating the worst effects of conflict-related disasters are acute. If international aid is contributing to the spiral of violence emerging across continents, should we simply stand back and watch the powerful develop new strategies of oppression and exploitation, and provide a permanent if minimal flow of resources to sustain those displaced from their homes within and across international borders? Clearly the answer is, No.

What is needed is a re-evaluation of the causes of conflict and the role of the international community in sustaining it. Out of this should grow more appropriate patterns of response by local and international institutions and agencies. Such a reappraisal touches at the heart of international relations and the current economic order; failure to address it promptly, in all its magnitude, will ensure that permanent and complex emergencies will persist.

References

African Rights (1993) "Components of a Lasting Peace in Sudan: First Thoughts", discussion paper no. 2, London, December.

Clough, M. (1992) *Free at Last?: US Policy towards Africa and the End of the Cold War*, New York, Council on Foreign Relations.

Duffield, M. (1981) *Maiurno: Capitalism and Rural Life in Sudan*, London, Ithaca Press.

——— (1993) "NGOs, Disaster Relief and Asset Transfer in the Horn: Political Survival in a Permanent Emergency", *Development and Change* 24 (1): 131–57.

Goulding, M. (1993) "The Evolution of United Nations Peacekeeping", *International Affairs*, 69 (3): 451–64.

Hanlon, J. (1991) *Mozambique: Who Calls the Shots?*, London, James Currey.

Jean, F. (1993) *Life, Death and Aid: the Médecins Sans Frontières Report on World Crisis Intervention*, London, Routledge.

Roberts, A. (1993) "Humanitarian War: Military Intervention and Human Rights", *International Affairs*, 69 (3): 429–49.

Scott-Villiers, A., Scott Villiers, P. and Dodge, C. (1993) "Repatriation of 150,000 Sudanese Refugees from Ethiopia: The Manipulation of Civilians in a Situation of Conflict", *Disasters*, 17 (3): 202–17.

About the Contributors

Lionel Cliffe is Professor of Politics and a member of the Centre for Development Studies at Leeds University. He has worked on and in Africa for over thirty years. He is founding editor of the *Review of African Political Economy*, and has written and edited many books, including (with Basil Davidson) *Eritrea's Long Struggle for Peace and Self-Determination*, and (with Martin Doornbos, A.G. Ahmed and John Markakis) *Beyond Conflict in the Horn of Africa*.

Mark Duffield has a background in anthropology and political economy. Between 1985 and 1989 he was Oxfam's country representative in Sudan. He now works for the School of Public Policy at the University of Birmingham. In recent years, Dr Duffield has published widely and completed a number of major consultancies in the field of complex political emergencies. His interests include the nature of war economies, the development and impact of international relief safety nets, and helping forge new directions for agencies working in conflict situations.

Judy el Bushra has worked mainly on and in the Sudan and Somalia. She has been concerned for some years with the challenges posed to development agencies by the emergence of the "gender and development" approach and by the prevalence of armed conflict in Africa. Since 1988 she has been Gender Officer in ACORD, a consortium of development agencies supporting programmes in Africa.

Reginald Herbold Green has been a student of the applied political economy of Africa for a third of a century, working, advising and researching in over thirty African countries. He is currently a Professorial Fellow at the Institute of Development Studies (University of Sussex) and a Senior Social Policy Advisor in the National Planning Department of Mozambique. He is a consultant to several national and international agencies including CIIR and UNICEF.

Barbara Hendrie is a social anthropologist with a professional background in development and relief programmes in conflict zones in the Horn of Africa. She is presently conducting social research on rural coping mechanisms in drought-affected areas of Tigray region, northern Ethiopia.

David Keen is a research consultant, specialising in the study of famine and human-rights issues. He has worked for Oxfam, Save the Children Fund, the United Nations, Africa Watch and the University of Bergen. He has a doctorate in sociology from Oxford University.

Joanna Macrae is a Research Fellow at the London School of Hygiene and Tropical Medicine. Her research interests include the effects of political violence on health and health systems, health policy and mental health in developing countries. She is currently coordinating a project concerned with health policy in post-conflict situations in Africa, Asia and Latin America.

Angela Penrose has worked in Ethiopia, Libya, Nigeria, Burundi and Zambia as a writer, teacher and journalist. She was the administrator of a relief and rehabilitation programme run by the staff and students of Addis Ababa University during the Ethiopian famine of the 1970s. She is co-author with Kurt Jansson and Michael Harris of *The Ethiopia Famine*, the story of the famine of the 1980s (London, Zed Press, 1987). She is currently Senior Overseas Information Officer with Save the Children Fund (UK).

Eugenia Piza-Lopez is coordinator of Oxfam's Gender and Development Unit. Her previous experience was as a researcher on images of the Third World in the UK, and in work on popular education with Central American women. In Costa Rica, where she was born, she was involved in a participatory research project with the University of Cost Rica, and produced films on development issues.

Hugo Slim has worked in humanitarian emergencies in Sudan, Ethiopia, Bangladesh and Iraqi Kurdistan for the United Nations and Save the Children Fund. At the time of writing he was the Senior Research Officer for Save the Children Fund (UK). He is currently the Director of the Disaster Management Centre at Oxford Brookes University.

David Sogge works as an independent consultant based in Amsterdam, Holland. Trained at Harvard, Princeton and the Institute of Social Science at the Hague, since 1970 he has been employed by local and northern NGOs to assess development and relief efforts in various countries, including Angola, where he has held seven assignments since 1985.

Katerina Tomasevksi is Senior Research Fellow at the Danish Centre for Human Rights, University of Copenhagen. She holds graduate degrees in international law from Harvard Law School and the University of Zagreb. She previously worked at the McGill Centre for Medicine, Ethics and Law, at WHO's Global Programme on AIDS, and at the Netherlands

Human Righs Institute. Her research interests include human rights in international development cooperation, particularly on the human rights of women, and prisoners and health issues.

Alex de Waal is co-director of African Rights, an independent human-rights organisation. He is the author of *Famine That Kills: Darfur, Sudan 1984–1985*, a major work on food security in Africa.

Ken Wilson wrote his doctoral thesis on the relationship between ecological stress, livelihood, social organisation, population, health and nutrition in an arid area of Zimbabwe. As Research Officer with the Refugee Studies Programme, University of Oxford, he undertook a number of research projects on issues of aid and livelihood in war and refugee situations in Africa, particularly in Mozambique. He is currently Programme Officer with the Ford Foundation, with responsibility for Mozambique and Angola.

Anthony Zwi is Senior Lecturer in Health Policy and Epidemiology in the Health Policy Unit, and a member of the Health Economics and Financing Programme (funded by the British Overseas Development Administration) at the London School of Hygiene and Tropical Medicine. Originally from South Africa, he has a long-standing interest in the impact of conflict on health, health systems and health policy, and has sought to advocate a greater awareness of these issues among public health practitioners. His current interests include on-going research into health and conflict, examining the public health burden and policy response to injuries and violence, and exploring the relationship between epidemiology, economics and policy-making.

Index

ACORD organisation, 151, 152
Afeworki, Issayas, 173, 174
African Rights organisation, 206
agriculture, 39, 41, 53, 72, 93, 97, 98,
    126, 152, 163, 177, 181; collapse of,
    129; depletion of resources, 165–7;
    Eritrean, 162; labour shortages in,
    101, 164, 165; mechanisation of, 223;
    technologies of, 93; traditional
    African, 94–5
aid *see* relief aid
Aidid, Mohammed Farah, 26, 139, 142,
    146, 149, 155, 217
Amin, Idi, 38, 39, 42
Amnesty International, 23
An-Na'im, Abdullahi Ahmed, 76
Angola, 9, 11, 12, 14, 15, 16, 20, 31, 37,
    39, 40, 42, 43, 44, 48, 65, 92–100,
    161, 177, 196, 205, 209, 222, 223,
    225, 229; aid to, 104, 105; elections
    in, 9, 29, 77, 107, 229; enclave
    economy in, 95–6; off-shore
    economy, 96; vulnerability of, 93–6
Anstee, Margaret, 205
assets, transfer of, 50–69, 170, 176, 182,
    210, 225

Baggara peoples, 53, 54, 113, 114, 117
banditry *see* looting
Barre, Mohammed Siad, 141, 184, 197,
    198; fall of, 141, 142, 143
Biafra, 29
Bosnia, 83, 209, 222, 228
Botswana, 44, 45
Boutros-Ghali, Boutros, 139, 152, 195,
    204
Bush, George, 150, 154

Cambodia, 75, 188
camps, relief, 27; as health risks, 217,
227; creation of, 218
CARE organisation, 28, 147, 148, 149,
    150, 153, 154, 158; attack on convoy,
    154
cassava, 102; mechanisation of
    production, 98
children: as soldiers, 226; deaths of, 38,
    41, 45, 85, 92, 104; malnutrition of,
    156; schooling of, 103
Cliffe, Lionel, 31
Clinton, Bill, 204
Cold War, 9, 52, 59, 78, 97, 194, 204,
    222, 224, 225, 227, 228
Combined Agencies Relief Team
    (CART), 118
Comitato Internazionale per lo Sviluppo
    dei Popoli, 151
Commission for Eritrean Refugee
    Assistance (CERA), 171, 172
communism, roll-back of, 92, 97
complex emergencies, 21–31, 50–69,
    222–6; international response to, 22,
    226; prevention of, 21–4; response
    to, 194–208
Concern organisation, 152
conditionality of aid, 22, 23, 25, 60, 76,
    116, 120
convoys, relief, 57; armed guards for,
    145, 155; attacks on, 13, 154; private,
    215
coping strategies, 7, 13, 15, 51, 52, 93,
    100, 102–4, 128, 140, 169, 176,
    182–3, 185, 223; failure of, 8; support
    for, 214
counterinsurgency, 9, 127, 163, 210, 217;
    famine as tactic, 113
cross-border operations, 125–38, 164,
    227
crossfire, killing by, 183
Cushitic Shebelle, 141
Cutler, Peter, 120

Darfur, famine in, 7, 13, 63, 112
Darod clan (Somalia), 141, 142; flight of, 142
de Reidmattan, Leon, 133
De Waal, A., 7, 8, 13, 14, 20, 24, 29, 112
deaths: from famine, 8, 11; from war, 37, 38, 48; in Mozambique, 26; in Uganda, 39; statistics, 92, 117, 152, 157, 214 (in Eritrea, 161, 162)
debt, Third World, 23, 50, 223
Declaration of Minimum Humanitarian Standards, 74
defence spending, 38, 41, 42
demobilised soldiers, 173–4; threat of, 189
Democratic Unionist Party (DUP) (Sudan), 56, 57
depopulation, 217, 218; functions of, 210–14
development, 231; models of, 24; right to, 76–8
diarrhoea, 38, 104, 156
Digil clan, 140
Dinka peoples, 53, 115, 121; attacks on, 113, 215; death rates among, 111; famine among, 53
Dir clan (Somalia), 141
disappearances, 74, 82
disaster tourism, 153
disease, 38, 45, 95, 140, 153, 156, 158; risk of, 8, 15, 27, 104
displaced persons, 19, 46, 62, 75, 84, 101, 102, 164, 170–3, 210, 212, 214, 218, 219, 220, 225
dollar trade, illegal, 56, 57
donor organisations, 113, 220; limited agendas of, 116–21
Dos Santos, President, 98
droit d'ingérence, 79–81, 86, 206
drought, 6, 7, 38, 106, 114, 125, 126–7, 135, 141, 160, 176, 213; and food security, 164–5; deaths from, 45
Duffield, Mark, 20, 21, 23

education, 46, 127, 172, 225; denial of, 21
Eide, Asbjorn, 71
El Mahdi, Sadiq, 113
elders, 216, 220, 224; importance of committees, 186
Eliasson, Jan, 148, 150, 203, 207

Emergency Relief Desk (ERD), 12, 131, 135
emergency: meanings of, 78–9; permanent, 50–7
enclave economy in Angola, 95–6, 107
environmental degradation, 8, 10, 53, 126, 160
Eritrea, 11, 12, 13, 14, 15, 16, 17, 20, 29, 31, 39, 40, 46, 47, 48, 60, 66, 183, 189, 224, 227; food security in, 160–78
Eritrean People's Liberation Front (EPLF), 17, 43, 161, 163, 164, 173, 174, 175, 176
Eritrean Relief Association (ERA), 28, 29, 131, 133, 167, 170
Ethiopia, 11, 12, 14, 18, 20, 25, 37, 38, 39, 40, 46, 47, 48, 54, 56, 60, 61, 66, 120, 125–38, 158, 160, 162, 167–8, 170, 173, 177, 189, 212, 227; access refused for food aid, 62; conscription into army, 164; exchange rate in, 61; migration to, 211
ethnic cleansing, 9, 52, 54
European Community, 105, 113
exchange rates: fixed, 227; manipulation of, 215
executions, 74, 82

families: dissolution of, 103, 224; separation from, 185
famine, 6–36; as collective experience, 7; as economic disaster, 111; as individual crisis, 24; causes of, 72, 116–18; conflict-related, 75; in southern Sudan, 111–24; man-made, 77–8; models of, 6–8; process of, 25; social nature of, 7
Famine Early Warning System (FEWS), 117
Farer, Tom, 206
female-headed households, 165, 172, 181, 188
flight of peoples, 21, 103, 117, 132, 142
food: and gender, 180–93; as weapon of war, 11–21, 25, 97, 129–30; functions of, 63 (in war, 10); imports of, 98; insecurity, 40; price of, 57, 145, 146, 148; right to, 6, 8, 12, 71–2, 86; self-sufficiency, 47
food aid, 12, 42, 43, 45, 46, 57, 73, 93,

137, 170, 176, 227; access denied, 224; attacks on, 17; dependency on, 157; distribution of, 105; diversion of, 19, 61–2, 227; leakage of, 105, 106, 121; looting of, 156; movement of, 155, 156; relief, subcontracted to NGOs, 58–9; role of, 13; undermining local markets, 30

Food and Agricultural Organisation (FAO), 148, 202

food systems, 40; attacks on, 9, 10, 13–14; post-conflict recovery of, 160

Foucault, Michel, 111

Fraser, Malcolm, 153

Garang, John, 112

garrison towns, 17, 19, 112, 118, 127, 211, 218; blockading of, 113

gender: and war, 180–93; transformation of relations, 224

General Agreement on Tariffs and Trade (GATT), 230

Geneva Conventions, 73, 83, 155

governance: good, as precondition of development, 230; integral to rehabilitation, 47–8; survival of, 50

grain, 131, 135, 168; distribution of, 219; imports of, 13; markets, 17, 98, 114; merchants, 128; price of, 6, 17, 62, 115, 214; production of, 177, 209; relief, 112, 117; reserves, exported from Sudan, 13; sale of, 20; speculation in, 62–3, 216; stores, 103 (attacks on, 14, 29)

Grant, James, 150

grazing, 169; changes in patterns, 15; destruction of, 170; restrictions on, 168

Green, Reginald, 31

guerrilla warfare, 163, 217

Hanlon, J., 213

Hawiye clan (Somalia), 141

health care, 30, 93, 127, 151, 161, 213, 219; attacks on, 9, 21; collapse of, 38; primary, 46

health services, 41, 43, 46, 151, 172, 197, 225

Henkin, Louis, 78

Hepburn, Audrey, 150

HIV/AIDS, spread of, 185, 224

hospitals, attacks on, 155

human rights, 10, 22, 60, 70–90, 76, 79, 116, 220, 230; abuse of, 70, 217, 227; monitoring of, 206; use of force to ensure, 85

Human Rights Watch, 28, 72

humanitarian aid: as part of political process, 65; object of, 63–4

hunger, and war, 70–90

Hurd, Douglas, 204

informalisation of economy, 24

InterAction group, 154

International Committee of the Red Cross (ICRC), 18, 28, 29, 81, 105, 118, 130, 133, 137, 139, 140, 143, 144–7, 149, 155, 198, 215; hospital attacked, 146

International Conference on Nutrition, 71

International Court of Justice, 85

International Covenant on Economic, Social and Cultural Rights, 71, 74

International Institute of Humanitarian Law, 81

International Medical Corps, 151

International Monetary Fund (IMF), 105, 117

international policy in Africa, 6–36

intervention, armed, for assistance, 86; risks of, 228

Iraq, 83, 85, 86, 199, 216, 217; agreement with UN, 84; Sudanese support for, 51

irrigation, 141

Isaaq clan (Somalia), 141

Islam, 54, 175; tensions with non-Islamic world, 78

Islamic banks, and grain speculation, 62

Isse, Dhahabo, 143, 144, 146

Jess, Ahmad Omer, 142

Johnston, Philip, 150, 153

Kassebaum, Senator, 150, 153

Keen, David, 27, 30

Kenya, 17, 55

Khatmiyya sect, 56, 57

Kitani, Ismat, 152, 153, 154

kitchens, set up in Somalia, 143, 146

Kurdistan, 32, 222, 228, 229
Kurds, 85, 86, 216; safe havens for, 84

land: access to, 171; confiscation of, 94, 141; control of, 94; distribution of, 171; intensive use of, 102; left idle, 165, 166; reform, 171, 174–6 (in Ethiopia, 163); rights for refugees, 175
land mines, 15, 31, 40, 45, 92, 97, 101, 106, 167, 183, 184, 214, 224; and loss of land, 161, 165; costs of clearing, 165; deactivation of, 31; effects on women and children, 184, 187; on grazing land, 168
Land Mines Protocol (UN), 15
law: collapse of, 78; humanitarian, 70, 74, 79, 80, 82; international, development of, 231; refugee, 70, 82
Liberia, 12, 20, 37, 46, 47, 48, 158, 196
Libya, 120
Life and Peace Institute (Sweden), 187
life, right to, 72, 73, 74, 86
livestock, 163, 164, 167, 168, 171; destruction of, 14, 127, 129; in Angola, 93; loss of, 114, 161, 168, 213; prices of, 64, 214; sale of, 117, 168, 169, 170; slaughtering of, 182; stealing of, 114, 164, 211; trade in, 114
looting, 17, 54, 140, 141, 142, 143, 145, 146, 147, 148, 152, 156, 173, 174, 182, 211, 226
Lutheran World Federation, 152

Mahdi, Ali, 142, 149, 154
malnutrition, 38, 41, 45, 48, 95, 103, 104, 158
marketing systems, 46, 94; breakdown of, 16, 96
markets, 181; attacks on, 128, 211; bypassing of, 213; distortion of, 217; held at night, 17
marriage, 186, 188; forced, 184, 185
Médecins Sans Frontières, 61, 80, 111, 112, 150
media, role of, in relation to aid agencies, 153
medical services, 15, 38, 184; collapse of, 48
Mengistu Haile Mariam, 11, 125, 127

middle class: loss of, 225; targeted for elimination, 224
migration, 8, 15, 128; absorption of, 129; as coping strategy, 128; drought, 136; famine, 7, 111, 114, 117, 126, 129, 140, 209, 210, 211, 214; labour, 51, 52, 95, 96, 165, 177, 224; to Sudan, 135
military intervention, 27, 65, 231; in Somalia, 152
millet, 102
Mogadishu port, 155; closure of, 145, 149, 154
Mohammed, Zahra Sheikh, 143
Morgan, Mohammed Hersi, 142, 143
mortality rates, 79, 158 see also children; deaths
movement of populations, 126, 170; controlled by relief, 121; restriction of, 16, 17, 21, 41, 56, 112, 168, 214, 223
Movimento Popular de Libertação de Angola (MPLA), 96, 97, 98, 99, 105, 106, 107; alliance with oil corporations, 97
Mozambique, 9, 11, 15, 20, 26, 29, 37, 39, 40, 42, 43, 44, 45, 46, 48, 92, 94, 158, 160, 161, 185, 196, 211, 212, 213, 214, 215, 216, 218, 225, 227
Mursal, Hussein, 151
Musse, Mohammed Abshir, 154

Namibia, 42, 47, 228
nation-states, 196; emergence of, 8
needs, assessment of, 209
Neto, Agostinho, 99
neutrality: active, 29, 145; of aid, 219, 229
Nnoli, O., 24
non-governmental organisations (NGOs), 12, 27, 62, 65, 66, 131, 132, 133, 134, 136, 137, 139, 148, 153, 155, 158, 197, 198, 216; and subcontracting of relief, 58–9; expansion of activity, 226, 229; loss of independence, 228; northern, role of, 27, 28, 29; placed in front line, 226–8; record of, 150–2; replacing state, 58; role of, 60, 64; US-based, 59
Norwegian Church Aid, 131

Novelli, William, 153
Nuba peoples, 62; eviction of, 54

Office of Foreign Disaster Assistance
(US), 135
Operation Lifeline Sudan, 61, 119, 121,
136, 211, 216, 228
Operation Rainbow, 228
Operation Red Star (Ethiopia), 16
Operation Restore Hope, 139, 154, 157,
158
oxen, 7, 177; loss of, 166; provision of,
172
OXFAM, 28, 152, 185, 201, 213, 214

pack animals, 172; lack of, 167
parallel exchange, regional, 56–7, 58
pastoralism, 168, 173, 214
Peace Aid Somalia, 143, 146
peacekeeping operations, costs of, 203–4
plough, 7, 126, 166, 172, 173;
introduction of, 93; use of, 94, 99,
101
Portugal, 93, 94, 97, 98, 205; settlers, 95
poverty, 225; levels of, 64; processes of,
176
Powell, Colin, 153
Prattley, Winston, 118
pregnancy, unwanted, 184, 185
Pronk, Jan, 77
prostitution, 102, 128, 183, 184

Rahanweyn clan, 140, 143
raiding, 112, 114, 116, 117, 210, 213, 215,
216 see also looting
Rangasami, Amrita, 7, 10, 111
rape, 9, 16, 183, 184, 190, 226;
counselling, 191
Reagan Doctrine, 78
recovery: strategies for, 167–70;
sustainable, 176–8
refugees, 8, 20, 46, 52, 75, 79, 101, 103,
129, 132, 142, 163, 164, 170–3, 177,
214, 218, 220; aid, 42; land rights for,
175; roundups of, 218; strafing of, 16
rehabilitation, 45–7, 48, 49; of Somalia,
157; post-conflict, 31; strategies, 225
relief aid, 76–8, 83, 115, 125–38; and
dynamics of violence, 214–19; attacks
on, 17, 18; appropriation of, 215;
delivery of, 27–30; diversion of, 216;

embargo of, 50; equal access to, 29;
geography of, 212–13; international,
50–69; manipulation of, 225;
obstacles to, 112, 211, 218–19;
reassessment of, 209–21; relation to
conflict, 209; timing of, 213–14; used
to control population movement,
121; weakening effect on state, 213
see also food aid
Relief and Rehabilitation Commission
(RRC), 119
relief operations: design of, 27; local,
143–7
Relief Society of Tigray (REST), 28, 130,
132, 133–5, 136
relief system, international, failure of,
139, 158
religious indoctrination, 111
Renamo organisation, 15, 26, 29, 40, 43,
44, 184, 211, 212, 213, 215, 225
Reordenamento Rural, 95
resettlement, 16, 25, 62, 129, 171, 172; by
UNITA, 40; forced, 18–20, 163, 211;
in Ethiopia, 18; in Sudan, 18
Rome Accords, 44
Rwanda, 1, 9, 38, 48, 222

safe havens, creation of, 32, 84
safety nets, provision of, 228, 229
Sahnoun, Mohammed, 152; resignation
of, 153
Samaritan's Purse organisation, 152
sanitary towels, provision of, 185, 191
Save the Children Fund, 28, 151, 158,
198, 202
self-respect, maintaining of, 185
Sen, Amartya, 6, 121
sexual oppression, 111, 211
sieges of towns, 17, 19, 40
slavery, 9, 19, 184, 214; prohibition of,
74
Sogge, David, 22
Somali National Alliance (SNA), 142,
143
Somali National Movement, 18
Somali Red Crescent Society, 139, 144–7
Somalia, 9, 10, 11, 12, 14, 15, 16, 17, 18,
20, 24, 26, 29, 30, 31, 37, 38, 39, 40,
43, 46, 47, 48, 52, 56, 58, 60, 61, 65,
79, 83, 186, 194, 196, 197, 198, 202,
204, 209, 215, 227, 228, 229;

diversion of food aid, 19; famine relief in, 139–59; rehabilitation of, 157; US presence in, 32, 65, 153, 155, 200

Somaliland, 184, 186, 197, 198, 216, 227

sorghum, 62, 102, 114, 130, 147

SOS-Kinderdorf, 151

South Africa, 9, 96, 97, 108, 212

sovereignty, 132–3; as obstacle to assistance, 78; defence of, 76; definition of, 76; disputed, 196; infringement of, 65, 212; of Ethiopia, disregarded, 60; of Sudan, 117; respect for, 11

Special Relief Programme for Angola, 12, 228

starvation, 86, 142, 152, 176; prevention of, 79; prohibition on imposing, 72–3; wars of, 70–90

state, buying of farm output, 100

structural adjustment, 59, 190, 230

sub-Saharan Africa, war in, 37–49

Sudan, 9, 10, 11, 12, 13, 15, 17, 23, 37, 40, 43, 48, 50, 52, 53, 54, 55, 58, 60, 61, 79, 83, 135, 170, 196, 210, 212, 213, 215, 218, 227; access refused for food aid, 11, 62; capital flight from, 56; exchange rate in, 60–1; famine in, 7, 111–24; migration to, 210; north, 62; parallel economy in, 56; southern, 13, 16, 18, 20, 24, 27, 39, 53, 54, 158, 215, 216, 225; sovereignty of, 117; weakening of social groups, 55

Sudan People's Liberation Army (SPLA), 54, 55, 57, 111, 112, 113, 115, 119, 120, 121, 211, 213, 215, 225; attacks on Nuer, 215

Sudan Relief and Rehabilitation Association (SRRA), 28

Swaziland, 45

sweeteners, use of, 219

Tanzania, 38, 39, 42, 44; invasion of, 40

targeting of relief, political problems of, 219

taxation, 211, 224

Taylor, Charles, 20

terror against populations, 13, 40, 224

Tigray, 11, 12, 13, 14, 16, 18, 20, 30, 31, 60, 125–38, 163, 183, 224, 227; migration from, 210

Tigray People's Liberation Front (TPLF), 125, 127, 128, 129, 132, 133, 134, 137

Tigray Transport and Agricultural Consortium (TTAC), 131

Togo, 37

Tomasevski, Katerina, 26

torture, 82

tractors, provision of, 101

trains, relief, 113–16, 118, 121; misuse of, 119

transport systems, 7, 18, 40, 96, 99, 103, 131, 134, 135, 145, 150; attacked, 147, 211; damage to, 44

Uganda, 9, 14, 37, 38, 39, 55, 57, 184, 187

UNAVEM II, 205

underdevelopment, 22; active, 21; structural, 226

underwear, provision of, 185, 191

assessement models of, 42

UNITA organisation, 9, 15, 16, 19, 29, 40, 43, 44, 96, 99, 103, 107, 225; use of terror, 97

United Kingdom (UK), 25, 228; charity laws in, 28

United Nations (UN), 10, 11, 12, 15, 28, 29, 32, 60, 62, 66, 71, 72, 74, 75, 76, 77, 79, 81, 104, 113, 117, 119, 120, 121, 130, 132, 133, 136, 139, 148, 149, 155, 158, 165, 171, 212, 215, 220, 227, 229; agreement with Iraq, 84; and NGO organisations, 201; changing role of, 228–9; in Bosnia, 32; intervention by, 229; limitations of Charter, 196; military operations, 207; numbers of troops deployed, 195; relief programme, 147–50; reform of, 194–208

UN Agenda for Peace, 32, 195, 198, 201, 204

UN Central Emergency Revolving Fund (CERF), 201

UN Centre for Human Rights, 23

UN Commission on Human Rights, 75

UN Department of Humanitarian Affairs (DHA), 199, 200–4, 207, 229

UN Department of Peace and Security Operations (PASO), 200

UN Development Programme (UNDP), 120, 148, 195, 198, 202

UN Economic and Social Council (ECOSOC), 199, 203

UN General Assembly, 80, 82, 83

UNICEF, 17, 44, 143, 150, 151, 198, 202, 212, 214; cost UN High Commission for Refugees (UNHCR), 18, 27, 79, 82, 84, 132, 148, 170, 202, 227

UN Office of Emergency Operations in Ethiopia (OEOE), 136

UN Operations in Somalia (UNOSOM), 154, 155, 197, 206

UN Security Council, 32, 83, 84, 85, 152, 154, 155, 195, 199–200, 204, 206; resolution 688, 84

United Somali Congress (USC), 141, 142, 143

United States of America (USA), 9, 92, 96, 98, 118, 119, 120, 152, 204, 205, 228; intervention in Somalia, 32, 65, 153, 155, 200

United Task Force (UNITAF), 154, 206

USAID, 25, 113, 117, 131, 135, 148, 214

vaccination, 156; of cattle, 64, 216

van der Stoel, Max, 85

victimisation, multiple, prevention of, 83–6

victims, rights of, 81–2

Vienna Conference on Human Rights, 75, 76, 81

villages: 'peace', 54; artificial, 211; protected, 95

violence, dynamics of, 214–19

von Braunmuhl, Joachim, 113

Wannop, Bryan, 120

war: economic costs of, 38, 39–40, 41, 48; impact on food security, 160–78; in Africa, 8–10; interaction with drought, 162; internal, political economy of, 50–69; relationship with hunger, 6; types of, 39–40

water supplies, 15, 46, 93, 104, 156, 157, 183; poisoning of, 15

Western economies, disengagement from Africa, 223

Western Relief Operation (Sudan), 62

wife-beating, 186

wild food, collecting of, 15, 16, 51, 112, 115, 211, 214

Wilson, K., 30

women, 127, 165; and carrying of water, 167; as household providers, 181–7; assault on, 16; burdens of, 224; disempowerment of, 190; education of, 189; execution of, 187; health of, 183–6; killed by crossfire, 183; murder of, 187; protection of, 186; re-evaluation of role of, 180; sexual exploitation of, 226; violation of, 9

World Bank, 58, 59, 117, 172

World Concern, 151

World Food Programme, 12, 27, 44, 148, 149, 202

World Health Organisation (WHO), 148, 156

Zaire, 9, 57, 96, 108

Zimbabwe, 29, 40, 41, 42, 44, 45, 47